PRODUCTION AND LOGISTICS IN MEETINGS, EXPOSITIONS, EVENTS, AND CONVENTIONS

PRODUCTION AND LOGISTICS IN MEETINGS, EXPOSITIONS, EVENTS, AND CONVENTIONS

George G. Fenich, Ph.D.

PEARSON

Boston Columbus Indianapolis New York San Francisco Upper Saddle River
Amsterdam Cape Town Dubai London Madrid Milan Munich Paris Montréal Toronto
Delhi Mexico City São Paulo Sydney Hong Kong Seoul Singapore Taipei Tokyo

Editorial Director: Vernon Anthony
Senior Acquisitions Editor: William Lawrensen
Editorial Assistant: Lara Dimmick
Director of Marketing: Dave Gesell
Marketing Manager: Stacey Martinez
Senior Marketing Coordinator: Alicia Wozniak
Senior Marketing Assistant: Les Roberts
Program Manager: Alexis Duffy
Senior Managing Editor: JoEllen Gohr
Production Project Manager: Susan Hannahs
Procurement Specialist: Deidra Skahill
Senior Art Director: Jayne Conte
Cover Designer: Suzanne Behnke
Cover Art: Cover Image Courtesy of Global Experience Specialists (GES)
Full-Service Project Management: Anju Joshi, PreMediaGlobal, Inc.
Composition: PreMediaGlobal, Inc.
Printer/Binder: Edwards Brothers/Malloy, Inc.
Cover Printer: Lehigh/Phoenix
Text Font: Adobe Garamond Pro

Credits and acknowledgments borrowed from other sources and reproduced, with permission, in this textbook appear on the appropriate page within the text.

Many of the designations by manufacturers and sellers to distinguish their products are claimed as trademarks. Where those designations appear in this book, and the publisher was aware of a trademark claim, the designations have been printed in initial caps or all caps.

Library of Congress Cataloging-in-Publication Data
Fenich, George G.
  Production and logistics in meetings, expositions, events and conventions / George G. Fenich, Ph.D.
     p. cm.
  ISBN-13: 978-0-13-313946-4
  ISBN-10: 0-13-313946-8
  1. Special events—Management.   2. Special events—Planning.   I. Title.
  GT3405.F46 2015
  394.2068—dc23

                                        2013042420

10 9 8 7 6 5 4 3 2 1

ISBN 10: 0-13-313946-8
ISBN 13: 978-0-13-313946-4

Dedicated to the "Fab Four" of academics in meetings, expositions, events, and conventions, without whom this book would not be possible.

brief contents

contents

1

Introduction 1

2

On-Site Meeting and Event Management 14

3

Designing, Organizing, and Producing the Environment for Meetings, Conventions, and Events 36

4

Managing the Technical Aspects of Meetings, Conventions, and Events 49

5

Managing Registration: What You Need to Know and Why 66

6

Food and Beverage Production 86

13
Public Relations 210

14
On-Site—Effective Event Communication 229

15
Epilogue 245

Preface

The meetings, expositions, events, and conventions (MEEC, pronounced like *geese*) industry continues to grow and garner increasing attention from the hospitality industry, colleges and universities, government officials, and communities. This book provides a comprehensive view of production and logistics in MEEC. It is meant to provide a hands-on or step-by-step method for producing and managing gatherings in the MEEC industry.

Production and Logistics in Meetings, Events, Expositions, and Conventions is based on the work of two task forces initiated and supported by Meeting Professionals International: the Meeting and Business Event Competency Standards Task Force and the Meeting and Business Event Competency Standards Curriculum Guide Task Force. This book should be of interest to practitioners, educators, students, and government officials. It is the most up-to-date book on production and logistics in the MEEC industry and covers a wide range of topics dealing with those two functions. This book can easily serve as the basis for a college course on the subject, for training sessions for new employees in the industry, and for educational delivery by industry associations. It should meet the needs of anyone interested in knowing more about production and logistics in the MEEC industry.

INSTRUCTOR'S RESOURCES

Instructor's Resources include an online instructor's manual, PowerPoints, and a MyTest.

To access the supplementary materials, instructors need to request an instructor access code. Go to www.pearsonhighered.com/irc, where you can register for an instructor access code. Within forty-eight hours after registering, you will receive a confirmation email, including your instructor access code. Once you have received your code, go to the site and log on for full instructions on downloading the materials you wish to use.

George G. Fenich, Ph.D.

Acknowledgments

I would like to thank Kathryn Hashimoto for her unabated support, patience, and encouragement; event professionals for sharing their knowledge; and adult learners everywhere for their interest in the MEEC industry. My thanks also go to the academics and industry professionals who contributed materials for this book.

About the Author

George G. Fenich, Ph.D., is a professor in the School of Hospitality Leadership at East Carolina University. Dr. Fenich worked in the hospitality industry for 15 years before joining academe in 1985. He teaches and conducts research in the area of meetings, conventions, and events and has written three books and over 60 academic articles. He has presented at over 100 conferences both in the United States and internationally. He has filled leadership roles in Meeting Professionals International (MPI), the Professional Convention Management Association (PCMA), Destination Marketing Association International (DMAI), and the International Council on Hotel, Restaurant, and Institutional Education (ICHRIE). He is the editor in chief of the *Journal of Convention and Event Tourism* and sits on the editorial boards of six other academic journals. He is also the principal of the consulting firm Fenich & Associates LLC.

Introduction

After the planning of the meeting and event is complete, it's time to put on the show. learchitecto/fotolia

Chapter Outline

The Importance of Production in Meetings, Expositions, Events, and Conventions

By

Greg Van Dyke,
Senior Vice President, Global Sales and Marketing
PSAV Presentation Services

Let's face it: planning a meeting consumes so much of your time and effort that it would be nice to think that everyone involved got the maximum possible benefit. Well, getting better results from meetings isn't rocket science. It isn't just about logistics; it requires a clear understanding of how your presenters and audience communicate.

At the most basic level, the point of a meeting is to communicate a message. The scary part is that your audience will take only about a minute (probably less time than you've spent reading this) to decide if a presentation is worth listening to. If they aren't engaged quickly, they let their minds wander. And all of the money you've invested in travel, catering, and planning can sink without a trace. When the audience arrives, they need to experience a professional and engaging atmosphere, which kicks off a positive feedback cycle through planned, rehearsed, and flawlessly executed staging and presentations. This is true for small and large meetings alike.

There is science behind this. Sensory stimulation is most effective when it is targeted and aligned. The more of the brain that is activated, the stronger and more widespread the learning. So in a meeting environment, an artful combination of audio and visual stimuli (multisensory cues) can help individuals perceive and retain information. When it's done well, you can create an experience that focuses the audience on the specific stimuli (your message) and provides your ultimate benefit (transferring the message into long-term memory for the attendee). Key considerations for audio and visual stimuli include:

- **Sound:** Walk-in music for your audience creates energy and anticipation. Volume changes help you manage your audience. Play-on stings—a short burst of energetic music—keeps the meeting moving while your speaker comes to the podium. Sure, you have to hear your speaker, but sound can provide a powerful emotional component as well.
- **Lighting:** Visual cues dominate our ability to absorb a message, so the speaker needs to be lighted and seen in depth. Color washes provide the desired color, and the intelligent use of moving lights adds atmosphere and energy.
- **Color:** From incorporating brand cues to aligning color the goal is to enhance your meeting. Blues and cool colors tend to calm; warm colors tend to stimulate.
- **Presentation Content:** Incorporate visuals and graphics (including video content) rather than written text alone. Match the ambient light and the size of the room with the projected materials.
- **Screen Size:** There are basic metrics for maximum screen size for a given audience and ceiling height. However, studies suggest that an audience will remember content on large screens. Edge-blending technology allows single wide screens with multiple inputs.

Clearly, you have tools at your disposal that will create a better meeting experience for your attendees. But remember an important caveat: your success requires an artful combination of multisensory inputs. More is not necessarily better. If you want your show to run seamlessly, it requires practice and skilled personnel to help you, including:

Show Producer: The show producers' role is to translate the client's communication brief into the best show possible. They design the look of the room and the stage. They plan the order of events and book performers and speakers. On-site, they supervise the working crew to ensure that their vision becomes reality; this includes managing rehearsals so that crew and presenters are comfortable and know what to expect. They will "call" the show, directing the crew through the individual video, sound, lighting, and staging cues that keep those sensory inputs targeted and aligned.

Technical Producer: As the most senior members of the technical crew, a technical producer will translate your requirements into orders that the crew can follow for large shows. Technical producers plan out the show in advance using CAD systems to ensure that all the details will work. They have the big picture in mind and can direct the crew during set and strike as well as support the show producer.

Lighting Designer: Lighting designers consider your stage design, the mood you want to create, your presenters, and your budget in order to create the best possible combination of lights to create your look. Their plan or show plot becomes the blueprint for the lighting crew to install. A few lights in the hands of an experienced lighting designer can create more impact than a ceiling full of lights installed without much thought.

Show Technician: Show technicians are responsible for installing the equipment and making it all work. Large shows may require separate operators for video, sound, lighting, etc. Smaller events allow one or two crew members to cover multiple tasks. Having a crew member provides a calm and steady hand that can save the day when unforeseen circumstances occur.

Finally: rehearse. A simple run-through guarantees that everyone knows what to expect, allows the crew to respond and react to your presenters, and keeps the positive feedback cycle flowing through the audience. The result is a meeting that delivers your message.

PSAV© Presentation Services Profile

PSAV provides the ideas and technology that inspire great meetings. This has made PSAV the leading provider of event technology for meeting planners and producers across the corporate, association, and tradeshow markets. PSAV provides an unparalleled range of event technology to support its customers' ability to create, collaborate, and communicate. With more than 1,200 partner locations around the world, PSAV provides highly trained technicians and advanced technology right where you want to have your meeting.

PSAV has built a reputation for supplying the very best in technology and up-to-the-minute resources. Our breadth of cutting-edge audiovisual, staging,

(Continued)

and connectivity technology is truly second to none. However what really sets us apart is our ability to collaborate. Event planners tell us we're more like creative consultants than vendors. From the first cocktail napkin sketch through to the final standing ovation we listen, engage, and promise creative solutions to problems you haven't even thought of yet. Popular innovations currently include:

Audiovisual

- **Video Mapping:** This allows for an unlimited amount of unique and creative video content to be projected on almost any surface. You can transform stages, walls, rooms, entire buildings, and any regular or irregular-shaped surface into a fluid environment of colorful movement.
- **Interactive Video Wall:** Consider this a large (wall-sized) iPad with two dozen apps to create maps, presentations, and games. It can be used as a presentation screen, interactive digital signage, 3-D visualization, and a real-time tool to send photographs to meeting attendees and enhance social media.

Digital Services

- PSAV has 300 videoconferencing centers around the world, allowing flexible options for virtual communication with minimal advance planning. PSAV has pre-certified a range of hotel locations with appropriate Internet bandwidth and available gear and technicians.
- Meeting Room Manager allows PSAV to manage Internet bandwidth at partner locations to ensure key meeting clients can secure the necessary Internet bandwidth they need for a successful event. PSAV created a bandwidth calculator available on the CIC website to help planners review their needs for dedicated bandwidth.

Traditional Services include:

- Full range of traditional services, including lighting, display, projection, and sound.
- Creative services, including graphic design, scenic elements, and video production.
- Staging services, including rigging, soft sets, and corporate theater support from concert sound to broadcast quality projection and seasoned producers.
- Interactive services, such as audience response and mobile applications.

For more information about PSAV, visit www.psav.com OR call 1.877.430.7728

PRODUCTION AND LOGISTICS IN MEETINGS, EXPOSITIONS, EVENTS, AND CONVENTIONS

Meetings, expositions, events, and conventions (MEEC, pronounced like "geese") are a part of the larger field of tourism. This is an exciting career area. Regardless of the attitudes and interests of the potential MEEC professional, he or she should be able to find a satisfying employment niche in MEEC. The reader of this book most likely has some knowledge of the MEEC industry. (Note that in some parts of the world, this industry is referred to as "MICE," which stands for meetings, incentives, conventions, and events. However, the "incentive travel" aspect of this industry has diminished in magnitude and has morphed to become much more like a meeting or convention, albeit more upscale. Thus, the acronym MEEC seems more appropriate.) While there are multiple aspects and theories in MEEC, its operationalization falls into two categories: planning and producing. Planning is considered to be determining or figuring out (in advance) what you want to do and how you want to do it. Producing, or logistics, involves the actual setting up of a meeting, event, or convention. This book focuses on the **production and logistical** aspects of the MEEC industry. (Planning of MEECs is beyond the scope of this text.)

THE MEEC INDUSTRY

Segments

The MEEC industry is quite diverse and multifaceted. The following provides some insight into MEEC divisions or segments:

a. Conventions and meetings
   i. National political convention
   ii. National Restaurant Association convention
   iii. Professional Convention Management Association annual conference
b. Expositions
   i. Where suppliers meet buyers
   ii. Educational
   iii. Entertainment
c. Corporate events
   i. Holiday parties
   ii. Annual dinner
   iii. Company picnics
   iv. Meetings
   v. Sales training
   vi. Conventions
d. Festivals
   i. Marketplace of ancient days
   ii. Community event
   iii. Fair (not for profit)
   iv. Festival (for profit)
e. Social events
   i. Wedding
   ii. Anniversary
   iii. Birthday
   iv. Reunion
   v. Bar mitzvah (bat mitzvah)
f. Religious events
   i. Papal inauguration
   ii. The Hajj (Mecca)
   iii. Easter
   iv. Kwanza
g. Special events may include:
   i. Civic events
   ii. Centennials
   iii. Founder's day

    h. Mega-events
        i. Olympics
        ii. America's Cup
        iii. Hands Across America
        iv. World's fair
    i. Retail events
        i. Long-range promotional event
        ii. Store opening
        iii. New product rollout
            1. Xbox
            2. iTunes
    j. Sporting events (occurring relatively infrequently)
        i. Super Bowl
        ii. World Cup
        iii. Yacht races

Along with the list above, there are jobs in many industries that support MEEC. For example, a company called Accent on Arrangements provides child care and activities for convention attendees around the United States. Its employees are people who have an aptitude for working with small children but are not interested in being schoolteachers who can travel extensively. The company regularly employs college students. Another example is a specialty service contractor that supplies floral arrangements for trade show booths. A third example is working as a princess or other character for a company such as Disney. These are examples of "putting on the show" or **production** in the MEEC industry. The work and career opportunities in MEEC are endless and available in every corner of the world.

    The individuals who work in MEEC are known by many different names: planner, meeting planner, corporate meeting planner, event planner, wedding planner, hotel or conference center salesperson, entertainment/sporting venue sales and services person, destination management employee, service contractor, and more (adapted from Fenich, 2012a). In this book, these individuals are referred to as **event professionals**.

Definitions

The definitions used in this book are based on a glossary developed by the Convention Industry Council that can be found at http://www.conventionindustry.org /StandardsPractices/APEX/glossary.aspx/.

    The following are four definitions that the event professional must know:

1. **Meeting:** An event where the primary activity of the participants is to attend educational sessions, participate in discussions or social functions, or attend other organized events. There is no exhibit segment. See also: consumer show, convention

2. **Exposition:** An exhibition that is open to the public, usually requiring an entrance fee.
   a. EXHIBITION: An event at which products, services, or promotional materials are displayed to attendees visiting exhibits on the show floor. These events focus primarily on business-to-business (B2B) relationships.

3. **Event:** An organized occasion such as a meeting, convention, exhibition, special event, gala dinner, and so on. An event is often composed of several different, yet related, functions.
   a. SPECIAL EVENT: A one-time event staged for the purpose of celebration; a unique activity.

4. **Convention:** A gathering of delegates, representatives, and members of a membership or industry organization convened for a common purpose. Common features include educational sessions, committee meetings, social functions, and meetings to conduct the governance business of the organization. Conventions are typically recurring events with a specific, established timing. See also: meeting, exhibition, trade show, consumer show

All of the above must be 1) planned and 2) produced. This planning and subsequent production are done by a meeting and event professional, sometimes called a meeting planner or an event professional.

Magnitude of the MEEC Industry

As can be seen earlier, the MEEC industry is quite broad and diverse. Thus, it is difficult to ascertain the size, magnitude, and economic impact of MEEC. According to the recent international statistics, in 2010 professional conference organizers planned events that had an estimated economic impact of over $55 billion and their average delegate spent over $2,500 at each meeting he or she attended. According to the *American Express Meetings & Events 2013 Global Meetings Forecast* (the "Forecast"), Asia Pacific, with its relatively strong economy, is likely to see the strongest growth among regions in both spending and the number of MEEC events held.

The *Economic Significance of Meetings to the U.S. Economy* study reveals that the U.S. meetings industry directly supports 1.7 million jobs, $263 billion in spending, a $106 billion share of the GDP, $60 billion in labor revenue, $14.3 billion in federal tax revenue, and $11.3 billion in state and local tax revenue each year. In the MEEC industry in the U.S. alone, 205 million attendees participate in the nation's 1.8 million conventions, conferences, congresses, trade shows and exhibitions, incentive events, and corporate/business meetings (CIC, 2010).

Trends in MEEC

MEEC is an ever-evolving industry. Thus, professionals must consider trends in MEEC when planning their events. A major trend is the growing globalization of the industry and the blurring of country borders and boundaries, i.e., the formation of the EU. With globalization comes growing concerns about safety, both physical and medical, and security. International travel is increasingly risky whether delegates are traveling *to* places with problems or coming *from* those places. Thus, event professionals must develop contingency plans, risk management strategies, and appropriate safeguards for their attendees. Staff must be trained to be ready to take action in emergencies (MPI, 2012a).

Another trend is the growing recognition that multiple generations are attending meetings and events that include pre-boomers, baby boomers, and Gens X, Y, and Z. They have very diverse wants and needs, so event professionals must vary the content and delivery of their events. Compounding the generational issue is that people from wider cultural backgrounds are also attending these events and have different expectations (MPI, 2010).

A third trend, albeit not necessarily new, is that corporate social responsibility is a continuing interest for meeting and event professionals' organizations and a potential differentiator for companies and associations that can demonstrate a strong commitment to effective CSR programs. CSR policies and initiatives within top-ranked, multinational companies have generated an expectation of CSR practice in *all* industries at *all* levels. In a similar vein, clients are expecting event professionals and events to be increasingly environmentally sensitive and a continuing of the "green movement" (MPI, 2012b).

These trends have an impact on how event professionals plan their meetings and events. Only those professionals who stay aware of trends in MEEC can be successful and create satisfied clients.

Evolution and Maturation of the MEEC Industry

It can be said that events and meetings have been around since the dawn of time. The Romans held meetings at the Forum and events at the Coliseum. Religious pilgrimages have taken place for thousands of years. In America, town hall forum–type meetings began in the 18th century. While someone had to plan all these events, there was neither formal training nor established sets of skills, standards, and abilities for MEEC professionals. However, like other industries such as law and accounting, as an industry evolves and matures, there is an increasing need among clients, employers, and governments to have a codified set of competency standards to which professionals must adhere. Until very recently, no common set of knowledge, skills, and abilities (KSAs) existed for events professionals.

This dearth of standards changed in 2011 with the release of the Meeting and Business Event Competency Standards (MBECS). **MBECS** contains the KSAs required of meetings and events professionals. It builds on previous work done by Silvers along with work by the Canadian Tourism Human Resources Council, where standards for special events professionals were put forth. MBECS is the result of almost two years of work by a task force consisting of both industry practitioners and academics supported by the MPI Foundation.

MBECS

The MBECS are divided into 12 domains or blocks with 33 skills and almost 100 subskills or subsegments. The domains and skills are listed below:

A. STRATEGIC PLANNING
   1. Manage Strategic Plan for Meeting or Event
   2. Develop Sustainability Plan for Meeting or Event
   3. Measure Value of Meeting or Business Event
B. PROJECT MANAGEMENT
   4. Plan Meeting or Event
   5. Manage Meeting or Event Project
C. RISK MANAGEMENT
   6. Manage Risk Management Plan
D. FINANCIAL MANAGEMENT
   7. Develop Financial Resources
   8. Manage Budget
   9. Manage Monetary Transactions
E. ADMINISTRATION
   10. Perform Administrative Tasks
F. HUMAN RESOURCES
   11. Manage Human Resource Plan
   12. Acquire Staff and Volunteers
   13. Train Staff and Volunteers
   14. Manage Workforce Relations
G. STAKEHOLDER MANAGEMENT
   15. Manage Stakeholder Relationships

H. MEETING OR EVENT DESIGN
  16. Design Program
  17. Engage Speakers and Performers
  18. Coordinate Food and Beverage
  19. Design Environment
  20. Manage Technical Production
  21. Develop Plan for Managing Movement of People
I. SITE MANAGEMENT
  22. Select Site
  23. Design Site Layout
  24. Manage Meeting or Event Site
  25. Manage On-Site communications
J. MARKETING
  26. Manage Marketing Plan
  27. Manage Marketing Materials
  28. Manage Meeting or Event Merchandise
  29. Promote Meeting or Event
  30. Contribute to Public Relations Activities
  31. Manage Sales Activities
K. PROFESSIONALISM
  32. Exhibit Professional Behavior
L. COMMUNICATIONS
  33. Conduct Business Communications

The list above represents all the KSAs that event professionals need to acquire, and be proficient in, during the course of their career. That these are, in fact, those KSAs needed by event professionals was validated when the Convention Industry Council (CIC) adopted MBECS as the primary basis for its new Certified Meeting Professional International Standards (CMP-IS) and for the CMP exam. The development of these standards marks a milestone in the MEEC industry. For the first time, all players have a common benchmark or point of reference. And moving forward, the industry, profession, academics, students, professionals, human resources staff, and others can work from the same base.

Uses for Meetings/Events Professionals

The MBECS represent the KSAs that a practitioner must possess in order to be successful in the field. Industry professionals can perform a personal "skills assessment" of those standards and skills at which they are and are not adept. The resulting "gap analysis" can help guide their professional and personal development. MBECS can also help plot career paths. Being able to provide an assessment that shows a broad mastery of the subject will enhance employability and mobility across sectors and countries. This also allows an industry professional to promote his or her KSAs to employers or clients.

The MBECS is of great value to employers and managers. The standards can aid in the development of job descriptions and job specifications. This leads to improvements in determining workforce requirements and producing worker solicitations. The standards can also help in developing a sequence of training for employees as well as a basis for performance assessment and feedback.

Uses for the Academic Community

The MBECS provides the internationally accepted basis for developing courses of study and their requisite content. It is up to a given program or institution to determine how the content is delivered: in specific meetings/events courses, in business courses, in general education, or a combination of those. The significant advantage of using MBECS is that it is not prescriptive: One size does not fit all. A companion "MBECS Curriculum Guide" has also been developed (see the MPI website). Existing programs can "benchmark" themselves against the standards with resulting global recognition. The MBECS also provide a platform for dealing with governmental authorities and accrediting bodies. Using MBECS, a program can show the relevance of its course offerings and justify the content based on an international body of knowledge. Students can use the standards to develop their educational pathways and to validate their "employability" to recruiters. They could also use the standards to determine which educational programs best meet their learning needs. For academics, the standards can help delineate areas or topics in the meetings/events world that are in need of research.

Uses for Associations

First and foremost, the MBECS provides recognition of the KSAs required by the industry. This can then help guide the development of program content and delivery that is consistent with international standards. MBECS can also be used by the members of an association to determine their educational or professional development needs and how the association can best fulfill those needs (Fenich, 2012b).

Translating MBECS into Educational Content

The MBECS are a tremendous resource and reference. However, given that they cover almost 80 pages in an outline format, they can be daunting to comprehend and understand. Thus, after the MBECS task force concluded its work, a Meeting and Business Event Competency Standards Curriculum Guide task force was created. Its charge was to translate the content of MBECS into ideas and tools that would provide relevant and quality programming for any individual or academic delivering MBECS-based content. This could apply to faculty in a university, trainers for an association, or CMPs who lead study groups in preparation for taking the CMP exam.

The Curriculum Guide Task Force reviewed the MBECS and analyzed each skill and subskill in terms of learning outcomes, depth of knowledge, and time to master the skill. The entire set of 100 MBECS skills and subskills fell into three categories in terms of depth of knowledge: what people employed at the meeting/event coordinator, manager, and director levels should know. Thus, MBECS can be covered in a sequential fashion that, generally, follows the career path of a professional from an entry-level position (coordinator), advancing to management (manager), and ultimately to executive level (director). The task force further determined that the coordinator- and manager-level skills could and should be possessed by someone graduating from an undergraduate college/university program. The director-level skills would be obtained through continuing education and professional seminars.

BOOK CONTENT

This content of this book is based on MBECS. It was developed using the output from the two task forces mentioned earlier. It is assumed that the reader has some basic knowledge of the MEEC industry and MEEC terminology. This knowledge can be obtained through a minimum of one or two years working in the industry or through formal education using books such as *Meetings, Expositions, Events, and Conventions: An Introduction* by George G. Fenich.

With this knowledge in hand, the reader can work through the content of this book. This book contains all the knowledge related to the **production and logistics** of

The Importance of Meeting and Event Production

By Robert Desautels

Visit Indy and 2013 President of Event Services Professionals Association (ESPA)

Meeting and event production is an activity that needs to be looked upon through the prism of the experience, not of functionality. The creativeness, effectiveness, and popularity of a meeting and its production are all gauged on how they are met by those in attendance. Regardless of discipline, convention and visitors bureaus (CVBs), hotels, convention centers, or special venues like stadiums and arenas, the manner—not just the actions in which the task is undertaken—will have a direct result on the end product. Given the multiple number of events, meetings, and other related activities that service managers undertake, the threat of standardizing how we prepare for and execute the servicing product is always out there. Avoiding the assembly line mentality of fulfilling our obligations as service managers is important to keep in mind. An imaginative presence in this work is always necessary. Bottom line: all meetings and events must be treated as unique and special activities that require individual attention.

Today's technology has changed the way we handle event management and production so much that it is tempting to lean or rely on technology to resolve issues and manage the process. The digital age is undeniably a massive aid in the function of meeting and event production, but it is not a "be-all" and "end-all." Familiarity with clients, paying close attention to their needs, and investigating new, improved, and outside-the-box thinking to improve the activity should be at the front door of providing quality service. Finally, it is the personal touch, the creative ideas, and ingenuity provided by the event professional that make all those served by not only notice and appreciate the event professional, but bring about the true success that the customer is trying to achieve for his or her constituency.

Courtesy of Robert Desautels, Visit Indy and 2013 President of Event Services Professionals Association (ESPA).

meetings and events that is expected of people who are to be employed at the coordinator and manager levels. This book does not address the knowledge of productions and logistics that should be possessed by an event professional at the director or executive level. A companion text, *Planning and Management of Meetings, Expositions, Events, and Conventions,* covers MBECS knowledge regarding planning meetings and events.

There are 14 chapters in this book. The topics range from managing the site to sales, public relations, and various aspects of marketing to human resources and training, food and beverage, and more. Each chapter begins with learning objectives and a chapter outline, both of which tie directly to MBECS. At the conclusion of each chapter, there is a chapter summary, chapter review questions, and a biography of the event professional who contributed the chapter content. Most importantly, there is also a checklist that indicates which MBECS standards and skills were covered in the chapter. Thus, after finishing this book, the reader can compile a self-assessment relative to MBECS standards and skills and determine what he or she knows and doesn't know. It is hoped that this book will provide content that helps prepare existing and potential event professionals.

Making the IT Fit

By

Celeste S. Anding,
CMP, Assistant Director of Events
Lisa Pedone, CMP, Senior Event Manager
Hilton New Orleans Riverside

It is the job of all great sales managers to show that their hotel is the best option for as many of the inquiries that come across their desk as possible. Most of the time, it truly is a natural fit of what the customer needs combined with what the hotel offers. But on occasion, the sales manager must complete the sale just to make the numbers and keep the hotel in business, regardless of the "fit." Then, the customer and the hotel will rely on the finesse and expertise of the event manager (convention services manager) to manipulate that contract and group into a "natural" fit that works for everyone. The key to this is knowledge and communication. Maybe the sleeping room process isn't as smooth as you would like because the client isn't well versed in housing; or maybe the language in the meeting room setup information is not the same as what you normally see. Or, maybe that sales manager sold something that just doesn't make sense! It is the job of the event manager (EM) to make it a success. The EM must ask the *right* questions, in the *right* way, to get the *right* information, from the *right* client. The foregoing can change from the time that the contract is signed to the time of the actual event. The EM must then reword, rework, and restyle the event plan so that it becomes workable inside the property with all of its quirks and idiosyncrasies. Most of this can be done with intense attention to detail during the planning phase and a vast knowledge of just about everything! Alas, many, many times, "it" is still something that is created onsite. "It" may be as simple as checking in with the customer each day so that they see you, and not just your operations staff. Sometimes, it is being the operations staff yourself—checking everything from the pillow fluff in each VIP's guest room to the direction of the logo on the pencils in each meeting room. Only the EM will know what will make for a "smooth-as-glass" meeting. And only the EM should communicate all of this information in as much detail and words as needed to the operating departments in a hotel or venue. No event could happen without us. Nor can an event happen without details, knowledge, communication, and changes!

SUMMARY

This chapter is meant to provide an introduction to the MEEC industry and to this book. It lends insight into the magnitude of the industry and the various career opportunities that exist. The chapter provides a basic underpinning for terminology and definitions used in MEEC. It also provides a discussion of the historical evolution of MEEC from the early days through the development of a common set of knowledge, skills, and abilities (KSAs) required of an event professional. There is an overview of the Meeting and Business Event Competency Standards (MBECS), which incorporates these KSAs; MBECS is provided as well as a discussion of how it can be used. The end of the chapter explains how the content in this book is based on MBECS.

About ESPA, the Event Service Professionals Association

In 1988, the Association for Convention Operations Management (ACOM) was founded as the first and only association to serve convention services managers. In September 2011, the association changed its name to Event Service Professionals Association (ESPA). The new name more accurately embraces the diversity of the roles that ESPA members play and their evolving responsibilities in their venues and cities.

ESPA is dedicated to elevating the event and convention service profession and to preparing members, through education and networking, for their pivotal role in innovative and successful event execution.

ESPA members hold many positions in convention and visitor bureaus, convention centers, conference centers, hotels, and resorts. Some of these include:

- Convention service coordinators, managers, and directors
- Event service coordinators, managers and directors
- Housing managers
- Operations managers, directors
- Directors of convention/trade shows
- Catering managers and directors
- Audio visual companies
- Decorator management companies

Through education and networking, members learn skills to be more effective service managers; gain a better understanding of the breadth of their role; and learn about meeting planners' expectations when hosting a meeting at their hotel, center, or city. Visit www.espaonline.org for more information.

Courtesy of Lynn McCullough, ESPA Executive Director

KEY WORDS AND TERMS

production   MBECS   production and logistics
event professionals

REVIEW AND DISCUSSION QUESTIONS

1. What is MBECS?
2. What led to the development of MBECS?
3. How can MBECS be used in career development?
4. What is CMP-IS?
5. What is planning?
6. What are some of the segments of the MEEC industry?
7. What is ESPA? What does the organization do?

REFERENCES

CIC. (2010). *The Economic Significance of Meetings to the U.S. Economy.* Washington, DC: Convention Industry Council.

Fenich, G. G. (2012a). *Meetings, Expositions, Events, and Conventions: An Introduction to the Industry* (3rd ed.). Upper Saddle River, NJ: Pearson Education Inc.

Fenich, G. G. (2012b). *The New Meeting and Business Events Competency Standards.* Published proceedings, AHTMM Conference, Corfu, Greece.

MPI. (2010). *FutureWatch.* Dallas, TX: Meeting Professionals International.

MPI. (2012a). *Future of Meetings.* Dallas, TX: Meeting Professionals International.

MPI. (2012b). *Business Barometer Annual.* Dallas, TX: Meeting Professionals International.

ABOUT THE CHAPTER CONTRIBUTOR

Kathryn Hashimoto, PhD, is an associate professor in the School of Hospitality Leadership at East Carolina University. She is a prolific writer, having authored over 10 books on different aspects of the hospitality industry.

CHAPTER 2

On-Site Meeting and Event Management

Learning Objectives

Upon completion of this chapter, the reader should be able to:

- Identify key players and understand on-site meeting/event roles and responsibilities
- Understand the importance of a communications framework
- Describe the communications procedures and protocols
- Explain the importance of timing and sequencing
- Explain the importance of knowing the physical resources of a venue
- List the tasks to include in a timeline for a production schedule
- Discuss the process of move-in and move-out
- Explain the importance of communicating with all stakeholders
- Identify what an event professional looks for during the final walk-through before the start of the meeting
- Discuss the importance of coordinating with colleagues and service personnel
- Discuss the importance of briefing all personnel
- Explain the need to monitor activities during the meeting/event
- List the things that a meeting event professional needs to review when monitoring the room block during the meeting
- Discuss why a production schedule is needed when the meeting ends
- Discuss the importance of leaving adequate time for teardown

A stage is an important element of the site at many events.
Photo courtesy of Freeman Audio Visual Solutions.

Chapter Outline

Introduction

Communications

    Identify Key Players and Understand Roles and Responsibilities

    Importance of a Communication Framework

    Follow Communication Procedures and Protocols

    Create a Flowchart of Communication

    Communication Resource

    Staff Training

    Monitor Communication On-Site

Logistics Plan for Setup and Teardown

    Timing and Sequence

    Availability of Resources

    Access to Site

    Detailed Production Schedule

    Drayage/Material Handling

    Plan for Human Resources

Site Move-In and Move-Out

Communication with Stakeholders and Constituents

Setting Up the Site

    Site Access

    Production Schedule

    Follow-Up

    Arrival of Related Groups

    Technical Rehearsal Time

    Equipment Check

    Receiving

    Interaction with Personnel

Keeping Track of the Site During Meeting/Convention/Event

    Monitor Meeting or Event Operation

    Analyze and Remedy Problems

    Need for Additional Resources

    Interaction with Appropriate Parties

    Delivery and Implementation of Services

    Hotel Room Blocks

- Explain who should be included in the final site inspection of the property
- Describe what happens in a post-con meeting
- Discuss the coordination of shipping

From the Venue CSM perspective

Julie Barnes, the Convention Services Manager (CSM) for a large hotel in Dallas, Texas, is amazed at how many event professionals are unprepared for the on-site meeting/event experience. Many don't plan ahead, and it becomes very expensive when they make changes on-site. Julie explains that some event professionals are outstanding. For example, Pat Jones, an event professional for a large association, requests that the hotel sales representative include the CSM in a review meeting before the contract is signed. During this meeting, the details are discussed and Julie can catch things that may be overlooked. Did Pat consider how much time it would take to set up the closing session? Who is she using for her audiovisual (AV) needs? How many boxes is she expecting to ship? For her AV needs, Julie suggests that Pat contact the hotel AV since she has a complicated production schedule and all her events will take place at the hotel. Another thing that Julie appreciates about Pat is that she shares a report that includes a complete history of her meeting/event, including the use of hotel outlets, fitness center, and spa. Finally, when the meeting/event is over, Pat sends the CSM and venue staff personalized thank-you notes containing a gratuity to show how much she appreciates that they go the extra mile for her.

Unfortunately, many event professionals treat the CSM like an order taker, do not return phone calls and e-mails, make constant changes to the banquet event orders (BEOs), expect the hotel to work with vendors that do not carry proper insurance, and never say thank you. Julie recalls a complicated meeting/event that required the staff to work very long hours. As a thank you, the event professional left the staff cheap-looking welcome bags with the conference brochures still inside.

"Most people have no idea of what my job entails," explains Julie. "On any given day, I may be working with five groups staying at the hotel whose meetings/events are in various stages of completion; meeting with event professionals who have meetings at to the hotel; and reconciling documents with event professionals who just finished their meetings. My job is very busy and stressful, but it changes each day and I love it!"

INTRODUCTION

After the event has been planned, the contracts signed, the marketing material finalized, and the attendees are starting to arrive at the meeting/event (synonymous with *event*), the event professional's work is beginning to take on a new focus: on-site meeting/event management. This requires skills in time management, communication, and problem solving. All the previous months of work are coming together and it is now *showtime*! Throughout the event, key elements must be carried out. The organization mission statement guides everything that is done, including on-site management. The mission statement for a religious organization will be very different from that of a large corporation. Think about how the event requirements will differ from food and beverage choices to entertainment for a religious group versus a corporate group. In addition to the mission statement, the meeting/event objectives will guide on-site meeting/event activities. Is the focus of the meeting/event to educate, network, launch a new product, reward employees etc.?

Another key component is the attendee profile. Who will attend the meeting—men, women, or families? What is the average age of the group? What areas of the venue will they use when they are not attending the meeting? Sharing this information with all the stakeholders is important to the success of the meeting/event. The operative questions regarding the group are 1) who are they and 2) why are they here?

The location of the meeting/event will dictate the types of activities and the processes to make them happen. Event professionals should consult with the convention and visitors bureau (CVB)/destination marketing organization (DMO) to identify legislation and regulations that may affect the meeting/event. This includes understanding tax structure, how to work with unions, how to obtain permits, and so on.

The event professional must create a safe environment so that attendees can focus on the objective(s) of the meeting/event. On-site, the event professional is assumed to be the one who can answer all the questions; this includes who to contact in case of emergency, the location of the nearest hospital, if the venue has defibrillators, and if the venue staff is trained to use them. The event professional should determine if emergency medical services (EMS) need to be on-site for the meeting/event and have a plan of action if there is a fire, flood, hurricane, or act of terrorism (for more detailed information, see Chapter 4 on risk management in *Planning and Management of Meetings, Expositions, Events, and Conventions,* by Fenich). Prepared event professionals have thought all of these things through and have a plan B and even a plan C for emergencies.

All the details listed above and more are located in the **Event Specifications Guide (ESG)**. The ESG is the preferred term for a comprehensive document that outlines the complete requirements and instructions for an event. This document is typically authored by the event professional and is shared with all appropriate vendors as a vehicle to communicate the expectations of services for a project. It is sometimes called a staging guide or resume (see APEX Glossary at http://www.conventionindustry.org/StandardsPractices/APEX/glossary.aspx.)

The ESG is in the form of a large binder with multiple tabs; it contains all the requirements for a meeting and outlines the instruction for each part of the meeting. All or a portion of this document will be shared with vendors. The ESG is critical in understanding how all the elements of the meeting/event come together. This document should be organized so that it is easy to follow; then, if something were to happen to the event professional, someone could review the ESG and continue with the meeting/event without any interruptions. The ESG will be used throughout the meeting/event; the guide holds the answers to the many on-site questions. As we begin this chapter on on-site meetings/events, the ESG will be referenced often. Details regarding **functions** that were agreed to months in advance are in the ESG and must be communicated to the on-site team.

This chapter attempts to encompass the on-site tasks that would be used for the production and logistics of a meeting/conference, a trade show/exhibition, and an event/special event; in other words, the MEEC industry (meeting, expositions, events, and conventions). The general term "meeting/event" will include meetings, expositions, events, and conventions; the term "event professional" will be used to indicate the role of the individual who is responsible for the planning, production, and on-site logistics of the meeting/event.

COMMUNICATIONS

Identify Key Players and Understand Roles and Responsibilities

The meeting event professional must establish a communication framework before the start of the meeting to ensure that each vendor understands his or her role in making the meeting a success. A pre-planning meeting organized by the event professional with all vendors should be scheduled one month to two weeks prior to the meeting to review the details of the meeting/event, build relationships among vendors, and establish communications protocols. Another "pre-con" meeting organized by the venue representative will be held a few days before the meeting/event to review any changes and to finalize the details.

The size and complexity of the meeting/event will determine the vendors used and the key players needed for the meeting/event. A conference of 4,000 that includes concurrent sessions, a general session, and an exposition may utilize all or some of the vendors listed below. Each vendor has a specific role in making the meeting/event a success; each has a point of contact and scope of authority that the event professional must understand prior to the meeting.

- Hotel venue(s) – Once the contract is signed, the event professional will work with the venue **Convention Services Manager (CSM)**; it is his/her responsibility to coordinate with all the hotel contacts that the event professional will need. This includes the banquet or catering department, shipping, rooms, bellman, electrician, audiovisual, and others.
- Convention center – The CSM plays a key role in helping the event professional coordinate all the departments needed to make the event a success; this includes electricians, shipping, loading docks, and more. If the meeting requires extensive food and beverage, the banquet/catering manager may be included.
- **Audiovisual contractor** – Will supply the technical staff and the audiovisual equipment, for example, projectors, screens, sound systems, video and staging (APEX Glossary http://www.conventionindustry.org/glossary).
- **Production company** – May be hired to implement all or part of an event. The company features special effects and theatrical acts (APEX Glossary http://www.conventionindustry.org/glossary).
- **Contractor** – A general term for the individual or organization that provides services to a meeting or trade show (APEX Glossary http://www.conventionindustry.org/glossary). The contractor may be called a decorator or general services contractor and may have an exclusive contact within a venue and/or operate as an independent. The event professional may hire specialty contractors to handle floral design, take care of event staging, produce a trade show, and so on. (For more detailed information, see Chapter 6 on service contractors in *Meetings, Expositions, Events, and Conventions: An Introduction to the Industry*, 3rd ed., by Fenich.)
- Destination management company – May be hired to assist the event professional with transportation, event production, and activities such as pre-, post-, and spouse tours and off-site events, such as museum tours, VIP tours, theme park outings, tours of historic homes, golf, cruises, etc. (For more detailed information, see Chapter 7 on destination management companies in *Meetings, Expositions, Events, and Conventions: An Introduction to the Industry*, 3rd ed., by Fenich.)

- Destination marketing organization/convention and visitors bureau – Is helpful for the pre-event and can help on-site with temporary staff and promotion of future meeting/events. (For more detailed information, see Chapter 3 on destination marketing organizations in *Meetings, Expositions, Events, and Conventions: An Introduction to the Industry,* 3rd ed., by Fenich.)
- Other companies may include a registration company to keep track of pre- and on-site registration; a **housing** company to assist with room block, a transportation company for handling transfers, a travel company, a security company, a floral company, postal and packaging services, an entertainment agency, translators, speakers' bureaus, temporary staffing companies, and so on.

Importance of a Communication Framework

Regardless of the size of the meeting/event, it is important that each vendor and staff member understand his/her role so that the meeting runs smoothly. Two pre-convention (pre-con) meetings are held. The first is a pre-planning meeting organized by the event professional that is held one month to three weeks prior to the meeting/event and may be in person or via phone. The second pre-convention meeting will be held on-site the day prior to the start of the meeting/event. The pre-planning meeting is an excellent time to build relationships and to review expectations. The event professional will run the pre-planning meeting; the agenda typically starts with a welcome and a review of the meeting/event objectives and the attendee profile. Each vendor will be introduced and will share with the team his or her role in the meeting. Once introductions are made, the group will review the **program book**, the printed schedule of events, the location of function rooms, and other pertinent information (see APEX Glossary www.conventionindustry.org/glossary). The program book may be referred to by event professionals as their operations manual and is a part of the ESG that is shared with vendors and staff.

During the pre-planning meeting, each vendor is able to communicate his/her needs to make his or her portion of the meeting/event a success. For example, the line may be working with an entertainment group that requires more electricity than is available at the host venue; the venue can address this issue by making more power available or can suggest a company that can provide generators.

Follow Communication Procedures and Protocols

The pre-planning and the pre-con will include a discussion regarding on-site protocol. If an attendee has an emergency, who should be called? If attendees report that a meeting room is too cold, who should be contacted? What if the AV in a room is not working? Who has the authority to order more coffee? Questions like this are addressed, and the protocol for addressing the issue is reviewed.

Create a Flowchart of Communication

Before the start of the meeting/event, the event professional will have a plan for communication. This may be illustrated as an organization chart or simply given in writing to the staff, venue, and contractors in advance. A clear understanding of team member role and scope of responsibility is needed for the success of a meeting/event. Because of the responsibility of the event professional, he/she will want to be kept informed of everything that happens during the meeting/event, especially things that will add cost to the meeting. On-site, the protocol may be for volunteers to contact a meeting sponsor staff member and for the staff to contact the AV technical with AV issues; the technician will then contact the event professional. With so many things going on during the meeting/event, a chain of command must be established to keep things running smoothly.

Communication Resource

Accessing information quickly will improve communication throughout the meeting/event. A document containing all contacts with phone numbers should be distributed to all staff and team members. The communication resource is included in the program book/operations manual and will include all vendors with names and contact information, board members, and company VIPs. Although most staff members will never have the need to directly speak to most of the contacts listed in the communication resource, the information is useful. For example, while a staff member is helping to set up the registration area, a representative from a floral company stops by and looks for the place to deliver centerpieces. The staff member recognizes the name of the florist from the communication resource and quickly contacts the event professional to let him/her know that the centerpieces have arrived and finds out what directions should be given to the florist.

Staff Training

On-site communications is critical to the success of the meeting/event. During training, staff members will receive the updated program listing all vendors and contact numbers. Training frequently occurs on-site in the staff room, which is sometimes referred to as headquarters, the day prior to the meeting. All staff should receive training on how to use communication systems (two-way radios and/or DataTel systems), answer the phone in headquarters and take messages, use the staff copier, printer, and any electronic equipment they may need to use. When using two-way radios, staff must be issued a radio and understand that they are responsible for keeping track of the equipment and recharging the radio each day. A daily check-in and check-out list is an easy way to keep track of radios. There is nothing worse than starting the meeting with dead batteries and losing communication with team members.

In addition, training should include what to do if communication fails—perhaps an emergency occurs and there is no radio communication. What is the plan if the team is unable to communicate with the meeting event professional? The plan should be discussed in advance of the meeting and reviewed on-site.

Monitor Communication On-Site

Once the meeting begins, it can take on a life of its own. One change in the program can affect multiple vendors. Communication on-site must be open and issues addressed immediately. The job of the event professional on-site is to keep the meeting/event flowing and ensure that things in the ESG are completed and that the meeting objectives are met. A morning meeting with all vendors gives everyone the opportunity to review the events of the day before and prepare for the activities of the current day. The event professional may set up meetings with vendors throughout the day to check on the progress.

LOGISTICS PLAN FOR SETUP AND TEARDOWN

Timing and Sequence

Regardless of the size of a meeting/event, a timeline is created to cover the procedures from setup to teardown. The **time line** includes detailed information as to each task that needs to be accomplished and is the core of the program plan (APEX Glossary http://www.conventionindustry.org/glossary). The time line will address the questions of who needs to come into the venue first to set up the ballroom for a general session and/or awards banquet. For example, the **rigging** and then the **trusses** must be set up first in order to hang the lights and the amplifiers. Directing the activities of a meeting/event can be compared with someone getting up in the morning. One does not wake up dressed and ready to go. There is sequence of things that must be done; select clothes, shower, put on clothes, put on shoes, and have a final look at oneself before going out the door.

Availability of Resources

Staffing is needed throughout the meeting for registration, as room monitors, function setup and teardown, deliveries, and so on. The event professional must work with the venue to determine the level of staffing. Although the venue is expected to provide labor to arrange the meeting rooms, it cannot be assumed that staff set up things like rented chair covers, linens, and centerpieces. The longer the time needed to set up a room, the fewer staff is needed. The opposite is also true: The shorter the time before the function starts, the more staff is needed.

Temporary staffing and CVB registration/temp staffing can be used for jobs like registration, room monitors, and **speaker ready room**. Many CVBs offer discounted or free staffing based on the number of hotel rooms used for a meeting/event. When hiring a temp staff from an agency, the event professional needs to check the minimum number of hours required and the cost of parking for workers. When planning a multiday meeting, the event professional should request that the same temp workers be available each day. This avoids the need for daily training.

Hotels only maintain a certain inventory of tables, chairs, rigging, linen, decorations, and so on at the property. The event professional should work with the hotel CSM to identify the availability of all equipment and décor needed for the meeting/event. If the event professional requires a room set with 30 chairs and 72-inch tables and the hotel does not have them or if the tables are being used by another group, the event professional will need to change the table size or make arrangements for tables to be delivered. This will be the case for all equipment used for the meeting/event. It is better to reserve equipment needed before the meeting/event begins rather than scramble at the last minute.

Access to Site

Depending on the complexity of the meeting/event, the move-in may start several days to a week before the start of the first function. Arrangements need to be made prior to the signing of the contract as to the date and time that the event professional may move into a space. In the months leading up to the meeting, the event professional should contact the venue to ensure that the space contracted is still available and to determine the time that vendors can arrive on property and the procedures for **load in/out**. A large trade show takes days to move in and set up prior to day one of the show. A typical convention with trade show will take two days to move in, three days for the convention, and one to two days to move out: This means the facility is booked for a solid week for a three-day convention.

Detailed Production Schedule

The event professional works with many vendors to create a time line for production. Each vendor in turn will create a time line for his or her staff to complete the task. The meeting/event function space is a blank canvas until the event professional works with the venue and/or contractor to create **floor plans**. Today, floor plans are created electronically using software such as Meeting Matrix and ExpoCad. Once the floor plans are created, they are sent to the event professional for approval. Functions for larger groups and/or those that require extensive rigging or include pyrotechnics will be sent to the **fire marshal** for approval. This process can take up to two weeks and should be built into the time line. Once the floor plans are finalized, they are sent to all vendors, audiovisual production teams, and others.

To produce a large event, the vendors will need to arrive at least three days in advance to begin their work. The venue will begin the process by setting up the stage and the rigging that will hold the trusses; the audiovisual company will then set up technical equipment that will be used. Once the staging and equipment has arrived, the technical crew can begin to set up the lights, screens, and sound and to prepare for the technical rehearsal and the show rehearsal. Once all equipment is tested for the technical rehearsal, the show rehearsal can begin. Allow 30 minutes per speaker for the show rehearsal. When the function is over, the items are removed in the reverse order. The last thing to be removed is the rigging.

The event professional must focus on the total meeting/event as well as each function. The room setup for the opening general session is just as important as the concurrent sessions for the meeting to be a success. The event professional uses the ESG to review each function sheet/banquet event order (BEO) and confirm the room setup; the setup will also include pre-function space, speaker ready room, staff room, hospitality rooms, and storage. Each room must be set up well in advance of the function and must be set to the specifications listed on the BEO. The event professional checks with the venue CSM to see how far in advance each room will be 100 percent set, how far in advance the AC or heat comes on, and how far from the start of the meeting/event the food and beverage gets set out.

The event professional will assess the complexity of the functions to determine how many personnel are required for setup and teardown. For functions that require complex décor, volunteers may be brought in to help with setup.

As the staff members, vendors, and volunteers come together, they must understand their individual roles and responsibilities. The event professional is the leader and will assist the team in defining roles and responsibilities and will oversee the production schedule. Each contact will work with the team at his/her company to ensure that the meeting/event is a success.

The venue CSM will work with his/her employees to ensure that all the activities that take place at the hotel, including function rooms, food and beverages, shipping, and so on are completed directed by the event professional.

The convention center CSM and staff will oversee the activities that take place at the convention center; this includes all the function space, food and beverage, shipping, and so on.

The general service contractor will allocate staff to work on functions that are held at both the hotel and convention center. This includes setup for exhibitions, registration, staging, audiovisual, and so on.

As mentioned before, the event professional will work with many contractors; each should have a clear understanding of his/her role and responsibility for the current meeting/event. Many contractors offer multiple services, and the event professional may not select all the services offered. For example, Freeman Company is known for exhibitor services but also has an audiovisual division. The event professional may select Freeman for his or her exhibitor needs and PSAV as the audiovisual provider for the meeting. The team must be aware which contractors are providing which services for the meeting/event.

Drayage/Material Handling

An important element in the setup and teardown of a meeting is the handling of supplies and creation of a system to ensure that all items shipped arrive on time and if needed are returned to their destinations.

During the site inspection, the event professional should identify the location and the number of loading docks and discuss their availability. Prior to the meeting/event, the event professional will work with the hotel to determine how the hotel will receive the shipments and how far in advance. Many venues limit the number of days prior to an event that shipping will be received. The venue may have secured space to store all items, but if items are not removed in a timely manner, the event professional will be charged; other venues will have a general area where all shipments are received.

Venues will charge to store and to move all shipping boxes. Cost may be based on weight (hundred weight) and/or per box. To keep track of shipping all boxes, the meeting event professional will create an inventory list that identifies the contents in each box. This inventory sheet is kept in the ESG. Many event professionals will provide guidelines for vendors that ship items for a specific meeting/event. One of the first duties when an event professional arrives at a venue is to check with shipping to ensure that all boxes have arrived.

Many items that are shipped for use in the meeting/event will need to be returned. The boxes in which the items arrived must be clearly marked and storage arranged in advance with the hotel or venue. If not, these items may be removed or destroyed. For example, during a particular awards night, an event professional wanted to display the awards for the function and later repack them to send to the recipients after the meeting. Subsequent to when the boxes with the awards in them were unpacked but before the function was over, the hotel staff destroyed the boxes. The event professional then needed to find an alternative way to re-box the awards and ship them back to the recipients safely.

Other shipping options used by event professionals include working with a general service contractor to pick up all shipping from the meeting sponsor, storing the items, and delivering them to the venue and/or using a third party to assemble and ship items like welcome bags. Shipping all welcome bag items to the venue for assembly on-site can be pricey and time-consuming. A third-party fulfillment organization is an option.

Plan for Human Resources

As the event professional assesses the need for staff, he/she must consider the setup, running of the meeting/event, and the teardown. The rule of thumb is that it will take more people and time to set up the meeting/event than to tear it down. When hiring labor, the cost must be considered for regular work hours or for Saturday, Sunday, and holidays, which will cost more. The event professional should also take into account the availability of labor at the location, the skill level of the labor, and if the venue's location requires using union labor. When working with labor unions, it is important to understand all the rules and regulations and to be prepared to create a plan that will include working with multiple unions. When working with temp staffing agencies, be sure to check on the minimum number of hours each temp is required to work. You would not want to pay someone for four hours when you only need help for two.

Site Move-In and Move-Out

The details of the move-in and move-out are mapped out months in advance of the meeting/event and are finalized at the pre-con. Many things must be considered when creating a process to move in and move out of a venue. The event professional must coordinate with the venue to determine when the loading dock is available; many venues have hours reserved for receiving food and beverage and are not open at this time. The number and size of the loading docks available, and number of trucks that can load and unload in a given time frame, must be considered as well as the location of the **marshaling yard** located in relation to loading dock.

When working with contractors, the event professional must coordinate with the contractor and venue on the move-in and move-out time times available. Everyone works best if the procedure is normal, but sometimes issues cannot be avoided. There should be a clear understanding of the process and the time line; this must be communicated in writing with clear and precise language.

When moving out, the condition of the space must be returned to the condition that it was accepted. The event professional must review facility rules and follow the guidelines. Many venues will have a weight limit for signs and may not allow the event professional to hang signs without permission. The event professional should ensure that all precautions are taken to protect the facility. If the meeting requires the use of liquids, then the floor must be protected by using **Visqueen**. Before leaving a venue, the event professional should conduct a walk-through with the CSM or designated representative of the venue to inspect its condition. The event professional and the venue representative should both "sign off" on a document to acknowledge the condition of the space before and after the meeting/event.

Communication with Stakeholders and Constituents

The details of the setup and teardown should be communicated orally during the pre-con and morning staff meetings. It is important that vendors work together to ensure that each piece is ready before the next action item is to occur. This communication helps to make everyone on the team aware of the things that need to be done. Because so many things affect each other, this awareness can help identify problems before they happen. If a problem should occur, such as the time to get into the ballroom to set up for the general session is delayed for several hours, the event professional needs to have a plan to communicate with all vendors and staff affected by this change. One small adjustment can quickly have a domino effect.

SETTING UP THE SITE

Site Access

The event professional will work with the venue CSM to review the rooms that will be used before accepting them. Once the event professional and his/her team take possession of the space, they are responsible for it. The event professional may be issued a key or a set of keys for access. If the keys are distributed to the staff, they should be assigned and include a check-in and check-out system. Lost keys will have to be replaced, and this can be pricey.

Production Schedule

Many things will come together during the setup of the meeting/event. For some things there is a set order; others can be done simultaneously, that is, multiple rooms can be set up at the same time. It is important for the team to know what is happening and the order in which it will happen. This is listed in the program book/production schedule. The following groups should be given a copy of the production schedule and be made aware of any changes:

- **Staff:** includes all members of the team
- **Suppliers:** rental companies, florists, venues, and any specialty companies used for the meeting
- **Service Contractors:** general service contractors if the meeting/event includes an exposition and/or audiovisual contractor, **security contractor** and other contractors needed for the meeting
- **DMC:** needs a copy of the schedule to coordinate all the services purchased; this may include, transportation, event production, audiovisual, and so on.

Follow-Up

During the setup, the event professional and his/her team will check and recheck to see that everything needed for the meeting has arrived. Checks will be made at the loading dock to see that equipment and all special deliveries arrive on time. If something does not arrive as scheduled, the event professional will need to follow up with the vendor to arrange a delivery before the event begins.

Arrival of Related Groups

In addition to deliveries, electricians and Internet vendors will arrive to set up power and Internet access; contractors begin setting up the registration and exhibition area; rigging companies raise banners and staging; audiovisual technicians set up sound systems and screens and create **gobos** (goes before optics); specialty vendors arrive (such as a balloon company to create balloon arches); temp companies arrive with staff; entertainers arrive to rehearse; and security and florist personnel arrive. All the function space moves from a blank canvas to a city that reflects the mission and objectives of the meeting/event. (For more detailed information, see Chapter 2 on strategic planning in *Planning and Management of Meetings, Expositions, Events, and Conventions,* by Fenich.) The event professional is the point person for all these groups and must communicate where things are located and then check and recheck that all is in place according to the ESG.

Technical Rehearsal Time

The ballroom area will transform from open space into a stage that will hold speakers and entertainers and will become the focal part of the meeting/event. Bringing this together takes time before the meeting/event begins. The concept and design are done in advance. On-site, the venue staff sets the rigging and the production company and/or the audiovisual company sets up the sound and lighting. At least one day is devoted for setup, a second day for the technical rehearsal, and a third day for the run-through. The **technical rehearsal** will include testing of all the equipment used for sound as well as the visual and special effects. The **run-through** (sometime referred to as the show rehearsal) will include a complete review of the general session and will include speakers, entertainers, and performers. Times for the rehearsal and run-through are included in the event professional's time line. Thirty minutes should be reserved for each speaker. In addition, each contractor will have a time line that is communicated to his or her staff as to when things need to be set up.

Equipment Check

Before the start of the event, the event professional will conduct a final walk-through with the suppliers to check the room setup, audiovisual equipment, power, and Internet access. Registration computers will be checked as well as the telephones, two-way communication systems, and the equipment in the staff office. Everything must be ready before the start of the meeting/event.

Receiving

Items will be arriving throughout the meeting/event. The event professional must communicate with the venue to understand the shipping and receiving rules and procedures. Most hotels have limited space and will charge for deliveries and storage. Items will only be accepted and stored for a short time period before the meeting sponsor will incur additional charges.

The event professional will work with the CSM and/or directly with the venue shipping and receiving department to check on items as they arrive. The storage for all

TABLE 1 Sample Move-In Schedule Prior to Start of the Conference

Monday: Day 1	MOVE-IN: Meeting Sponsor Staff/ Freeman/ J&S AV/Hotel/HBGCC	Loading Docks for Hall C, 615 S. Bowie
8:00 am–5:00 pm	Freeman marks exhibit hall floor	Exhibit Hall C
8:00 am–5:00 pm	Freeman to set up registration and exhibitor registration	East Registration
10:00 am–5:00 pm	Set up sponsor office (lock up) & water service	207 A
	Freeman to transfer boxes of materials, freezers, shoulder bags, proceedings to HBGCC (Stage in Hall C)	216 A & B & 207 A; East Registration
	J&S Audiovisual, Inc. Office move-in, delivery and setup	215
11:00 am–12:30 pm	Delivery of pres. letter to each hotel	

Tuesday: Day 2	MOVE-IN: Convention Center	
	SWVS Office (set up office)	**207 A**
7:00 am	Emergency medical	
7:00 am	Security begins	Exhibit Hall C
All day	HBGCC & J & S A V Boneyard setup and delivery; assign radios (23)	215
All day	J Spargo to deliver computers, equipment, and set up reg. area	East Registration
All day	JSA & meeting sponsor staff set up registration area thru Wednesday	East Registration
All day	Freeman Electric Company to set up electricity	Exhibit Halls C, East Registration
7:00 am–5:00 pm	Smart City to set up phone lines; T-1	East Registration; Exhibit Hall C (VIN); 205, 207A, 207 B, 209, 216A
7:00 am–Noon	Freeman set up freezer, refrigerator, and lab office	216 A & 216 B
	Freeman set up LABS (lock up rooms)	217A, B, C, D; 218
	Freeman set up exhibit hall	Exhibit Hall C
	Freeman set up exhibitor registration	East Registration
	Freeman set up REGISTRATION AREA & MIS lock up OFC	East Registration
	Freeman set up speaker-ready Room	207 B
All day	Freeman set up 4 table tops; CVB; Dallas CVB; creative dining concierge	East Registration
All day	Freeman to hang sponsor welcome & banners throughout Convention Center	Street, Level, Concourse, Level 2
All day	Pre-set room for computer software demos	205
10:00 am–5:00 pm	Continue to set up Meeting Sponsor Ofc., J&S to install computer, printer, fax, copier	207 A
2:30 pm–3:00 pm	Pre-con meetings all hotels & housing (Bitsy)	207 A
3:00 pm–4:00 pm	Pre-con meeting with Convention Center, RK Group, JSA, housing, all vendors, hotels, meeting sponsor staff,) J & S to assign radios (get 23 radios)	**207 A**

Wednesday: Day 3	SETUP: CONTINUED	
6:00 am	SWVS Staff Office (cont. breakfast)	207 A
All Day	Continue setup - Freeman - LABS by Thurs. 10:00 am	217A, B, C, D; 218;
All Day	Continue setup - Freeman - registration, exhibit hall	East Reg, Hall C; Concourse
by Noon	Continue setup phone lines, electric	East Reg, Hall C; Concourse
6:00 am	Security (schedule on separate page)	East Reg, Hall C; Concourse

(Continued)

TABLE 1 (Continued)

Wednesday: Day 3	SETUP: CONTINUED	
8:00 am–5:00 pm	Emergency medical	
8:00 am–4:00 pm	Continue setup HQ Office, J&S computer, printer, fax	207 A
8:00 am on	Freezer from Lowe's to be delivered (move to 216 A)	Docks Bowie St.
8:00 am–5:00 pm	Exhibitor registration/information open	East Registration
8:00 am–5:00 pm	EXHIBITOR MOVE-IN	Exhibit Hall C
All day	Set up speaker ready room & lost and found (water cooler)	207 B
All day	Set up technician lounge & water cooler	209
All day	HBGCC / R K Group set up water coolers	Exhibit Hall C, Concourse, Ballroom levels
All day	J&S AV boneyard	215
All day	LAB setup continued	216 A, 216 B; 217A, B, C, D; 218;
All day	Communication center & cyber café set up by VIN	Exhibit Hall C, # 200
All day	Set up hospitality area, hang banner by Freeman & RK Group	Concourse Corner

Wednesday: Day 4	Registration Open Setup A	
6:00 am	SWVS staff office (cont. breakfast)	207 A
All day	Continue setup - Freeman - LABS by Thurs. 10:00 am	217A, B, C, D; 218;
All day	Continue setup - Freeman - registration, exhibit hall	East Reg, Hall C; Concourse
by Noon	Continue setup phone lines, electric	East Reg, Hall C; Concourse
6:00 AM	Security (schedule on separate page)	East Reg, Hall C; Concourse
8:00 am–5:00 pm	Emergency medical	
8:00 am–4:00 pm	Continue setup SWVS Office, J&S computer, printer, fax	207 A

items related to the meeting is one of the first things that event professionals will check upon arrival at a venue. A count is taken to confirm that all shipments have arrived and in what condition they are.

Interaction with Personnel

An event professional's primary point of contact at a venue is the CSM, who typically arranges the meeting/event specifications with all hotel departments. Once the event professional arrives at a venue, the CSM will meet with him/her to review the details of the meeting/event. When possible, the CSM will arrange for the event professional to meet with the venue staff that the event professional will be interacting with, including hotel rooms' manager, front desk personnel, banquet staff, bellman, shipping, security, and others. In order to simplify the communication process, the CSM should be the first point of contact when something related to the meeting is needed. If the CSM is not available and the event professional must contact a department immediately, he/she should inform the CSM after the issue is resolved.

As mentioned in the meeting setup, the event professional must not only interact with representatives of the venue but with *all* contractors, specialty vendors, VIPs, and others. The event professional becomes the focal point for answers to all questions: ranging from what to do with an attendee who said that he registered online but does not have confirmation to a data projector that's not working in one of the breakout rooms. The event professional must know the status of the meeting/event at all times.

Even with all the months of planning, the event professional must be prepared for the unexpected. Examples might include: 1) the venue sold one of your meeting rooms, 2) the keynote speaker becomes ill, 3) construction is blocking the place that you planned to load and unload your attendees. The key to handling changes is to remember the safety of the attendees and what can be done to achieve the meeting/event objective(s). The event professional must show confidence in the decisions made and communicate changes with the staff and everyone who will be affected.

All staff and team members must be updated on the progress of the meeting/event, including setup, showtime, and teardown. A briefing meeting each morning before the first function of the day is an excellent way to ensure communication. The previous day should be reviewed to go over the problems that occurred and how they were handled; the events of the current day should also be discussed. With all the key contractors in the room, problems can be discussed face to face and quickly resolved. The briefing meeting is also a time for the meeting/event event professional to give everyone an update as to the registration numbers, review what people are saying about the meeting, and praise the team for making the meeting a success.

KEEPING TRACK OF THE SITE DURING THE MEETING/CONVENTION/EVENT

Monitor Meeting or Event Operation

The meeting/event begins; the event professional depends on the entire team to help monitor all activities and ensure that functions start and end on time. Because the event professional cannot be everywhere at the same time, the CSM and her/his team work with the meeting/event planning staff to monitor all aspects of the meeting/event, including meal functions, breaks, any special deliveries, and so on. Staff from the meeting sponsor may be delegated to monitor rooms, assist exhibitors, remove or add signs, and assist with the departure of tours.

Before each activity, the event professional will check the room's setup and audiovisual requirements and compare the room setup with the BEOs. If any changes are needed, the venue's CSM and/or service contractor will be contacted. After the activity takes place, the event professional will make notes about whether the correct menu was served, the number of people that attended, and any changes that were made on-site. The event professional will save these notes for future reference.

Various techniques are used to monitor activities during the meeting/event. Walking around to double-check meeting setup and to handle on-site problems is the most common technique used. Staff can communicate with the event professional via two-way radios or Data Tel to quickly discuss issues like a room being too cold, food not arriving on time, a lost package, a major sponsor needing help, incorrect signage, and so on. The event professional may also ask leaders of the organization to communicate anything that needs to be changed. When the staff meets for lunch, the event professional is always asking how things are going and what needs to be addressed. The event professional constantly monitors all areas of the meeting/event.

Analyze and Remedy Problems

During the meeting/event, the event professional will be faced with many problems on-site. Each problem must be reviewed to determine if it is something that needs to be solved immediately or if it can wait, and what the cost of the decision is.

Some potential problems include natural disasters. Others are man-made and must be addressed by the venue (electrical needs, food and beverage, service issues, etc.).

For instance, the band selected for the closing banquet decides to add additional amplifiers but does not tell anyone that the amplifiers will require more electricity. On the closing night, the power goes out in the room and no one knows why. Event professionals need to have an understanding of how much electricity they need to order and to communicate the availability of power to vendors. A major issue today is broadband capability in a meeting room or venue. With some many people using portable devices, bandwidth can be overloaded easily. The AV company PSAV has developed a bandwidth calculator for use by event professionals. Another true story: Eight hours before a trade show was about to begin, a cherry picker broke down in the middle of the front row aisle of the exhibit floor. When attempting to move the cherry picker, it spewed black smoke and oil, creating a mess for all the exhibitors near the picker. After a long night of problem solving, the cherry picker was removed by using two vehicles to lift it up and slowly move it out of the exhibit hall.

Other challenges relate to personnel. There are times when people do not get along, and the event professional becomes a counselor. An attendee is not happy because his or her name does not show as being preregistered, so the registration desk insists that the person must pay the higher on-site price. The event professional must decide if the attendee will pay the pre-registration fee on-site fee. A celebrity speaker demands a private room, caviar, and special vodka but has to share the speaker ready room and gets cheese and crackers and water. It's another problem that the event professional must try to solve. The list goes on and on. Ask any event professional—he or she will be more than happy to share some on-site meeting/event stories.

Need for Additional Resources

Event professionals frequently need to come up with ways to do more with less. If a problem comes up that will cost money or will require additional people, where will the resources come from? What are the ramifications of increasing cost? Was money budgeted for contingencies? An event professional's ability to negotiate and make on-site adjustments is critical.

Interaction with Appropriate Parties

Throughout the day of the meeting/event, the event professional interacts with meeting sponsors and supporters, the facility/venue representatives, and local authorities. The event professional must use various communication skills to interact with each group. (For more detailed information regarding on-site communication, see Chapter 5 of this book.) The event professional must listen to the needs of the meeting sponsors to make sure that their needs are met and to ensure future funding. The interaction between the venue and the event professional may include a review of the day's events as they unfold or collaborating to solve a problem. Finally, the event professional may interact with local authorities, including the police, government officials, the fire marshal, and customs officers to provide permits, security, and medical assistance.

Delivery and Implementation of Services

Throughout the meeting/event, the event professional will review the ESG to identify the expected time that rooms are to be set and who is involved. The facility will determine how far in advance the room will be set. The event professional will check each room to confirm that it is set as listed in the BEO. The event professional will meet with the in-house and/or independent contractors, including audiovisual, production, decorations, and security, to ensure that each function will run smoothly. If the meeting/event includes an exposition, the event professional may work with a show manager and a general service contractor to view the show layout and address any issues that may concern exhibitors.

Hotel Room Blocks

Up to this point in this chapter, we have focused on the responsibilities of the event professional as they relate to the function and meeting rooms. The event professional is also in charge of the hotel room block. Each day, the event professional will meet with the CSM or housing bureau representative with a checklist of items to review that relate to the room block.

- Check the room pick-up to see if the meeting sponsor is subject to any attrition fees.
- Check the hotel reservations to see if any conference attendees booked outside the block. If attendees can be identified as staying in the hotel, then the meeting sponsor's room block should be credited with the room. The viewing of the hotel guest list must be negotiated in advance, and the venue may require that their personnel do the audit.
- Check to see if the hotel was overbooked and if any meeting attendees were walked (relocated to another hotel at hotel's expense). The event professional will work with the hotel to make arrangements for the displaced attendee to enable him or her to attend all meeting functions.
- Complimentary rooms will be confirmed and checked that they are not charged.
- VIP rooms will be confirmed.
- Amenities will be reviewed with hotel CSM to check that items will be sent to the allocated room(s) and that the cost for delivery is correct.

DISMANTLING THE SITE

Just as when the meeting/event was set up, an organized time line/production schedule must be followed to dismantle the site. To keep the teardown on schedule, the event professional will consult the ESG to make sure that he/she has communicated the information with colleagues and outside service personnel so that everyone is able to quickly work together to remove items from the event. This schedule must be shared with staff, venue personnel, and contractors. The meeting/event does not end until the venue is returned to the same condition in which it was acquired. Staff members will have tasks that must be done: These include taking inventory of items and repacking and labeling boxes. Venue personnel will focus on tasks related to the facility, such as removing tables and chairs from a room. Contractors will disassemble audiovisual equipment, including lighting, audio, and screens. They will follow a schedule set by the venue and the event professional as to when to load items.

The items are removed in reverse order of the setup; this will take much less time. As soon as the awards banquet or musical performance ends, the dismantling begins. The first to be removed are the things on the table: centerpieces, glasses, plates. Linens are removed, followed by chairs, tables, AV equipment, and rigging. (Note: If the linens and chair covers are provided by a third party, the event professional will want to count and inspect the linen and chair covers for damage). If an exhibition was part of the meeting/event, the general service contractor and/or decorator will begin the teardown as soon as the show is over. The exhibit hall is dismantled in about half the time it takes to set up.

At the end of the meeting/event, the event professional, staff, and the team are tired and ready to leave. However, the event professional is responsible for returning the venue to the condition in which it was acquired. Either the event professional or the production company will stay until everything is removed. Time and staff must be allocated for the teardown.

The event professional must review the teardown production schedule to identify the human resources needed and cost. Everyone on the team should be assigned tasks. Understanding the scope of the teardown will help determine the number of people needed.

Before finalizing staffing, the event professional should check with the CVB and venue to determine which, if any, unions operate at the venue; nonunion workers may work in the banquet department and union workers at the bell stand. When working in states with unions, the event professional will need to coordinate with the union hall to ensure that staffing is adequate. Further, event professionals cannot reprimand a union worker; they must go through the "on-site union rep." Further, each union worker has a strictly defined set of activities in which he or she is allowed to engage: A carpenter can take the nails and wood cover off a crate but cannot take the contents out of the crate—that is the responsibility of a materials handler. You need a "plumber" to erect the frame for "pipe and drape" since pipes are involved, but someone from the seamstress union must put the "drape" on the pipe. Extra time and money should be allocated when working with unions.

Some meetings/events will require specialized equipment that must be removed. Boat shows require special cranes to move boats in and out of the venue; medical meetings may use needles and surgical equipment that must be disposed of in a specified manner. Arrangements should be made in advance and monitored on-site.

Just as when packing the boxes for shipping to the meeting, care should be taken to return items. An inventory should be taken of what is in each box and shipping labels used to return boxes to their destination.

Any missing or damaged items should be reported to the event professional. If possible, any damaged items will be repaired. To collect items, event professionals use a check-in/check-out system. Staff should turn in items such as uniforms, two-way radios, and keys and mark that they were returned and in what condition.

Any items that were rented need to be returned prior to the event professional's departure from the venue. Although arrangements should be made prior to the meeting/event, the event professional will want to check and make sure that all rented items are returned and in a timely manner. A delay in returning items will cost the meeting sponsor.

Small items, such as decorations, glass bowls, or easels, that were borrowed from the venue will need to be returned and stored.

The meeting/event contract will include a clause as to how the space used must be returned. Every effort should be made to leave the property in the same condition (if not better) than when the event started. Before equipment is picked up by the vendor, it should be checked to see that it is working. All printers, computers, copiers, two-way radios, and so on should be checked before their return.

A walk-through of each function room used must be conducted to ensure that suppliers have removed equipment and that the room is in its original condition.

If the meeting/event required using hazardous chemicals or installation, care must be taken to ensure proper removal. Often strict guidelines must be followed. Dangerous chemicals must be stored in special containers and cannot go into the normal waste stream or landfill. For example, conventions of medical surgeons work with (dead) body or animal parts. When the convention is complete, the parts must be disposed of in a special way since many are considered "medical waste." Event professionals will hire authorized companies to handle this removal to ensure that all rules and regulations are followed.

Meetings/events generate a lot of waste, from the boxes that carried items, name badges, and gift bags to the decorations. All must be removed before the event professional leaves the venue. Event professionals are making an effort to recycle. Waste should be evaluated to see if it can be recycled. Check with the venue to see if they have recycle policies, and contact the CVB to locate groups that could use unused welcome bags and centerpieces. Locate businesses that will pick up paper items for recycling.

Final Meetings with Key Facility Personnel

Before leaving the venue, a thorough site inspection should be made with the personnel of the key vendors, including the CSM, audiovisual company, production company, DMC, and general service contractor. The space will be inspected to confirm that all equipment has been removed and that the space is in the condition that it was before the meeting/event began.

Once all site inspections are complete, the event professional then arranges a post-con meeting with the venue CSM. Another post-con will be arranged either in person or via videoconference with all vendors to review the meeting/event and identify areas of success and those that need to be improved. The post-con with all vendors should take place within a week or two after the meeting. Memories fade quickly, so a debriefing should be made in a timely manner and organized with the same detail used for the pre-con.

The meeting with the venue CSM will include a review of the room block, function space, and all details of the meeting/event and contract obligations. When possible, an event professional should request a **post-event report (PER)** with detailed information on the meeting as it relates to rooms and food and beverage usage. The PER can be used to show meeting history when arranging future meetings/events. This process will be repeated with each venue where the event professional used sleeping and/or meeting rooms and/or food and beverage.

The CVB/DMO will meet with the event professional and may even require that the event professional produce a report that includes hotel **room pickup**, area vendors used, attractions visited, and so on. The information is gathered so that the CVB/DMO can measure the value of the meeting/event to the city.

Finally, the venue should have a preliminary bill to review that identifies expenses and the date they are to be paid. A face-to-face review of the bill is best to ensure that any corrections can be made and additional expenses clarified. The bill should be finalized two to four weeks after the meeting/event.

Documents and Records

Complete all relevant documents and records according to the organizations procedures. This may include post-con reports listing room pickup and usage history of attendees and the ICW's shipping documents, manifest, and signoff on the contracts for the **Exposition Services Contractors (ESC)**.

Outbound Inventory Counts and Shipping

One of the event professional's final activities is to make sure that items return to the home office or to suppliers. Some items (such as extra gift bags) may be shipped to suppliers. The event professional will have a checklist that notes where boxes will be shipped and the expected date of arrival. This effort to remove all boxes needs to be coordinated with a shipping company.

All computers and electronic equipment will need to be checked and an inventory taken before shipping is arranged. This is done to make sure that no items were stolen or damaged during the meeting/event.

Shipping is expensive. To get the most for the money, the event professional needs to know what will be shipped and when it needs to arrive. Recycled name badges may not be needed for months, while computers and office supplies may be needed immediately. When possible, event professionals should identify ways to decrease shipping needs by only shipping what is needed for the meeting and/or using technology for meeting evaluations and speaker handouts.

The Pre-Planning Pre-Con

One month before the annual conference for the ABC Association, the pre-planning meeting is called to order. Representatives from the following companies are in attendance:

- Meeting sponsor staff: the event professional, executive director, director of programs, director of labs, exhibits manager, marketing manager, and accountant
- Association chapters: Dallas, Louisiana, Arkansas, Oklahoma, and New Mexico
- Audiovisual: J & S
- Exhibits: Freeman Decorating Company
- Exhibits: Move-in, move-out manager
- Registration: J. Spargo & Associates
- Housing: J. Spargo & Associates
- Tours and shuttle service: Production Transportation, Inc.
- Photography: J. Woods
- Golf: City Wide Country Club
- Convention center: Dallas
- Convention food & beverage: The PK Group
- Internet network/telephone services: Smart City
- Electrical provider: Freeman Electric Services
- Security provider: City of Dallas Off-Duty Employment Unit
- Convention and visitors bureau: Dallas
- DMC: PRA
- Temporary staffing
- Hyatt Hotel
- Marriot Hotel
- Omni Hotel, (host venue)
- Sheraton Hotel

The meeting begins with a welcoming from the executive director, followed by the meeting event professional, Sue Jones. Sue shares with the group the mission of the organization and the objectives of the meeting. She asks that people make a brief introduction and tell the group their role in the meeting and how many years they have been a part of this annual meeting.

Each person is given an operation manual/program that includes all contact information, floor plans for the convention center, and a time line, starting with move-in. For the next five hours (including lunch), each page of the operations manual is reviewed. This gives each member of the team an opportunity to ask questions and make recommendations. At the conclusion, the group is invited on a tour of the facility to further understand the flow of the meeting and to identify any potential problems.

Sue is convinced that the pre-planning meeting is one of the most important things that contribute to the success of the conference. "The face-to-face time together helps build relationships and trust. On-site we must work together as a team to ensure that the attendees have the best possible experience," explains Sue.

TABLE 2 Sample Production Schedule for Awards Banquet

Imagine that you are the meeting planner. You are working with your production team to set up the closing event for 500 people. This includes entertainment, a keynote speaker, and an awards ceremony.

The production company tells you they will need six to eight hours for setup and four for teardown. The setup and time will look something like this, assuming that all goes well with the rigging and that there are no problems.

Activity	Time needed
Unload and sort all equipment	30–60 minutes
Pre-rig process. Sort, assemble all shackles, truss, bolts, span sets, and motors, and mark floor.	30–60 minutes
Begin audio pre-set. Establish placement of speakers, front of house location, cable runs, power source, signal flow.	30–60 minutes
Begin lighting pre-set. Unpack gel, lens, all fixtures. Establish signal flow and cable runs. Location of FOH. Discuss lighting look with designer.	30–60 minutes
Begin video pre-set. Unpack, establish locations of screens, projectors, FOH, camera location, and sources discussed with project manager.	30–60 minutes
Work with in-house banquet team to establish size and locations of all risers, tables, chairs, buffets, wait staff entry, and special supplier rules.	60–90 minutes
Begin first tests of all systems (audio, video, lighting)	60–90 minutes
Work out any signal flow problems or faulty equipment issues.	60 minutes
Rehearsals for band. Introductions of main A1, monitor engineer, and master electrician.	60 minutes
Full test of all systems without client.	90 minutes
Full test of all systems with client.	60 minutes
Rehearsals for presenters. Camera rehearsal, lighting cues finished. Audio to ring room out based on presenters' voices and videos.	30 minutes per presenter
Correction of "show flow" documents. Document printed and distributed to all technicians and posted back stage and FOH.	30 minutes
Paper show flow review with all technicians. Technical director and client must be present and approve.	30 minutes
Begin pre-show walk-in looks and sound. Begin pre-roll for any video. Give client approval to open the doors.	30 minutes
Show GO.	

SUMMARY

The key to a successful meeting/event is the execution of all the plans made prior to the start of the meeting/event. An event professional's ability to communicate the organization's mission and meeting/event objectives to all parties involved in the meeting/event is step one. On-site, the event professional's job can be compared to that of an orchestra conductor whose music involves a variety of musical instruments. Each musician has rehearsed and knows his or her instrument. When the music is performed, the musician looks to the conductor for direction. The conductor depends on each musician to follow the conductor's direction to create a beautiful piece of music. The event professional depends on each venue and contractor to perform his or her job to create a memorable meeting that achieves the meeting/event objectives. It's showtime!

The ESG, program/operations manual, and time line are tools used by the event professional to keep track of all the meeting/event details. The on-site experience for the event professional is demanding; he/she must use skills in communication, negotiation, patience, and time management.

Now that you have completed this chapter, you should be competent in the following Meeting and Business Event Competency Standards:

MBECS Skill 22: Select Site

Subskills	
22.01	Determine (and select) site
22.02	Identify and inspect sites

MBECS Skill 24: Manage Meeting or Event Site

Subskills	
24.01	Create logistics action plan for setup and takedown
24.02	Set up site
24.03	Monitor site during meeting or event
24.04	Take down site

MBECS Skill 25: Manage On-Site Communications

Subskills	
25.02	Determine and acquire required communications equipment and resources
25.03	Specify communication procedures and protocols

KEY WORDS AND TERMS

Event Specifications Guide (ESG)
functions
Convention Services Manager (CSM)
audiovisual contractor
production company
contractor
housing
program book

time line
rigging
trusses
speaker ready room
load in/out
floor plans
fire marshal
marshaling yard
Visqueen

security contractor
gobos
technical rehearsal
run-through
post-event report (PER)
room pickup
Exposition Services Contractors (ESC)

REVIEW AND DISCUSSION QUESTIONS

1. Why is it important to understand the mission statement of the organization and the meeting objectives when planning a meeting/event?
2. Who are the key players that make an on-site meeting/event a success and what is their role and responsibility?
3. What is included in a logistics plan for meeting/event setup and teardown?
4. What types of activities/tasks must an event professional do when setting up the site for a meeting/event?
5. Describe the things that an event professional can do to keep track of all the activities that take place on-site.
6. When a meeting/event ends, what are the activities that an event professional must do before leaving the venue?

REFERENCE

APEX Glossary: http://www.conventionindustry.org/StandardsPractices/APEX/glossary.aspx

ABOUT THE CHAPTER CONTRIBUTOR

M. T. Hickman, CMP, is in the Travel, Exposition and Meeting Management Program at Richland College in Dallas, Texas. She began her career at the Convention & Visitors Bureau in Irving, Texas, where she worked in many departments, including tourism sales, convention sales, and special events. Over the years, she worked as director of marketing for the National Business Association and as a proposal writer for WorldTravel Partners. She is active in MEEC industry associations, including MPI, PCMA, and IAEE.

CHAPTER *3*

Designing, Organizing, and Producing the Environment for Meetings, Conventions, and Events

Learning Objectives

Upon completion of this chapter, the reader should be able to understand:

- Theming and branding in event design
- Functional requirements of event design
- Securing and installing décor and furnishings
- Knowing the importance and effectiveness of signage

Part of the environment at a recent MPI convention was entertainment provided by a troupe that danced on the glass-shrouded side of a building.

Photo courtesy of George G. Fenich, Ph.D.

Chapter Outline

INTRODUCTION

The production of an event through **event design** is a critical element that will determine the success of the event. Whether event design as both an integral and discrete activity is included depends on many factors and should influence each stage of event planning and event production. The process of designing an event environment is also referred to as staging an event = showtime! This process involves combining all the elements into a single unit. Event design can also refer to the organization of a venue within a much larger event. The main elements of designing an event environment include:

- Theming and event design
- Target audience
- Legislation and regulation within special effects
- Capacity limits
- Sensitivity to local culture
- Regulations of event venues

CONCEPTS AND THEORIES RELATING TO EVENT DESIGN AND ENVIRONMENT

Theming and Branding in Event Design

When staging an event or meeting, determining what the event theme will be is a crucial artistic and creative decision. This theme will differentiate the event from others. The theme is often determined by the client's needs. Theme design is when a visual spectacle is created by artifacts and symbols that imaginatively reinforce a special atmosphere. Themes can range from casino nights to Hollywood and cabaret. For this purpose, the event space itself may require several elements, which might include:

- Decoration
- Scenery
- Artists, entertainers, speakers
- Sound and lighting
- Audio visuals and special effects
- Venue setting
- Catering

Theming an event is essential to creating an event atmosphere; however, an event professional should also take into consideration the image of the event in the minds of the target market.

It is important for event professionals to integrate a brand into their events. This **branding** could be simple, such as a logo, or complex, such as corporate identity (company name and product or positioning statement). The image of an event is emphasized by branding. Companies with strong existing brands should maintain dominance and positioning, while those that lack brand recognition need to utilize their competitive space in order to make a name for their brand.

Target Audience

Target audience refers to the people who would potentially attend an event or meeting. The target market can be influenced by the event theme and branding. Marketing is important: It helps attract a target audience without which any event will turn out to be a nonevent (see Chapter 12 in this book for more detailed information). The event audience makes decisions relating to costs and efforts to attend and weigh these against the benefits of attending the event. Developing and implementing an integrated marketing strategy will enhance the quality and quantity of the people who attend an event. When choosing a target audience, an event professional needs to segment the market according to where the following criteria ought to be met:

- The market should be measurable in terms of socioeconomic status, gender, age, and others.
- The market should be economically sustainable.
- The market should be accessible to marketing communication channels.
- The market should be realistically actionable by the event organizer, taking into account the marketing budget and event resources.

LEGISLATION AND REGULATIONS IN THE PRODUCTION ENVIRONMENT

Many legal requirements must be adhered to when staging an event or meeting. Bear in mind that the larger, more complicated, or innovative the event, the larger the range of requirements is that needs to be adhered to. In order to avoid contravention of the law, it is necessary to conduct vigorous and up-to-date research to determine the legislative requirements within the area where the event is to be staged. **Legislation** and regulations differ across geographic borders, from country to country and state to state. Although there is a wide spectrum of legislation regulations, they may be grouped into the following four main groups; special effects, capacity limitations, sensitivity to local culture, and regulation of event venues.

Special Effects

The uniqueness and excitement of an event may be influenced by the **special effects** used to entertain and create a specific atmosphere. Examples of special effects may include smoke, sound, bubble machines, water fountains, pyrotechnics, foam machines, revolving stages, and laser lights.

In order to promote safety standards, it is essential to use experienced contractors when employing special effects and to ensure that the necessary safety precautions are followed. Event professionals should consult with local authorities to obtain the necessary permits and licenses, should these be required.

In some areas, the use of special effects are regulated by relevant government agencies in order to ensure that the effects are properly operated and that they do not pose a threat to the safety of attendees or spectators. In the case of South Africa, the South African National Standards for Health and Safety regulates the use of special effects at events in areas near old-age homes, schools, religious sites, and other sensitive areas (SANS, 2006).

Gyro Pyro

A convention was held at the Opryland Hotel in Nashville, Tennessee. The organizers decided it would produce a "wow" factor if they included indoor pyrotechnics. The fireworks began. One of the attendees standing near the back of the crowd was really wowed when one of the fireworks sailed off the stage and over his head in a blaze—until he turned around and saw the palm tree behind him on fire. Luckily, there was fire equipment nearby and the fire in the tree was extinguished before anyone got hurt.

Capacity Limits

Capacity limits refers to the number of people who can safely enter, circulate, and exit an event or meeting space. Legislation and regulations govern the entrances, access, exit, and venue capacity requirements. In the South African context, the SANS (2006) document stipulates that the capacity of a venue generally depends on the available space for all on-site and the number of emergency exits. In the United States, it is usually the local fire marshal who establishes and enforces capacity limits. Furthermore, there should be a sufficient number of entrances to cope with peak demand, supervision at event entrances, and exit signs that are free of obstruction and clearly marked.

Sensitivity to Local Culture

Event professionals may belong to an association within their own country that is bound by its own code of ethics and governed by legislation and regulations. Associations in each country require organizers to adhere to the guidelines of the country concerned. These guidelines are often created to minimize the negative impact of these events on host communities. Host communities may have a unique heritage and culture that might be affected by the activities associated with the hosting of an event. As such, an event professional should ensure sensitivity and respect for issues that may include religion, dietary requirements, use of colors and symbols, and use of language. In India, most people do not eat meat, and English is the official language in the United States. Although guidelines, ethics, legislation, and regulations differ in order to manage these impacts, event professionals in most countries must adhere to common principles:

- Deal with visitors and exhibitors with professionalism, integrity, and courtesy
- Foster mutual respect and trust in all dealings
- Embrace integrity and transparency in business conducts
- Respect client confidentiality
- Exhibit a sensitivity to local culture in terms of the use of language, national symbols, and alcohol, to name a few examples

Regulations of Event Venues

Regulations governing event venues are twofold: those that govern the venue itself and those that are influenced by the type of event hosted at the venue.

With regard to the venue design, regulations and legislation will be determined by a number of factors:

- **Location** – The venue could be located in an environmentally sensitive area, and event greening principles may be encouraged.

- **Accessibility** – The relevant impact studies may need to be conducted in terms of traffic management and parking to conform to legislation.
- **Building material utilized** – The range of building materials may be controlled by legislation in terms of their use. Other building material (such as timber and thatch) can pose risks and require specialized management regulations.
- **Size of the venue** – This relates to the volume of the specific structure. The larger the venue, the more regulations may be imposed.

THE FUNCTIONAL REQUIREMENTS OF EVENT DESIGN

The event industry encompasses a variety of different types of events, each with its own unique functional requirements. This section will discuss the development and production of meetings, conventions, and events and the fulfillment of stakeholder obligations.

When designing and organizing an event, event professionals should take into consideration the attractiveness, functionality, theme, and enhancement of performance and experience of the event or meeting.

Attractiveness

The **attractiveness** of a meeting or event will be determined by the event's target audience/customer. In some cases, a customer may approach an event professional to plan and produce an event (such as a conference or meeting) according to detailed specifications; in other cases, an event may require a more complex approach (such as the planning of music or art festivals). In order to manage the attractiveness of the event, the event professional may take into account the following:

- **Event history** – Event professionals should consider where the event has been held previously and what the advantages and disadvantages of hosting the event at the desired location are.

Sandton Convention Centre (SCC)

Sandton Convention Centre is South Africa's leading and most prestigious, multipurpose exhibition and convention center. Situated in northern Johannesburg in the heart of Sandton's business, hotel, and entertainment district, Sandton Convention Centre offers easy access to over 5,000 hotel rooms and is adjacent to the country's top shopping and entertainment complexes. SCC has over 22,000 square meters (234,000 square feet) of convention, exhibition, and special event space. This 12-story structure was designed to provide convention, exhibition, and special event space over five main levels. The Convention Centre offers the most advanced conferencing and exhibition technologies available today, under one roof.

The technologies used by the SCC are supported by highly skilled technicians and a dedicated support staff contingent. The combination of cutting-edge expertise and the passion of team members means that the Sandton Convention Centre is able to host conferences, exhibitions, and special events of almost any kind.

- **Event location** – Decisions should be made where to host an event; this considers the location and venue type. The choice of location may be used to reflect the event theme, brand, and ambience of the event or meeting. The SCC is considered a premier location for large conventions/conferences and exhibitions in South Africa. This venue has successfully hosted a number of prestige events, including the United Nations World Summit on Sustainable Development in 2002, Miss World Pageant in 2008, SADC Summit in 2010, and the 60th FIFA Congress in 2010.
- **Event audience** – Different events may attract different target audiences that are dependent on size, scope, and purpose of the event. A sports event may attract spectators and athletes, while a convention may be aimed at a specific membership group and exhibitors.
- **Event transport and parking** – This is essential to the accessibility of the venue. The more accessible the venue, the greater the attractiveness of the event. The SCC was constructed during a period of rapid growth around the area of Sandton, which is today the financial hub of Johannesburg. As a result, the center was planned with growth in mind. Today, it is centrally situated with sufficient transport infrastructure, including roads, parking, and a subway linking the center to the international airport in Johannesburg as well as the capital, Pretoria.
- **Event timing** – It is fundamental for the event professional to take into consideration the timing of the event in relation to any other event that may be competing for the same target audience. Seasonality could also have an impact on the attendance of the event. School, university, and public holidays may either be a blessing or a curse for an event professional.

Functionality

Event professionals should work closely with facility staff to use meeting space correctly and effectively. This requires a consideration of the **functionality**, configuration, dimensions, ceiling heights, and capacity of the selected venue.

Enhancement of Performance and Experience

Enhancement is the total immersive outcome that combines all the various elements that are experienced by individuals or a group. It essentially amounts to the holistic event experience.

The visitor experience may differ from individual to individual. An event professional can use an experience matrix that identifies the different experiences that may be encountered by an event visitor, such as sensory, tactile responsive, flowing, visually pleasing, colors, photographs, auditory mystical, enticing, intellectual, emotional adventurous, intimate, authentic, functional resources, geographical, information, product information, cultural self-actualization, aspiration, and personal image.

Ensuring That the Event Fulfills Stakeholder Obligations

When planning an event, it is no longer sufficient to meet just the needs of the event audience. The event professional must also take into consideration numerous other stakeholder requirements. These stakeholders may include, among others, the host organization, host community, sponsors, media, and coworkers (see Exhibit 1).

The successful event professional should be able to identify the relevant stakeholders in an event and to determine and manage their individual needs, which in some cases overlap and may cause conflict.

EXHIBIT 1 Stakeholder Matrix

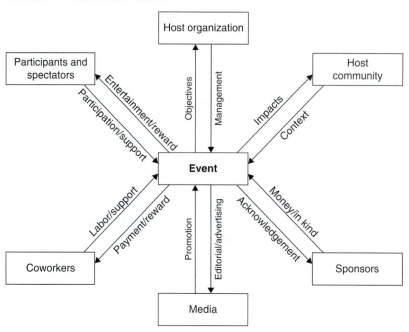

FULFILLING FUNCTIONAL REQUIREMENTS FOR FACILITIES/VENUES

Often the meeting or event objectives and physical and **functional requirements** may dictate the general area and type of facility where the meeting or event should be located. Political, economic factors, or organizational policy may also influence the choice of location.

Types of Venues

There are numerous types of venues, from hotel ballrooms to football stadiums; events can be held in country clubs or even streets. Compared to hotels, convention centers are more likely to be used for exhibitions. Exhibit halls are usually larger and often used for large events such as trade shows or concerts. Conference centers, on the other hand, are smaller with well-appointed facilities to enhance the needs of the meeting environment. When selecting an appropriate venue, it is important to consider **setup** aspects such as audiovisual needs, refreshment break areas, stages, and podiums for speakers as well as the layout of seating to be used. Off-site events can be challenging as far as designing and producing are concerned and are highly demanding of the event designer and decorator (see Exhibit 2).

Your motivation for choosing a particular facility or venue may include practicality, financial viability, facilities, uniqueness, layout, location, and perception.

Site Inspection

When selecting a suitable venue, the venue must be able to meet the needs of the event or meeting and its audience. Prior to selecting a venue, a **site inspection** may take place. The event professional arranges to visit the venue to inspect its suitability according to a set of criteria relevant to the specific event. A checklist may be developed listing the particular requirements of the event in terms of the venue. The venue should be chosen that best matches the criteria.

EXHIBIT 2 Venue Finding Checklist

EVENT: _____ DATE: _____

NAME OF VENUE _____ ADDRESS: _____

TEL NO: _____ _____

FAX NO: _____ _____

E-MAIL: _____ EVENT CONTACT: _____

What are the objectives of the event in relation to the venue?

_____

What factors are critical to the success of the event in relation to the venue?

_____

Site inspection: Venue environment and location:

Location: _____ .

Access (general comments):

Road: _____ .

Air: _____ (nearest airport) _____ .

Rail: _____ . (nearest station) _____

Identify any access problems related to lading/mobility of passengers/parking limitations

_____

SITE INSPECTION: VENUE FACILITIES AND SERVICES:

Capacity of main area: _____ Capacity of parking: _____
Capacity of support areas: _____

SCALE PLAN OF THE VENUE:

Ceiling height _____ Door height _____
Door width _____ Air conditioning/heaters _____

COMMENT ON OVERALL IMPRESSION OF THE VENUE

_____

Site Selection

Site selection is probably one of the most important aspects of the development phase of an event. In some cases, an even organizer might know exactly which venue to select. In other cases, the choice may be extremely limited. The first question an organizer often asks is about the location; the second is what available venues are within that location. What we know about the audience and the event itself will assist with the judgment of a suitable event: Who are they? Why are they here? For example, if the event is an exhibition, then the venue should probably be large and central. If the event is a festival or carnival, then the venue may cover several locations in the town.

There are numerous types of venues—from hotel ballrooms to football stadiums. An events can be held in a country club or even on a street. Compared to hotels, convention centers are more likely to be used for exhibitions. Exhibits halls are usually larger and often used for large events such as trade shows or concerts. Conference centers, on the other hand, are smaller, with well-appointed facilities to enhance the needs of the meeting environment. It is often more expensive to host events at unique or less commonly used sites.

Some of the considerations to be taken into account include:

- **Event History** – Where has the event been held in the past? What were the pros and cons of holding it there? Are there any benefits in changing the venue? Are there other elements being added to the event that require additional facilities or space?
- **Venue History and Reputation** – What venue(s) fit with the qualities and principles of the event? Are certain venues synonymous with your individual event type? Will a particular venue give added benefits to the event?
- **Location** – Does the event need to be located in a specific area? Are there necessary facilities nearby, such as transport links and accommodation?
- **Budget** – Will the budget support the choice of venue? Have all the possible costs been considered?

Other factors to consider may include matching the venue with the theme, venue configuration, availability, facilities, accessibility, amenities, climate, communication, transportation and parking, timing, services and resources, infrastructure, layout, restrictions for closing times, and emergency facilities.

DÉCOR AND FURNISHINGS

The theme of an event can be further established with the use of décor. **Décor** may include props, backdrops, lighting, balloons, and any other materials used to reinforce the theme and add to the atmosphere of the event. Skilled use of these elements can make the attendees feel as though they are part of an imaginary world.

Two rules of décor include being consistent and using the space. The look should be reflected in linen, floors, décor, entertainment, and even on the menu. Using your space means finding elements that are proportionate to your available space.

Atmosphere

Creating the environment and atmosphere can be one of the most enjoyable tasks in staging an event or meeting. Whether creating an upscale ambience for a gala, or a casual farewell dinner, the appropriate environment will support the goals and objectives of the event.

Floor Plan and Space Management

Use the venue **floor plan** as the foundation of the event's design. This will enhance the logistics and the flow of the event. Plot out the various elements of the event; for example, where the stage and dance floor will be, key décor elements, and interactive activities. It is important to note that the number of people who will attend the event or meeting will determine the size of the venue and the event space requirements. A challenge facing an event professional may be a venue that is too small because of limited alternatives. However, the event organizer can be creative to solve this problem. Options may include incorporating outside space, such as the erection of tents or marquees or the use of terraces. In this case, the event organizer must also consider potential health and safety risks. Venues that are too large may create the appearance of wasted space, poor attendance, and the underutilization of resources.

Flow

Flow is the movement of the guests or attendees within the event environment. All events should make provisions for entrance and exit space. There should be sufficient space for the efficient flow of the guests into the room as well as around the room to engage in various activities, such as networking or making use of the buffets, dance floor, and rest rooms.

The Haj

The pilgrimage that all devout Muslims are expected to make once in their lifetime is called the Haj. Hundreds of thousands of people flock to the Middle Eastern city of Mecca and converge on its small and ancient street layout. This city was never designed for this many people; flow is a problem. Bottlenecks occur as people try to move through tunnels on foot to get from one religious ceremony to another. It is so bad that in some years, attendees have gotten crushed or trampled and died.

Lighting

Lighting enhances the desired ambience and transition of space effectively. Including "up lighting" to light props and features and "down lighting" to highlight food, decorations, and centerpiece displays creates an ambience. Lighting can also be used to project company logos or theme messages onto a wall or banner.

Lighting

Justin Glickman is a lighting specialist at DeLight Events in South Africa. He mentions that lighting is both an art and a science. As people often experience it on a subconscious level, the event professional needs to assess and understand each individual and his or her function at the event along with the visual quality of the lighting and the surrounding environment.

He mentions that lighting can be used to make the ordinary look beautiful and the beautiful look even better. However, if lighting is done incorrectly, then it can create the opposite effect. Glickman points out that lighting can be used to draw attention to certain objects by increasing the contrast in brightness between the object and its surroundings. It is also important to note that spectators and attendees do not like to sit in brightness, but would rather see brightness.

Signage and Audiovisual and Technical Equipment

All events require signage; this can range from a basic idea to specialized signage specifically adapted for the purpose of the event. Three main categories of signage are prominent in event design: risk management signs, information signs, and decorative signs.

The term *audiovisual* refers to all the elements relating to sound and visual support equipment. An audiovisual technician usually manages equipment that requires expertise and technical skills; this may include microphones, speaker systems, recording equipment, projectors, LCD screens, video equipment, and lighting.

Creativity

In events such as festivals, weddings, parties, celebrations, award ceremonies, and stage shows, the major features of the event are creativity and creative resources, such as food, drink, flowers, centerpieces, objects, sounds, and smells. Creativity at such events is limitless, and a truly amazing visual setting can be created.

Budget

The first step in successful event management is to determine the financial objectives of the event or meeting. The types and sources of this finance are determined by the client's needs and are the responsibility of the event professional. Budgeting is a useful tool for an event professional, as it provides clear guidelines for the management of finance. Items often included in the budgeting process are venue charges, food and beverage, décor, incidental entertainment, show production, equipment rental, sound, staging, lighting, and transportation (see Chapter 11 in this book for more information on managing finances).

SECURING AND INSTALLING DÉCOR AND FURNISHINGS

Having formulated an event plan, it is now important to secure the selected décor and furnishings for the event or meeting in order to put the plan into action. This process involves three major steps: setting up (before), implementing the event (during), and event closing (after).

Setup

At this stage, the event professional has determined the objectives and identified appropriate furnishings and décor as well as the event venue. It is now necessary for the event organizer to negotiate with the relevant in-house and out-house suppliers to provide the required products and services and set up the necessary contracts. Contracts bind the two parties to a mutual agreement that stipulates each party's responsibilities and requirements.

Implementation

Implementation involves the actual staging of the event and ensuring that the event runs according to the established objectives and scheduling. At this stage, the delivery process (moving goods in and out) would have already been established, and the contractors and suppliers would have determined the layout of facilities and delivery requirement (for more information, see Chapter 8, Designing the Environment, in *Planning and Management of Meetings, Expositions, Events, and Conventions* by Fenich). Event professionals should take note of essential logistical operations that may need to be installed on-site, such as communication networks, water and sanitation, and waste removal. These should be carried out in accordance with the health and safety requirements.

Event Closing

This refers to the "shut down" of the event. While a site is being shut down, it may also be prepared for the next event. During this stage equipment, furnishings and décor are removed and returned to suppliers. It is imperative that stakeholders adhere to the schedules; failure to do so may have financial and safety implications. Event professionals will review the contracts to ensure that all roles and responsibilities as well as financial commitments have been fulfilled by all relevant stakeholders.

Communication and Approval of Décor Plan

The successful staging of an event or meeting is intrinsically related to excellent communication. This process starts during the planning of the event, when precise expectations are conveyed among all stakeholders, including the client, meeting managers, site managers, and service contractors. During the event, communication entails the review of logistical details while post-event communication entails feedback from the various stakeholders.

Effective communication minimizes barriers to the successful hosting of an event. These minimized barriers and greater understanding should result in a timeous and complete approval of the plan.

In order to reduce unnecessary resource pressure, it is important to obtain approval of the décor plan. This will assist in controlling the event and minimizing any risks. The approval of the décor plan may occur prior to, or concurrent with, the organizing of the event. This approval should be obtained from all necessary stakeholders, who may include the owners/board of directors of companies involved, clients, and government authorities (for more information, see Chapter 14 in this book).

SIGNAGE

All event signs fulfill one or more of the following functions: to identify, to inform, or to direct. It is imperative that signage is done correctly; bear in mind the specific objective of each sign and how it functions for your audience.

It is also important to include the location of all signs on the site map. It should be noted on the event schedule when signs will be put up and taken down. It is essential to ensure that signage creates a corporate feel, looks professional, and is consistent in the appearance.

Identification Signs

Identification signs are used to identify the event's name and the names of places and features within the event. For example, the Sandton Convention Centre at the entrance of the exhibition hall will display the conference name in progress.

Informational Signs

These signs provide background data or information to the reader. Sometimes information signs advise the attendees of any late changes to the program.

Directional Signs

Directional signs assist attendees to move throughout the facility. Directional signs can make use of arrows or symbols.

More than one function can often be presented on a sign. The Sandton Convention Centre often houses a number of events simultaneously. A company's logo on signs may be used to draw the attention to the relevant attendees.

SUMMARY

Producing a memorable and successful event is a long process that often requires input from a variety of people. Ideally, the meeting or event should exceed the attendee's expectations. In order to achieve a well-designed and developed event, clearly defined objectives must be set. Within the event framework, the design is an integral activity and depends upon many factors. Art in an event is achieved through design and decoration. Event design is the conceptualization of the structure that expresses the concept visually. Decoration and design combined gives the event or meeting synergy.

Now that you have completed this chapter, you should be competent in the following Meeting and Business Event Competency Standards:

MBECS: Skill 19 Design Environment

Subskills		Skills
19.01	Establish functional requirements	
19.02	Select décor and furnishing	
19.03	Coordinate meeting or event signage	

KEY WORDS AND TERMS

event design	attractiveness	site inspection
theming	functionality	site selection
branding	enhancement	décor
legislation	functional requirements	floor plan
special effects	setup	implementation

REVIEW AND DISCUSSION QUESTIONS

1. Identify the major elements that should be dealt with when designing an event environment.
2. Which factors will determine the regulation and legislation of venue design?
3. Briefly identify and describe the features that an event professional should take into account when determining the attractiveness of the event.
4. What attributes should an event professional consider when choosing an event venue?
5. When selecting décor and furnishings, which six factors should an event professional consider?
6. Identify and describe the three phases of securing décor and furnishings.
7. The use of signage will be determined by the purpose of the signage. Briefly identify and describe the different types of signage utilized during events.

ABOUT THE CHAPTER CONTRIBUTORS

Uwe Hermann is a faculty member in the Department of Tourism Management at the Tshwane University of Technology (TUT) in Pretoria, South Africa. He holds a master's degree in tourism and hospitality management and is currently completing his Ph.D. Hermann has been involved in various research projects and has published in the fields of sustainable tourism, heritage tourism, events curriculum development, and mega events.

Lisa Welthagen is also a faculty member at the Department of Tourism Management at TUT; she is the course coordinator for the Diploma in Events Management. She has been involved in lecturing tourism and event management for the past 14 years at TUT and further education and training colleges in South Africa. Prior to this, she was actively involved in the tourism industry in South Africa and the UK, coordinating and managing inbound and outbound group, conference, and incentive travel. Welthagen holds a master's degree in tourism and hospitality. Her research is based on event and festival management.

Managing the Technical Aspects of Meetings, Conventions, and Events

CHAPTER 4

Chapter Objectives

Upon completion of this chapter, the reader should be able to:

- Link technology design to client's goals and objectives
- Recognize basic terminology
- Discuss current trends in meeting and event technology
- Identify human and equipment needs in specific environments
- Determine basic budget expectations

GES turned the world upside down with their upside down booth.
Image Courtesy of Global Experience Specialist.

Chapter Outline

The task of translating vision and design into an experience that achieves the client's objectives requires that the event producer have a well-planned approach to managing all the technical aspects of a program. Often referred to as "herding cats," or wrapping one's arms around the entire scope of the project, well-managed technical elements can serve to enhance the experience and message of a meeting or event.

INTRODUCTION

As the tastes of attendees and audiences have become more and more sophisticated, expectations of the levels of technology they will experience have also been on the rise. Overhead projectors and flipcharts are no longer the staples of the audiovisual department: LCD projectors and plasmas or LED/LCD monitors have become the norm. The event professional must work with the client, the venue, and the vendors to ensure that the technology used accomplishes the desired objectives and creates a memorable experience.

Client's Goals and Objectives

When producing events, whether choosing equipment, determining a food-service style, or planning the program, the foundation for all decisions always comes back to the client's objectives. Listing those goals and objectives at the very beginning of the planning and production process can keep the event producer on track. The success of the technical manager will hinge on how completely those objectives were met and how smoothly all aspects of the meeting or event were produced.

Objectives are not always financial; with many corporations today, their event objectives are strongly tied to the concept of **corporate social responsibility (CSR)**, or how the company is giving back to the community. Other objectives address atmosphere, interaction, and sending a certain message to the audience.

Current Trends

One of the more recent challenges to managing the technical aspects of meetings and events is the trend toward utilizing nontraditional venues. Clients are always looking for ways to design something new, something with a "wow" factor that will create a memorable experience for their attendees. As a result, semipermanent tents, airplane hangars, rooftops, giant cranes, and the like are becoming event venues, thus creating additional concerns for adhering to basic engineering principles and safety guidelines. Installing trade show elements in a convention center that was constructed specifically for trade shows is a walk in the park compared to converting a Quonset hut–type structure into an exciting, working trade show. How about producing an entertainment element 50 feet in the air, at the top of a crane? The demand for highly trained labor, with well-developed problem-solving skills, increases dramatically in these challenging environments.

Another trend that is having a profound effect on both the technical management of meetings and events, as well as on many event budgets, is the move toward energy-efficient equipment and policies. For example, it is no longer always necessary to secure, and pay for, massive power draws for entertainment production lighting; today's newer lighting elements are almost exclusively low-energy, LED fixtures that use a minimum amount of power.

For the producer assigned to managing the technical aspects of today's meetings and events, the role can be divided into four parts: (1) determining equipment requirements, (2) selecting appropriate vendors, (3) I&D (installing and dismantling), and (4) managing human logistics.

TECHNICAL REQUIREMENTS IN SPECIFIC ENVIRONMENTS

Although each trade show, special event, or concert will be unique in its specific needs, the technical elements to be considered can usually be divided into distinct categories:

- Design requirements
- Contractual requirements
- Standard AV items
- Staging
- Lighting fixtures
- Sound equipment

Because of continually emerging technologies, the innovative management of AV, lighting, sound, and special effects has become the skill that can determine the success or failure of an event production.

Site Feasibility

Starting with the overview design, the technical manager must determine the strengths and limitations of the space that has been chosen, for example, ceiling minimum and maximum heights, availability of power, and a long checklist of site characteristics. During the site visit, a technical checklist is a great tool to list what is and isn't available to produce the design elements required. Take the example of an event in an aircraft hangar; believe it or not, this type of site is requested frequently for media events and for "adventure-themed" occasions. In many instances, this type of nontraditional venue was not built with special events in mind and may not have many of the amenities found in a more traditional space, such as air conditioning or heat, restrooms, storage space, and sometimes even running water! This is information that the event professional/technical manager needs to discover in advance in order to be able to determine how the requested design elements can be implemented in the space.

The Convention Industry Council, with the APEX Initiative, has developed useful tools to aid in analyzing a particular site. Checklists are available for hotels, resorts, convention centers, and conference centers, along with pertinent questions to ask about in-house exclusives, union labor, and outside contractors. Every venue will have its specific rules and regulations; each city, county, and state will also have certain fire regulations, along with licenses, and permits that will be required. Gaining this information early in the management process will save time, money, and frayed nerves as the events begin. It is up to the event professional/technical manager to gather information about the actual structure and amenities of the venue, any in-house exclusives, and labor contracts that are in place.

Once the site has been evaluated in light of the design requirements, the next step in the process is deciding what equipment will best translate the design ideas into the event experience that is being requested. The process includes assessing the need for standard AV equipment, what lighting opportunities would work, which fixtures

Some of the items to consider when evaluating a site are:

Space Capacity	Dimensions, ceiling height, occupancy limits based on specific layouts, e.g., capacity varies with rounds of 10 vs. theater seating
Site Access Conflicts	Elevated dock, dock schedules, elevator sizes, route/distance to site
Venue Contracts	Exclusive suppliers, union labor requirements, in-house providers
Services Included or Excluded	Activities that are included with rental of the site, such as technical services, setup, and teardown
Equipment Available	Example: venue may have moving lights and house speakers already installed in a theater; can they be included in the rental or for just a minimal extra charge?
Additional Venue Charges/Fees	If the venue has exclusive or in-house providers of certain commodities, you may be charged a fee if you bring in an outside supplier; specifics will be in site rental contract
Storage	Sound and lighting elements are usually transported in heavy, durable road cases that need to be stored while the equipment is in use
Electrical Supply	Enough individual power circuits to handle the equipment that is being recommended
Fire Marshal Regulations	Required floor plans submitted, fire retardant certificates for all fabrics and decor items
Required Permits, Licenses	Permits needed for use of any public space, alcohol service license, or permit
Security	Control access to all areas, aid in crowd control, emergency staff
Rigging Points	Reinforced structural points in a ballroom or convention center from which heavy items can be hung; each point is "rated" for a certain amount of weight (weight load limit), usually a minimum of 500 pounds

are best suited for the space and design, and how expansive a sound system is necessary to accomplish the goals of the event.

Standard Audiovisual Equipment

Over the years, the industry has standardized some categories of equipment, and certain terms have become commonplace in technical management. The most commonly used term is AV, which stands for audiovisual requirements. The current use of "AV" indicates equipment used in support of a meeting/event or as a teaching aid. The equipment can be either used for sound or visual presentations and includes video projection and screen, overhead projection, flip chart, write board, and public address system.

Two of the most commonly requested pieces of AV equipment items are:

- **Liquid Crystal Display (LCD) Projector.** This technology utilizes sets of red, green, and blue panels to produce brighter, more saturated colors on the screen. The higher the light number, or lumens, the better the quality of the image; typically, a 5200-lumens projector will produce a bright, sharp image.
- **Front and Rear Projection Screens.** When the projector is placed somewhere in front of the screen, either hung from the ceiling, or on a cart, there is usually brighter illumination and a nice sharp picture. One of the drawbacks to front projection is the necessity to either have a high support structure, or a visible cart in front of the screen, to accommodate your projection device. There may also be issues with attendees crossing in front of the projected image. Rear projection, placing the projector behind the screen, is a neat and orderly way to accomplish a large projection. This method hides the equipment and provides a more updated look. What sometimes makes this technique impractical is the need for the projector to be at least 14 feet behind the surface of the screen to get the best images; this distance is referred to as "throw space."

Lighting

In many ways, great lighting can be the most important element in the success of a meeting or event. Imagine an educational session that is too dark for the attendees to take notes, or a rock concert without the energy, atmosphere, and mood created by the explosion of intense colors and images colliding across the stage. What about a guest speaker standing at his/her lectern on the stage, totally in the dark?

Lighting requirements can be a considerable part of the event budget, and sometimes it is difficult for the client to see the value received. In most applications, lighting instruments are either mounted on the floor, hung from a ceiling or rafter, or flown from a rigging system overhead. The instruments need a connection to a power source and control center. Installation of all lighting systems, hung or flown, requires the skill and experience of professional riggers and electricians. When dealing with overhead installations, safety is always a concern. Extra precautions are generally taken, like the use of additional clamps, safety chains, and heavy duty motors to hoist a structural **truss** holding dozens of lighting instruments to their places overhead. Uplights and other floor mounted lights should be seamlessly incorporated into the décor of the space, for both aesthetic and safety reasons.

Some basic lighting fixtures used in most lighting installations:

- **Dimmer (Control) Board:** Computer-driven, gives lighting operator control, sends an instructional signal to each lighting instrument
- **Par Can:** Produces a broad flood (wash) of light, covers large areas with a wash of light, color **gels** (thin plastic sheets used to change the color of the light) may be inserted
- **Ellipsoidal Spotlight:** Commonly called a **leko**, contains shutters, can focus narrowly, cylindrical, horizontal, vertical format, accepts a metal or glass gobo, die cut with a logo or image through which light passes, projecting the image unto a desired surface
- **Follow Spotlight:** Manually operated, can be focused, meant to follow performer or speaker, color may be added with cellophane gels
- **Intelligent (Robotic) Lighting:** Robotic, or computer-controlled lights, moveable, color changing, image (gobo) changing, programmable, fog is added for special effects, more expensive than static lights

Once a lighting package is installed, the process of designing the movement and changes in the lighting patterns begins. Here, the talents of a lighting designer, and then a lighting director, come into play:

- **Lighting Designer**
  - Plans the lighting design
  - Designs the light plot for the room
  - Creates the lighting cues
- **Lighting Director**
  - Supervises on-site installation
  - Makes on-site adjustments
  - Supervises the show
  - Programs final lighting cues

Some final tips: When lighting flowers or other décor, sit in the chair or stand where the guests will be standing to make sure that the lighting will not be in anyone's eyes. Everything you do with lighting, every decision you make, should have a reason or it will look inappropriate or out of place.

It is difficult to find out where this list came from, and who Monroe is; nevertheless, these are good rules to follow when lighting meetings and events.

Rules of Lighting
Warm white or light pink is a flattering color for people
Blue is romantic but not flattering
Dim is romantic but hard to eat or talk by
Backlighting is always romantic
A blend of pink and blue generally works well for events
Too much light is as bad as too little
Only white light should be used on food or flowers
White is an excellent accent color when surrounded by colored light
Spotlights draw attention
Green light makes greenery look artificial and people look dead

Sound

The use of sound equipment in meetings and events runs the gamut from a single microphone attached to a lectern for a speaker's presentation, to all the arrays of main house speakers, monitors, amplifiers, and **mixing boards** that are needed for large scale musical entertainment. Even that single speaker's microphone requires a public address system (PA), an electronic sound amplification, and distribution system, consisting of the microphone, an amplifier, and at least one speaker. The term is also used for systems that may also have a mixing console, amplifiers, and loudspeakers that could be used for music as well as speech.

Some of the standard sound equipment items used for meetings and events are:

- Mixers or mixing boards are used to blend sounds from different inputs, with large-scale boards capable of handling dozens of input sources (such as a 26-piece orchestra). The blended sound is then sent out through a central output (such as a speaker system or monitors). Musicians and vocal groups require this type of process to create a uniform, amplified sound. Mixing boards are particularly useful when combining live and recorded music.

- Lectern or speaker microphones—these tend to be **unidirectional microphones**, only picking up sound from one direction. Those that are used for gathering sounds from multiple directions are considered to be **omnidirectional microphones**. The **perimeter zone microphone (PZM)** is flat in shape and picks up sound from a 180-degree radius. Choirs and other large vocal groups typically use this type of microphone.
- Wireless microphones, like the **Lavalier**, are made for hands-free operation, and use FM transmitters to send signals to the mixing board. Lavaliers are small microphones that are worn on the body, usually fastened to clothing with a clip, pin, or magnet. The lavalier cord may be hidden by clothes and either run to an RF transmitter in a pocket, be clipped to a belt (for mobile use), or run directly to the mixer (for wired applications).
- Sound consoles or racks are multicomponent systems, stacked in a vertical configuration, and are the control centers for microphones, amplifiers, speakers, and monitors.
- Monitors, both stage monitors (wedges) and in-ear wireless monitors, allow performers to hear each other and to communicate with the sound engineer. The concept behind the use of monitors is that they allow the performers to hear what the audience hears.

As with all event elements, sound and lighting decisions are not just for effect; rather, they need to be based on the goals and objectives of the client. If the objective is to allow attendees to network, your lighting design and sound levels will create a more casual, relaxed atmosphere; conversely, if a more celebratory environment is desired, changing lights, moving images, lots of colors, and energetic music will do the trick. And all of these ideas need to fit within the parameters of what's possible at that particular site. With all the technical options available, adding excitement and production value are the realistic goals of a sophisticated lighting plan as well as a well-configured sound system.

In order to determine what sound and lighting equipment is needed, one does not have to be a roadie or skilled technician; what is required is the ability to determine what end experience is expected by the attendees or guests. Research and exposure to all types of productions is key to knowing what is possible. Relationships with vendors and suppliers can be enormously helpful when it comes to new technology ideas and how they might be adapted to specific meetings, events, and venues.

Power Distribution

After determining the feasibility of the design, and the equipment that will be used, power requirements will be the next element on the technical management checklist.

Power distribution, or "power distro," is the function of carrying the required amount of electricity from a main source to the event space. Once the power arrives in the space, it is run through a distribution board, which then divides the power into individual circuits, and equipment is plugged in. Circuits carry a certain load, or amount of power, and the total of each event element will determine the overall power needs. It is always a good idea to utilize your participating vendors, and their knowledge and experience with the equipment, to give a good overview of power requirements and capabilities. It is important for the technical manager to find out the power requirements for each of the chosen AV, sound, and lighting elements. As mentioned earlier, newer LED and energy-saving equipment technologies are reducing the overall power needs of today's conventions, meetings, and events.

Staging Needs

The term "stage" or "staging" can refer to both permanent and temporary structures. If you're lucky enough to have a permanent, built-in stage in the space being used, it will translate into savings in your budget, time, and logistics. When a venue is built with a permanent stage area, some of the ancillary equipment is already installed: This may include fly rods, trussing, even a minimum number of **luminaires** (light fixtures). As an example, when determining what equipment and services are included with the space, ask about a static "stage wash"; that is, will the venue turn on the existing lighting fixtures, at a minimal charge? Permanent stages definitely offer some overall savings.

Portable or modular stages are used in situations where a built-in stage is not available. Indoor stage sections, sometimes called risers, are usually available in a variety of section sizes, with legs that can be installed at 12 inches, 24 inches, and 30 inches, with steps, ramps, and guardrails provided (it is important to check both local codes and venue rules to decide when handrails are required). An outdoor venue may require a self-contained mobile stage, usually delivered in a trailer, and opened right on the spot.

Depending on the activities to take place, stage height, flooring material, and weight limits will need to be taken into consideration. A factor such as audience size might also be a determinant in the height of a stage; an audience of 5,000 to 10,000 concertgoers needs to be able to see the performances from a distance, so concert stages tend to be four- to five-feet high, for visibility and security reasons. A meeting of 300 to 500 sales reps, viewing a PowerPoint presentation and listening to next year's financial forecast, probably only needs the presenter's stage to be raised about two feet for good visibility. Flooring material makes a vast difference to dancers in a production show…please, no carpeting! It can actually be dangerous for dancers to perform on carpeting, as the pile of the carpet may act as nonskid brakes on their movements. When permanent stages are built, they are required to provide the weight limitations to anyone producing an event on that stage. Portable stages are usually the ones that cause the most problems. Dangerous situations can occur when the technical manager of a production does not consider all the equipment that might be needed on a portable stage, not just the performers and speakers. There are many documented instances where disaster could have been averted if the weight load of equipment and people had been properly calculated. Some situations have resulted in injury to staff.

Safety and Security

By definition, when we discuss safety, we are talking about keeping the event environment free from potential hazards or risks to the attendees. Everything from the design and layout of the site, to the equipment and décor that is brought in, needs to be considered in any safety analysis. A standard risk assessment chart can help determine what hazards could affect staffers, volunteers, and attendees, and how likely it is that an oversight will create a safety issue. Some questions to be considered include:

Equipment and Décor

- Is all equipment and décor in structurally sound condition?
- Has everything been properly installed?
- Have all rigging and staging elements been properly rated for weight loads?
- Have all overhead elements been properly rigged?

Attendee Movements

- Are all aisles clear of obstacles?
- Have all cables and electrical wiring been secured and ramped, if necessary?

- How will attendees move throughout the space? Will this change as the event goes on?
- What activities during the event will affect how the crowd changes?
- Are there any special effects that need to be considered for safety issues? (e.g., indoor use of fog machines or **pyrotechnics** requires that smoke alarms be disconnected, and that a Fire Marshall stand watch for fire issues.)

Security deals with a separate issue: the protection of property. The term is also commonly used in reference to the personnel that carry out the tasks of overseeing and protecting the property and assets of a meeting, convention, or event. Even though each type of event will need to address specific challenges and concerns, the general categories of a security plan deal with the following responsibilities: controlling attendance, observing behavior, preventing realized risks, guarding assets, and dealing with emergencies. With such a wide array of issues to cover, the ability for the technical manager to communicate with security staff is extremely important. Technologies such as two-way radios, cell phones, headsets, and concealed microphones aid in transmitting information to the appropriate parties. The technical manager and the event producer have the responsibility of creating a safe and secure environment and maintaining it throughout the production.

SELECTING VENDORS

Equipment Specifications

A good working relationship with vendors, suppliers, and contractors, along with aggressive negotiating skills, usually leads to successive and memorable meetings and events. Since no technical manager produces any event without interacting with a multitude of other companies, knowing the products and services of many different suppliers is definitely a positive attribute.

The vendor selection process begins with a comprehensive list of equipment and services needed to accomplish the event objectives. Elements such as trash disposal or photographers can have fairly general specifications, while the instruments for a musical rider may need to be specific brand names, model numbers, and have certain capabilities, as requested by the performers.

The Care and Feeding of Riders

In law, a rider is an additional clause, amendment, or stipulation added to a legal document. Think about your homeowner's or renter's insurance; if you want to have your jewelry or high-end electronics covered on your policy, you need to add an additional document specifying those items: a rider. In the hospitality industry, it is an addendum to any service contract.

For example, a technical rider might be given to show management when they rent a space for a trade show or convention. This type of rider will spell out all the specifications of the space, including its dimensions, power capabilities, and all the technical equipment currently available there. It will also contain rights and restrictions for the renters of the space as well as their event professionals and outside vendors. It is crucial that the event professional review the contract rider early on, so there are no surprises when the final bills come in. Preset fees and charges may be applied, and specific labor may be required, depending on the design of the event.

(Continued)

Another type of rider, one that deals with speaking engagements and other performance genres, is commonplace in entertainment contracts. Entertainment riders tend to cover a variety of categories, technical equipment, and services included. Typically, a performance rider will address:

- Transportation, accommodations
- Hospitality, food and beverage
- All technical equipment and services before, during, and after the performance
- Rehearsals, dressing rooms
- Personal services, specific products

In the contract, the length, content and actual cost of the performance is agreed upon; the rider includes all the required elements for the performer(s) and their staff or support crew. The cost of the technical requirements of most performance riders can be equal to or more than the cost of the entertainment itself. Executing the technical portion of a performance rider is just as important as paying for the performance. Speakers, celebrity guests, and performers can refuse to appear at a contracted event if the agreed-upon elements of the rider have not been met.

Take care to dissect and digest every section of a rider. When you sign the contract, you are agreeing to the rider, so tackle the rider as soon as you have an idea of the site selected or the entertainment chosen. Proper review may save you time and money in the production of the event.

Resources for the technical production will vary in price, quality, and availability; all three of these variables must be weighed against the human, financial, and temporal limitations of the event. Once the technical manager has assessed the meeting or event needs, certain questions must be answered. Do I have enough time, money, and staff to utilize a particular technical element? If so, which supplier can provide the equipment or service within the resource guidelines? The answers will aid in selecting the right vendor, supplier, or contractor. Of course, previous working relationships and recent references help in narrowing the search.

In-House Providers and Exclusive Contractors

One aspect of vendor selection that needs to be considered is the use of in-house providers and exclusive contractors. In-house providers are usually retained by the facility, or can be an internal department within the venue, and have an excellent working knowledge of the capabilities of the site. Contracts for meeting and event space may refer to the need to use the products and services of these providers. With some venues, hefty surcharges and fees are applied if the technical manager or event producer decides to hire an outside vendor for products and services that are available from an in-house provider. For example, if a venue has an in-house AV department, bringing in an LCD projector and screen might incur additional charges, usually in the neighborhood of 50 percent of the revenue that the department would lose. Exclusive, or outside, contractors have a similar role: They are the only companies that are authorized by the venue to provide a particular product or service; basically, they have been approved and are recommended by the venue.

The good news is that it is common to negotiate pricing and terms on equipment provided by an in-house or exclusive contractor; in many cases, the departments or companies actually own the equipment to be used and have a great deal of leeway in discounting the prices. Labor and staffing prices tend to be less flexible.

Union Contracts

One of the questions that a technical manager must ask early on is whether a venue is a union or nonunion house. If union contracts are in place, the effect of these contracts on the technical labor force needs to be clearly understood. Sometimes hourly rates, breaks, and other required working conditions will be spelled out; duties and responsibilities are clearly outlined—resulting in a list of do's and don'ts for the event professional to follow. Since every contract, every union, and every venue has different guidelines, it is not a good idea to generalize about what limitations the technical manager may have; read and ask questions about the union contract. In trade shows, the exhibitors are provided with a manual, or guideline and resource book, either printed or in digital form, which delineates what the exhibitor can and cannot do as well as the in-house and exclusive vendors they are required to use.

Supplier Contracts

Once the research has been completed, and estimates have been obtained from various vendors, the selection and contract process begins. Most vendors have a standard contract; this is usually a good starting point. As with any well-written contract, insure that it spells out the benefit for each party (offer), there is a place for both parties to sign (acceptance), items of value are exchanged, like services and payments (consideration), and it gives the assurance that the person signing has authority to sign (legality). To make sure that your interests are protected when signing a vendor or supplier contract, look for the following:

- Detailed description or list of products/services
- Key dates, start and end times
- Terms of delivery
- Payment schedule
- Liability and insurance
- Key contacts

Completed supplier contracts can serve to provide historical and evaluative information: How was the quality of the product? Was the service what you expected? Was the vendor easy to work with? This type of review helps to expand your roster of good working partners.

General Services Contractor (GSC)

Here is one last word on trade show vendors. The most important vendor relationship during exhibits and trade shows is the **general services contractor (GSC)**. In most destination or convention cities, this is a company that handles all aspects of installation and dismantling (I&D), from booth structures to power drops. The GSC is also responsible for securing and implementing all permitting, licensing, and Fire Marshall Guidelines for the site. The GSC signs off on all union contracts in force during the trade show, and is required to ensure that stated union rules are followed.

LOGISTICS AND THE HUMAN FACTOR

When the design and planning have been completed, the technical manager must prepare to orchestrate all the elements of the event. This process can be the most challenging, especially when working with multiple vendors, suppliers, and contractors as well as the venue itself. This is the "herding cats" syndrome mentioned earlier. The production schedule and the event or show flow are tools that allow the manager to put plans in writing, in a chronological manner, and communicate these timetables to all key players in the event production process.

Production Schedule

An updated **production schedule** (see Exhibit 1) provides an accurate, chronological history of the event installation and dismantling, whether for a special event, concert, or trade show. The period of time covered by a production schedule begins with the first item being loaded into the site and ends with the last element loading out, or leaving the event. Each step of the process is scheduled, taking into account what has been discovered about the site, its loading facilities, and traffic flow. Of course, this is a projection of what should happen and is subject to change at any time.

The production schedule serves a few other purposes, as well. Once a schedule has been created, you can see how you are allocating event resources and any improvements that might be made. Another benefit to a well-developed production schedule is that it keeps all stakeholders on the same page and requires their input to be realistic.

When developing this type of schedule, based on what is known at the time, it is important to include key information, such as day/date, start/stop times, and details of the activities to be completed. Much of the schedule will be based on common sense. For example, dining tables must be put in place before linen is added, and so forth. The rest of the information will depend on the site and its delivery policies and schedules and on the vendors' availability for deliveries and installations. Some production schedules consist of a one-page working document for staff and volunteers during the setup, the event times, and the teardown; task supervisors, along with their contact information, can be included. A production schedule should be prepared several weeks before the event, even though there will be changes right up to the event date. Early preparation allows any and all stakeholders to contribute their input, and allows the technical manager to institute changes as they occur and make decisions as they are needed. Another benefit to this type of schedule is that it highlights the need for any ancillary equipment. For example, scheduling the load in and rigging of the lighting equipment may require the use of a lift or other machinery; common logistics sense ensures that the ancillary equipment is on-site when it's needed. The production schedule utilizes all the facts and insights gathered by the technical manager during the site visits, and from the design discussions with the vendors, suppliers, and contractors.

EXHIBIT 1

the STELLAR EXPERIENCE infinitepossibilities						
				Show Name:	Big Fame Weekend 2010
				Client:	Planet Hollywood
				Client Contact:	Dan Reeves
					Suzi Waltos CSEP
				Event Location:	London Club/Celebrity
				Venue Contact:	Dan Reeves
Shirley Fugazotto				**Event Date:**	Fri/Sun 02/05, 02/07/10
				Event Times:	Fri 8p-10p, Sun 2p-6p
				Room Ready:	One hour prior

EXHIBIT 1 (*Continued*)

Event Production Schedule				Event Producer:	Shirley Fugazzotto CSEP
Thursday February 4, 2010					
Start	Completion	Activity	Supervisor Contact	Contact Cell #	Floorplan Location
AM	PM				
4:00 PM	11:00 PM	Stellar Staff Schedule	Shirley Fugazzotto		Conference Center/Celebrity
5:00 PM	6:00 PM	Load In - Big Fame Entrance/ Backdrop	Juan Suarez		Conference Center
6:00 PM	10:00 PM	Install Entrance	Juan Suarez		Conference Center Glass Doors
7:00 PM	9:00 PM	Install Backdrop & Drape	Juan Suarez		Celebrity VIP Riser
Friday February 5, 2010					
Time		Activity	Supervisor Contact	Contact Cell #	Floorplan Location
AM	PM				
9:00 AM	2:00 PM	Stellar Staff Schedule (AM)	Shirley Fugazzotto		London Club/Celebrity
9:00 AM	10:00 AM	Load In - Chalk Talk Desk/Chairs	Donna Sandoval		London Club
9:30 AM	10:30 AM	Load In - Astroturf	Bob Reinecke		Celebrity Ballroom
10:00 AM	11:00 AM	Set Chalk Talk Desk/Chairs	Donna Sandoval		London Club Riser
10:30 AM	1:30 PM	Install Astroturf	Bob Reinecke		Celebrity VIP Riser
11:00 AM	12:30 PM	Load In Live Trees/Plants	Mark Hill		London Club/Celebrity VIP Riser
12:01 PM	1:30 PM	Install Vinyl Graphics - Desk	Scott Wellington		London Club Riser desk
5:00 PM	8:00 PM	Stellar Staff Schedule (PM)	Danielle Wagner		Celebrity Ballroom
5:00 PM	6:00 PM	Load In - VIP Recliners	Mark Ketchum		Celebrity VIP Riser
6:00 PM	8:00 PM	Build/Install Recliners	Mark Ketchum		Celebrity VIP Riser
Event Production Schedule - Page 2				ph Big Fame Weekend 2010	
Saturday February 6, 2010					
Time		Activity	Supervisor Contact	Contact Cell #	Floorplan Location
AM	PM				
8:00 AM	5:00 PM	Stellar Staff Schedule	Shirley Fugazzotto		Celebrity Ballroom
8:00AM	9:00 AM	Teardown Chalk Talk Desk/Chairs	Donna Sandoval		London Club Riser
8:00 AM	9:00 AM	Load In - VIP Furniture	Donna Sandoval		Celebrity Ballroom
9:00 AM	9:30 AM	Load In - Linen/Referee Caps	Shirley Fugazzotto		Celebrity Ballroom
9:00 AM	9:30 AM	House Blk & Wht Linen - 50 each	Kevin Shepherd		Celebrity Ballroom
9:00 AM	11:00 AM	Install VIP Furniture	Donna Sandoval		Celebrity VIP Riser
10:00 AM	1:00 PM	Drop Linen - House Blk/Wht, Overlays	Danielle Wagner		Celebrity Ballroom
2:00 PM	4:00 PM	Set Live Trees/Plants	Shirley Fugazzotto		Celebrity VIP Riser
Sunday February 7, 2010					
Time		Activity	Supervisor Contact	Contact Cell #	Floorplan Location
AM	PM				
6:00 PM	10:00 PM	Stellar Staff Schedule	Shirley Fugazzotto		Celebrity Ballroom
6:00 PM	8:00 PM	Teardown Linen Overlays	Danielle Wagner		Celebrity Ballroom
6:00 PM	8:00 PM	Load Out - Furniture	Donna Sandoval		Celebrity VIP Riser
6:30 PM	7:00 PM	Load Out - Trees/Plants	Mark Hill		Celebrity VIP Riser
7:00 PM	8:30 PM	Load Out - Entrance/VIP Backdrop	Juan Suarez		Conference Center/Celebrity
7:30 PM	9:00 PM	Load Out - Astroturf	Bob Reinecke		Celebrity VIP Riser

From The Dock to Dessert!

Ryky Patterson, union steward and lead rigger for International Alliance of Theatrical Stage Employees (IASTE) Local 720, likes to tell the story about a load-in that did not go exactly as planned, mainly because of a lack of communication between all interested parties. The job was to produce a headliner concert at the pool of a Las Vegas Strip hotel. This was a regular occurrence at this particular property, especially during the summer months, so the local sound and lighting crews were very familiar with the odd path and tight spaces from the dock to the pool. It always took a coordinated effort with all departments to efficiently bring all the equipment to the pool.

For one particular concert, the headline performers brought their own production crew, a crew who knew the needs of their group very well. What they failed to realize was how limited the back-of-house space was, and how many hotel departments needed to move through the areas at any given time. As the load-in crew started moving the 45 road cases full of sound and lighting equipment through the back halls of the property, it started to look like a Three Stooges movie. The crew first encountered a dozen circus performers getting ready to make their entrances into a ballroom from the back hall service doors. Just as the crew had made their way through the circus acts and turned a corner in the service corridor, they were met by about 100 food servers, some with blow torches, plating 900 individual desserts for another ballroom! Needless to say, the load-in of equipment for this concert took much longer than anticipated, and cost the client more in union labor. The surprising thing is that all the interruptions, slow-downs, and confusion could have been avoided if the technical manager had communicated his/her plans to the other departments; adjustments could have been to either the schedule or the load-in route.

Event Flow or Show Flow

The event flow or show flow document is another tool in the technical manager's arsenal. The event flow covers the time from the opening of the doors until the guests or attendees leave, or "doors closed." This schedule outlines the sequence of everything that will happen in the space during the event. When properly detailed, the event flow helps the on-site vendors keep things moving, and ensures that the client's objectives are met within the time frame of the event. For the sound and lighting engineers, the venue staff, and the speakers and performers, the event flow allows them to be ready for stage cues and visual changes.

Production Professionals

The right crew is vital to the technical manager's success at producing an event. It is quite okay to ask a vendor what team members it is sending to handle your event and to question their experience.

When it comes to structural or technological installations, the event professional must feel comfortable in the knowledge of the crew; in most destination cities, union workers seem to be the most qualified. The International Alliance of Theatrical Stage Employees (IATSE) is the oldest and largest union in the United States and Canada, serving members from the motion picture, theatrical, and audiovisual disciplines. IATSE provides ongoing training, both locally and internationally, to keep its members up-to-date on the newest technology. This union also sponsors educational sessions preparing members for the Certified Technology Specialist (CST) designation. Experienced and rated riggers, who have some of the most potentially dangerous jobs, usually belong to IATSE and are required to take recertification classes regularly. The International Brotherhood of Electrical Workers (IBEW), usually responsible for power distribution at most urban convention centers, requires similar continuing education for its electricians. It is best to ask other managers about the skill level and competence of the workers in your area, union or nonunion. Personal references can be the most telling. Someone who has worked with a crew previously knows firsthand the quality of their work as well as the quantity. Of course, you can gather information from the venue, too.

Managing both union and nonunion workers requires providing staff with a well-developed production schedule so that everyone is on the same page. The technical manager is also responsible for maintaining a safe and comfortable work environment for all workers and scheduling appropriate breaks and mealtimes.

THE MANAGEMENT ROLE

Typically, a technical director or technical manager is part artist and part director, and responsible for all the technical aspects of a meeting, trade show, or special event. He or she must be critically aware of the specifics of the site as well as the needs of all parties involved; it is an all-encompassing role that requires someone with a good overall understanding of event management. The skill that is sometimes overlooked or missing in a technical manager is the ability to lead and motivate the production team. This means wearing many hats, such as:

- Team builder
- Liaison with the equipment operators, in-house staffs
- Rehearsal director
- Risk manager
- Stage manager

Of all of these roles, stage management is the most exacting. This refers to the practice of organizing and coordinating a production, or putting on the show! It encompasses a variety of activities, including controlling communications between various personnel and ensuring that all technical elements are smoothly executed. Stage management may be a role that the event professional or technical director performs in small productions, while larger productions typically have a stage management team consisting of a head stage manager and one or more assistant stage managers and talent coordinators. The responsibilities and duties of stage management vary depending on the type of production and the setting. Generally, it is the stage manager's duty to ensure that the event producer's and client's objectives are realized in the technical aspects of the event. Once "doors open" for an event, the stage manager controls all aspects of the performance by calling the cues for all transitions (this is known as "calling the show") and acting as communications hub for the speakers, cast, and crew. Other team members operate backstage to ensure that actors and crew are ready to perform their duties.

Risk assessment and risk plans must be part of any discussion about the management of a production. Event professionals will discuss having contingency plans, or "backup plans," for certain aspects of a meeting or event. Properly managing the technical aspects of events also requires that the technical manager take into account the various risks that could affect production. The process starts with a risk analysis or assessment that asks the following questions:

- **risk/hazard** = what could happen?
- **probability** = how likely is it to happen?
- **impact** = how bad could it be if it happens?
- **mitigation** = how can you reduce the probability, that is, strategy?
- **contingency** = how can you reduce the impact?

It is important to keep in mind that risks or hazards are not always about safety and security; equipment failures, speaker cancellations, and last-minute changes to layout are all possible hazards, above and beyond safety and security issues. Hazards or risks can usually be grouped into four categories: human, technological, natural, and environmental. Some examples of these are:

- **human** – type/size of crowd, performer cancellation
- **technology** – mechanical, audiovisual, electrical
- **site** – physical location, site conditions
- **environment** – weather, outside noises/smells

Once the risks have been determined, the event professional must plan methods to handle each situation, should it arise during production of the meeting/event. The solutions fall into five categories of action. We can look at the risk of rain at an outdoor wedding, to show three examples of plans to manage that risk:

- **elimination**: removing the problem – nothing we can do about the weather
- **substitution**: replacing with problem with a less risky product or process – not practical
- **engineering**: changing the design so the problem no longer exists – installing a tent over the entire ceremony and seating area
- **administrative**: changing a procedure to avoid the problem – moving the ceremony indoors so weather will not be an issue
- **PPE**: personal protective equipment – this could be as simple as providing umbrellas to guests

Being prepared for the likelihood of a realized risk is a vital part of the role of the event professional or technical manager. If plans are already in place, dealing with the situations as they occur is quite a bit easier (for more detailed information, see Chapter 4 on risk management in *Planning and Managing Meetings, Expositions, Events, and Conventions*, by Fenich). The experienced event professional will take the time to use the risk management plan that has been developed and that can be distributed to all stakeholders; if everyone on the team knows what to do if a situation arises, the production will appear seamless to the attendees and objectives can still be met. Exhibit 2 shows a simple risk management plan form that can help organize the potential hazards as well as their solutions.

EXHIBIT 2   Event Risk Management Plan – Template

Name of Event:				Exact Location of Event:		
Date and Time of Event:				Expected Number of Attendees:		
Event Producer: Name/Company, Address, Phone, Email				Person Completing Risk Assessment		

Task/Issue/Hazard	What Could Happen?	Affected Persons	Priority Rating	Risk Control Measures	Who/When	Notes

SUMMARY

The process of managing the technical aspects of any meeting, convention, or event definitely has its challenges. The responsibility for procuring the required equipment is only the first step. Knowledge of the site and how the design elements will translate at that site is a large part of the manager's role; this is where the event professional or technical manager needs to be part artist and part director. Common sense, aesthetics, knowledge, and previous experience all come into play when making the many decisions about the technical products and services to be used. The person filling this role must also have the communication and leadership skills to work as harmoniously with sound and lighting technicians as with the banquet managers and staff. The manager must also have the vision to foresee the possibilities, problems, and solutions that come up in the production of all meetings, trade shows, and events.

Now that you have completed this chapter, you should be competent in the following Meeting and Business Event Competency Standards:

MBECS Skill # 20: Manage Technical Production

Sub Skills		Skills
20.01	Determine requirements for staging and technical equipment	
20.02	Acquire staging and technical equipment	
20.03	Install staging and technical equipment	
20.04	Oversee technical production operation	

KEY WORDS AND TERMS

corporate social responsibility (CSR)
truss
par can
gel
leko
intelligent (robotic) lighting
lighting designer

lighting director
backlighting
mixing board
unidirectional microphones
omnidirectional microphone
perimeter zone microphone
  (PZM)

Lavalier
power distribution
luminaire
pyrotechnics
general services contractor (GSC)
production schedule

REVIEW AND DISCUSSION QUESTIONS

1. Pick a nontraditional venue that could serve as the site for a special event. What challenges would the event producer face in managing the technical aspects of this site?
2. Explain why a technical manager might choose rear projection over front projection.
3. How does the role of the lighting designer differ from that of the lighting director?

4. Name at least two unions that might be involved in the production of a convention or trade show. What tasks would these union crew members be assigned to accomplish?
5. Give an example of each of the following categories of risk: human, technology, site, and environment.
6. If utilized properly, how can a well-developed production schedule help the event professional?

ABOUT THE CHAPTER CONTRIBUTOR

Shirley Fugazzotto has a 22-year background in the management and sales end of the fashion and merchandising industry. Over a decade ago, she drew on her sales and merchandising skills as she entered the Las Vegas events arena, specifically in weddings, catering, and corporate events. Fugazzotto is owner and creative designer of the Stellar Experience, a boutique event design and production company serving corporate clients for the past 10 years in the Las Vegas market. Before creating Stellar Events and the Stellar Experience, she held director and management positions in several prestigious Las Vegas properties, in the areas of weddings, catering, sales, and convention center special events.

Fugazzotto has also served for several years on the board of directors of the Las Vegas Chapter of the International Special Events Society (ISES) and is a past present of ISES Las Vegas. She has earned both the certified special event professional (CSEP) designation, as well as the certified hospitality educator (CHE) credential. Since 2008, Fugazzotto has also been on the faculty of The International School of Hospitality (TISOH), in Las Vegas, and has been an active mentor for those considering advancing in the hospitality industry.

Member of ISES *International Special Events Society*
Member of NACE *National Association of Catering Executives*

CHAPTER 5

Managing Registration: What You Need to Know and Why

Chapter Objectives

Upon completion of this chapter, the reader should be able to:

- Determine and standardize appropriate policies and procedures for registration
- Seek approvals as required
- Communicate to stakeholders as required
- Determine computer systems and hardware required
- Write a request for proposal (RFP) and assess the proposal to contract an online registration company
- Design a registration form
- Design a standardized confirmation letter
- Create standardized name badges and data lists for use at the conference
- Design and manage on-site registration
- Analyze registration numbers, revenue, and fee structures after the event for inclusion in conference historical documentation

IGNITE Business Event Expo;iBE, June 2012, Toronto Canada.
Debbie van der Beek/IGNITE Business Event Expo: iBE, June 2012, Toronto, Canada. STRONGCO Group of Companies.

Chapter Outline

> ## Prologue
> According to Mark Turner of dotcomyourevent, the true purpose of online **registration** is to create a one-to-one relationship between the event professional and the registrant without them actually meeting. Through a properly designed registration website, registrants should be fully informed about the event before they get there and be able to communicate to the event professional what their personal desires and needs are. The event professional in turn, should pay attention to those wishes on an individual basis and be able to deliver them.

INTRODUCTION

In this chapter, the strategies required for successful registration, both during the process of pre-conference and on-site, will be reviewed. The impact of what can happen within the following elements, if the correct information is not collected, will be addressed:

- Cash flow
- Confirmation letter (particularly as it impacts an international conference)
- Food and beverage
- Room setups
- Handouts (or any printing)
- Shuttle services
- Increased on-site costs
- Marketing
- Risk management
- Speaker satisfaction
- Attendee satisfaction

Historically, the collection of **attendee** data has been done in a variety of ways, including telephone call-in, mail with checks, and others. The collection of registration data progressed in step with technology. The introduction of Excel and other database management systems meant that the event professional could keep track of those who registered. Registrations could now come in from fax machines and be entered into the database, and then through e-mail and credit cards. The challenges with these methods are human error: An employee of the organizing committee had to transcribe all the information, and the margin for error was great; attendees often didn't complete the form and event professionals would have to make phone calls to get the information; if a credit card was declined, it could take some time to track down the attendee and rectify this (and similarly for a check that was not good). Most important was the lack of security: Forms could be lost in the mail or faxed to the wrong location, e-mails could be hacked into and credit cards misused.

Much of this has been rectified with the use of web-based registration systems. Credit cards are encrypted; if they are not acceptable, the attendee is notified immediately. Drop down menus and "must complete" fields ensure the correct information is input by the attendee. All this happens in the blink of an eye in today's world. As this was written, mobile registration apps were just beginning to hit the conference world. What does the future hold for registration technology?

THE PLANNING ORGANIZATION

By now, the event professional, registration manager, or organizer should be familiar with the general structure of the entity planning and producing the conference. Some questions that need to be answered include:

- What is the organizational structure? Who reports to whom?
- Where do I have to go for confirmation and/or approval?
- What is the organization's policy on registration? What legislation has to be referred to and adhered to?
- What record keeping is essential within the confines of the conference/organization?
- Who has signing authority on purchase orders and/or expenditures?
- What computer systems and software will be required? At a minimum, they should include Word, Excel, and a database management system. What will be required on-site? At a minimum, there must be a computer loaded with all the registration information, Internet access, a printer, and badge materials.
- What policies and procedures have been agreed upon? How will reporting back to stakeholders happen? How often?
- What are the financial targets for revenues from conference attendance? What if the targets aren't met?

POLICIES AND PROCEDURES FOR GATHERING INFORMATION FROM REGISTRATION FORMS

Once these questions have been answered, it's time to determine and standardize registration. It's assumed that the event professionals will be using a web-based registration process (either customized for the organization, or managed by an outside company). This must be a seamless transition from the main website. (The development of the website is outside the scope of this chapter; for more information, see Chapter 12 on technology in *Meetings, Expositions, Events, and Conventions: An Introduction to the Industry* 3rd Edition, by Fenich.) The website must include all the information that a potential attendee needs to know (benefits of attending, where, dates, program, speakers, costs, booking accommodations, and transportation). The focus will be on the form itself and the confirmation letter will be sent back to the attendee.

Set Fee Structures

Working with the budget (for more information, see Chapter 6 on financial planning in *Planning and Management of Meetings, Expositions, Events, and Conventions,* by Fenich), the number of days of the conference, and the variety of conference events, a **fee structure** must be determined and made very clear to potential attendees. These can include:

1. As a rule of thumb, a one-day or two-day package, when taken alone, costs more than a three-day package. This is done to encourage full-package purchases.
   a. Full package
   b. One-day package
   c. Two-day package
2. Could be broken down to purchasing individual workshops. Purchase one, and the price is X; purchase two, and the price is XX; purchase 3 or more and save!
3. Purchase "add-ons" to a full package, such as:
   a. Opening reception
   b. Awards dinner
   c. Dine-a-round
   d. Pre- and post-conference tours

4. Price cut-off dates:
   a. Early bird (substantial savings, helps organizers with cash flow)
   b. Regular (up to 48 hours before the conference, enables organizers to manage on-site requirements, such as food and beverage guarantees, shuttle services, and room setups)
   c. Premium on-site should be 30 to 50 percent more than regular pricing. (Please refer to the impact on services in the case study when event professionals don't implement a premium pricing.)
5. Savings for multiple registrations from one company paying at once.
6. If the conference is provided by an association, use higher pricing for non-member attendees. Consider offering attendees member pricing if they purchase a membership.

Set Cancellation and Administrative Fee Charges

Determine how far out (in advance) people can cancel their registration. What will the cancellation fee be? If they cancel within 10 days, will they lose the entire fee? What administrative fees will accompany a cancelled registration? There are costs to the organization to cancel a registration. Credit card fees prevail (both ways); as does staff time to do the work.

Substitutions

Will substitutions be allowed? Does the original registrant need to send a note in writing? Will substitutions be allowed on-site? Will there be a cost to this? Each of these policies has an effect on attendee satisfaction and the conference budget.

Methods of Payment

What credit cards will be accepted? If registration is outsourced, what percentage will be paid to those companies for credit card processing? Will PayPal be accepted? If accepting checks, what currency will prevail? As a rule of thumb, currency is that of the home country of the conference organization. Be sure that the credit card management system is set up to accept cards from different countries if the marketing strategies include targeting other countries.

When calculating expenses for registration, don't forget to calculate expected credit card processing fees.

On-Site Payments

Will only credit cards be accepted? What if someone wants to pay cash? Will there be computer kiosks where on-site registrants can register themselves?

Once these decisions have been made, it's time to look for either a customized registration system or to contract a web-based registration company.

FINDING THE RIGHT REGISTRATION COMPANY

Before contracting with a company, know what the registration company wants and needs. Basic services from the supplier include:

- Helping guide the event professionals to ensure that they have all the information required
- Helping build the website
- Managing the collection of funds
- Having back-of-the-site services to provide required data in a readable and usable format
- Answering all questions

Start by asking around. Check with colleagues. Check with industry associations. What companies do they suggest? Prepare a request for proposal (RFP) that, at a minimum, includes the following questions and information:

- History of the organizer
- Anticipated numbers attending the conference
- Possible variety of fee structures
- Payment methods
- Cost per registration
- Cost of credit card processing
- Cost of web design
- Types of data programming provided to the organizer
- Can a mobile application be designed?

A note about technology: The event professional must know and understand the demographics and psychographics of potential attendees to the event or conference. In 2012, some associations still existed that allowed phone/fax registrations and payment by check. The event professional must determine what applications are appropriate for the attendees.

Once proposals are received, review them all, comparing apples to apples. Check references for those companies submitting RFPs. Review RFPs with decision makers in the organization. Be sure to complete an analytical summary for the decision makers, including recommendations from the registration manager.

THE REGISTRATION FORM

For another example, refer to the Convention Industry Council APEX glossary.

Information to Impart

The conference/meeting/event program is the marketing piece of the conference. What are the benefits to the attendees if they attend? What is the educational value? Will attendees obtain continuing education credits? What are the networking opportunities? What's the return on investment for attendees? A program is for attendees. The organization benefits when it gives the attendee reasons to attend.

As the event professionals determine what information is to be gathered on the **registration form** (see Exhibit 1), it is important to know how that information will be used. If there's no reason to know if the attendee is going to a trade show attached to the conference, then don't ask the question. If the organization wants to compare the numbers on the trade-show floor to the number of attendees who said they would be going to the trade show, then it is an important question to ask. If there are ticketed events, ask each attendee how many tickets he or she wants; do not assume spouses, or so on. Would not want to attend the event.

Please keep in mind that it's not legal to ask certain personal questions (gender, age) in the United States or Canada, while it is legal to collect this data in many European and South American countries. If the conference is being co-organized with a country where it is legal, a decision needs to be made about which of the two countries will be the "host" and which laws are pertinent.

Be sure to include:

- Conference dates
- Conference location
- Conference venue (address and website)
- Registration fee schedule (refer to section on set fee structure)

EXHIBIT 1

This is an example of information that can be requested on a registration form. Used with permission of Michelle Wilson, Registrar, Toronto, Ontario, Canada.

REGISTRATION FORM

[LOGO]

Conference Name
Conference Date(s)
Venue
Venue Address

Thank you for registering for the conference. We look forward to your participation! Please complete the following registration form and click "submit" at the bottom of the page.

Should you require registration assistance, or have any questions, please contact [   ].

Your full conference registration includes [here you could advise if all sessions/breakfasts/breaks/lunches/dinners are included, as well as any evening functions].

Registration Fee Table

Registration Type*	Early Bird (By)	General (After)

* Please review the registration categories/fee types and ensure that you select the appropriate fee below under "event fees." All registration types/fees will be reviewed, and an adjustment to your rate will be made if necessary. Students eligible for the reduced student rate must be enrolled as full-time students. Students may be required to show valid full-time student identification at the conference registration desk when picking up their registration package.

Getting There:

By air: _____
By train: _____
By car: _____

Staying There:

Special conference rate = $ _____ + taxes (single/double occupancy)

Reservations can be made at the _____ by:
Calling _____
Emailing _____
Website _____

(Continued)

PERSONAL INFORMATION

First Name

Last Name

Title

Company/Organization

Address 1

Address 2

City

Province/State

Country

Postal Code

Telephone Number
(include area code)

Email

Confirm Email

ATTENDANCE

Please indicate the
day(s) you will be
joining us at the
conference.

CONCURRENT SESSION – Date/Time

*Please select the concurrent
session you wish to attend:*

MEALS/FUNCTIONS – Please indicate the meals/functions you plan on having/attending.

Date

Breakfast – Day

Lunch – Day

Networking
Reception – Day

Date

Breakfast – Day

Lunch – Day

MEDICAL/DIETARY RESTRICTIONS

Special
requirements

If other, please advise

PRIVACY LEGISLATION – Due to privacy legislation, we require your approval to print your name and contact information in a participants' list for distribution at the conference.

Please indicate:
1. Include my name and contact information
2. DO NOT include my name and contact information

EVENT FEES – Please select the appropriate fee type below. All registrations will be reviewed and registration rates modified if necessary.

Student Information:

FULL-TIME STUDENTS: Students eligible for the reduced student fee must be enrolled as a full-time student in the supply chain program. Students may be required to show valid full-time student identification at the conference registration desk when picking up their registration package. If registering at the full-time student rate, please provide the following information:

Institution:

Student number

Event Fees – Early bird rates are available until "date":

Fee 1
Fee 2
Fee 3

Discount/Promotion Code: If you have a discount or promotion code, please enter it here:

With thanks to Michelle Wilson, Registrar, Toronto, Ontario, Canada

- Information on transportation (air/train/driving, with links as appropriate)
- Information on booking bedrooms (with link and phone number to hotel)
- Personal information
  - First/last name
  - Title
  - Company/organization
  - Address
  - Telephone numbers (business/cell)
  - E-mail
- Attendance fields
  - Days registrant is attending
  - Concurrent sessions registrant plans to attend
  - Meal functions registrant plans to attend
  - Pre- and/or post-conference events or workshops
  - Companion and/or children's programs
- Special requirements
  - Medical challenges
  - Dietary challenges
  - Emergency contact information

- Privacy legislation: When collecting personal information (special requirements), refer to the province/state/country where the organizer is incorporated and registered. A **privacy statement** in Ontario, Canada, might read as follows:

The personal information you were asked to provide on this form will be used to register you for this event as well as for associated administrative purposes, such as meal preparation, emergencies, hotel, travel, and additional event information. The business contact information is normally provided to all participants and sponsors. Questions regarding the usage of personal information can be directed to the chief privacy officer at XYZ e-mail address.

- Method of payment
  - Credit card information
  - Currency
- Discount/Promotion Codes: This is defined by the organization. It could be for speakers, staff, contest winners, and so on.

Impact of Information Collection

On cash flow   Early bird registrations allow the organization to have funds in place to enable payment of deposits as required. Since funds are coming in right up until the conference, the event professional should always be aware of revenues from registrations.

On confirmation letters   By enabling the system to immediately send a confirmation letter (see section on confirmation), attendees have a receipt of their registration and all the information they require before the conference. This is particularly helpful to attendees coming from another country.

On food and beverage   Event professionals can begin to plan for meal guarantees and special meal requirements. Always having up-to-date registration lists makes this a simple process.

On room setups   Event professionals can plan for the most effective use of space for concurrent sessions and the most effective setups for keynote and meal functions.

On handouts   Though fewer materials are printed today, it's important to maintain an up-to-date registration list. Items are often printed at the last minute, so having immediate access to numbers means that it can be done in the host city with very little overprint and no shipping charges.

On shuttle services   As a result of knowing the numbers on a daily basis, event professionals can arrange shuttle services as appropriate—not too many buses and not too few.

On increased on-site costs   There are always unanticipated costs incurred on-site. By knowing attendee numbers, there are fewer costly on-site surprises. (Refer to the case study to see what happens when on-site numbers increase substantially.)

On marketing   By being able to review the number of attendees on a daily basis, event professionals know if they're meeting their target goals. If not, event professionals can develop new marketing strategies to improve registration sales.

On risk management   Knowing who is coming and what their needs are helps the venue employees and caterers prepare for any special food and beverage requirements. If any of the attendees have physical or other challenges, that information can be presented to all those delivering the conference or event and plans can be put into place ahead of time. By asking for an emergency name and contact number, the event professional can immediately contact someone who knows the attendee should a medical or other emergency happen on-site.

On speaker satisfaction   Particularly for breakout sessions, putting a speaker in a suitable room (not too big, not too small; not a cavernous room with just 20 people in it) allows that individual to better relate to his/her audience. (See the section on room setups in the previous page.)

On attendee satisfaction   The more information an attendee has, the more comfortable he or she will be on-site. Because event professionals can view numbers on a daily basis, they can make changes in room setups, food and beverage details, handouts, and others. This will ensure a smooth delivery of the meeting or event, which equals satisfied attendees, which can lead to testimonials that can be used for marketing the next conference.

Access to Information

Not everyone should have access to attendee information. The payment information is encrypted by the registration company and banking institution. Checks should immediately be deposited into the organization's bank.

The following details need to be shared with specific conference suppliers:

- Dietary restrictions (with caterers)
- Physical and other challenges (shared with suppliers such as venue meeting space managers, hotel/accommodations, shuttle services, and perhaps technical support)

Under no circumstances should emergency contacts be shared with anyone unless it is required in an emergency.

The organizations need to decide internally who needs to see the list of attendees, the number of registrants in each fee category, and so on. These lists are designated "back of the house" by the registration company and will be dealt in more detail later in the chapter.

THE CONFIRMATION LETTER

Once attendees have input their information, the back of the house obtains credit card approval, and the required information has been completed (remember, this happens in a matter of seconds), an automated **confirmation letter** (see Exhibit 2) is sent to the attendee at the e-mail address provided. This letter must contain all the details required by the attendee. It's very important for the attendee to be ensured that his or her needs are met. This is the event professional's opportunity to welcome the attendee to the conference or event. If social media is being used prior to the conference, let the attendees know how they can connect to other attendees.

If an attendee is from another country, be sure that he or she is aware of the documentation required to enter and exit the country. Provide the URLs for pertinent websites (for a passport, visa, etc.). Be sure that the attendee is aware of what documentation will be required when he or she registers on-site. Is a copy of the confirmation or photo ID required?

Be sure to repeat the information on accommodations and transportation that is already included on the website. If attendees are traveling by air, how will they get from the airport to the host hotel?

The confirmation letter also includes:

- Conference dates and location
- Branding (logo used on website)
- Cancellation policy

EXHIBIT 2   Confirmation Letter.

Here's an example of a confirmation letter sent to attendees after payment was confirmed. Used with permission of Michelle Wilson, Registrar, Toronto, Ontario, Canada.

Confirmation Email:

Conference
Location
Dates

Thank you for registering for the _____ conference. We look forward to your participation!

Please check your information below for accuracy. Should any changes be required, or if you have any registration questions, please email _____

Cancellation Policy:
Notification of cancellation and requests for refunds can be made by emailing _____ before _____.
Cancellations will be subject to a $_____ administrative fee. No refunds will be issued for cancellations received after that date.

Substitute Delegate:
Substitute delegates are permitted with advanced notification to _____.

Please Note:
[Under this tab, you can list any important information that you want to pass on to the registrant, such as main conference website, travel, accommodation information, passport information, etc.]

Please print this page for your records.

First Last
_____

Reference Number: _____

Registration Information
_____

[All registration information is outlined here]

Event Fees
_____

Fee

Payment Summary
_____

Subtotal
+ Taxes
= Total

Amount Paid
Balance Due

With thanks to Michelle Wilson, Registrar, Toronto, Ontario, Canada

---

- Substitution policy
- Sessions attendee signed up for (concurrent, social, etc.)
- Confirmation of attendee's dietary or special requirements
- Confirmation of name (ask attendee to advise if there is an error; the software automatically prints what the attendee input and this will be the name printed on the name badge)
- Fees paid and **method of payment** (including taxes)
- Reference number (to be used if attendee has any changes)
- An e-mail address to be used if attendee has any questions

NAME BADGES AND DATA LISTS

About 72 to 48 hours before the beginning of the conference, it's time to start thinking about name badges. The name badge provides information about the attendee to other attendees and to security personnel, as the badge indicates what the attendee has paid for. Think of the name badge as external information being shared on-site. It should be branded with the conference logo. The positioning of the names must be consistent. Will the company name be included? The font needs to be clean and large enough for other attendees to read the name.

The badges can be printed directly from the data list provided by the registration software. Because the attendees input their own names, there should be no spelling errors (unless the attendee input the wrong information). The badges, for multiple fee structures, must also indicate what the attendee has paid for. Generally this is done with either colored badge paper or colored dots. For example, a full registration may be a white badge; a two-day registration a yellow badge, and so on.

Badges may also have ribbons attached. The variety is endless and can include first-time attendee, board of directors, student, speaker, member, and others. Badge holders today come in a wide variety. They can carry a logo with or without a sponsor. If using lanyards, be sure the length can be adjusted to suit the person. Some badges are clear plastic to allow for the insertion of printed material, while others are laminated plastic. Some badges are even imbedded with radio frequency identification devices (RFID), which allow for automated electronic tracking of attendee movements.

It is at this point that those with dietary requests need to have a ticket; this is generally inserted into the badge to be used at meal functions. Any other tickets (perhaps special tickets to the gala) should also be included with the badge at this time.

The data lists, on the other hand, are the internal information required on-site. At a minimum, a list of attendees by last name should be printed and be quickly accessible on whatever computer systems are being used. Caution: What if those computer systems fail for whatever reason? It is still good to have a hard copy. The list of attendees should include the following:

- Payment status (does registration staff have to collect funds on-site?)
- Days attending (full conference, one day, two days, etc.)
- Sessions and meals being attended
- Any dietary or other special needs
- Emergency contact information

Each list can then be broken down into speciality lists. For example, lists could include those attending one day only, those with special meal requirements, a full breakdown of who is attending which workshops, and so on. The special meal requirements can then be given to the banquet captain and they can distribute internally as required.

DESIGN AND MANAGE ON-SITE REGISTRATION

At this point, 80 percent of the work has now been done! An additional 10 percent is the delivery of the conference and 10 percent is "post-conference." Up to now, attendees have had only good experiences as they registered, received confirmations, and received answers to their questions in a timely matter. It's time to strategically plan the on-site registration process. How many on-site registrars are needed? How will people register on-site and receive their materials? How will payment be managed on-site? How will questions be managed on-site? The registration area is often the hub of the conference.

As a rule of thumb, there should be one registrar per 75 attendees. It is also preferable to have one or two staff (depending on the numbers) to manage any on-site registration issues, such as substitutions, errors on name badges, on-site registrations, managing credit cards, and so on. The scheduling will be heaviest at the beginning of the conference and less so as the conference moves through several days. It is very important to train registration staff, as they are the first people attendees encounter and are the go-to people throughout the conference.

Finding Registration Staff

Many organizations will use volunteers from their organization. While it is important for employees and volunteers of organizations to meet with attendees, the registration desk is not the best place for this to happen. It is often quite hectic. Find a local college with a hospitality or special events or conference program. Often, students must have completed a specific number of hours of volunteer work to attain their certificate or degree. Make plans to go to the college about two months before and speak to one of the classes. Explain the conference and what the needs are at the registration desk. It is at this point that the collection of names/phone numbers and e-mails is important. As the conference gets closer, confirm which students are prepared to work the registration desk. These students are very appreciative of getting "real-life" experience.

Develop On-Site Registration Policies and Procedures

Policies and procedures for on-site registration include:

- Payment for on-site registration can be handled in two ways. Determine which is best for the conference:
  - Have a registrar dedicated to this. Registrars should have a computer that has a Wi-Fi connection and a printer. They can register the attendee with the software provided by the conference organizer. Once the payment has been processed, the on-site registrant receives a confirmation. Registrars can print a name badge and give the attendee any conference materials required.
  - Set up a kiosk with computers (the number of computers will depend on the size of the conference and historical knowledge of on-site registration numbers) where attendees can input their own registration information. (Note: The software needs to be adjusted to allow premium pricing only.) After payment has been made, a confirmation letter will be printed out. That letter can then be taken to a specific registrar in exchange for a name badge and conference materials.
- Determine the setup of the registration area. Will people line up by last name? Will it be a single queue or multiple queues? Will people come to the first open registrar?
- Determine if people will receive the conference materials along with their name badge or receive their name badge and then go to another area to get the conference materials (this generally happens in larger conferences).

- Determine where speakers, VIPs, and the likes, will check in. Will it be at a separate desk? Will it be with the lead registrar, who is also managing on-site registrations?
- Determine how questions about payments, or payments on-site from outstanding invoices, will be managed. Will they go to the lead registrar?
- Determine how substitutions will be managed. Will they go to the lead registrar for a new name badge?
- Determine how general questions will be answered. Each registrar will be given a list of general questions with answers (see more about this in the training of on-site registration staff). What about a question that can't be answered by the registrar? What will the attendee be asked to do? Or will the registrar get the answer from the lead registrar (using communications) and respond to the attendee?
- Determine when scheduled breaks will happen.
- Determine chain of command if a person can't make his or her shift.
- Determine payment, expenses reimbursed, and letters of reference for on-site registration staff.
- Determine the dress code.
- Determine if food can be kept at the registration desk for on-site registration staff.
- Determine a policy on the use of smartphones by on-site registration staff while on duty.
- Determine what cross-training of roles will take place.

Write an On-Site Manual

The on-site manual will be used for training purposes and as a guide for on-site registration staff. It should contain:

- The name of the conference
- Conference dates
- The history of the conference
- The conference location
- A map of the venue
- The conference agenda, with an outline that includes presentations, social events, trade show hours, and speaker biographies
- A risk management plan
- A contact list that includes the name, home phone, smartphone, and e-mail for:
  - The direct contact
  - The lead registrar
  - Each on-site registration person
- Job descriptions for:
  - The lead registrar
  - On-site registrars
  - Other roles that on-site registrars may fulfill (room monitor, speaker help, trade show work, etc.)
- Answers to "what if" scenarios, such as:
  - What if a person hasn't paid
  - What if a person hasn't registered
  - What if an attendee gets ill (this will be covered in risk management)
  - What if a name badge is incorrect
  - What if you can't answer a question
- A schedule for each on-site staff member
- Policies for:
  - What to wear
  - What if a person can't make his or her shift

- ◦ Food and beverage at the registration desk
- ◦ Payment
- A sample name badge
- The materials to be given to each attendee
- What each dot or color of badge indicates (full, partial registration, etc.)
- What each ticket added to badges indicates (dietary, reception, etc.)
- What to say to attendees as they come up to the registration desk. The following is an example:
  - ◦ "Welcome to our conference. What's your last name? May I see some photo identification? Thank you. Here's your badge and any extra tickets. The yellow ticket is for your special dietary meals. Please show it to your server. Your conference bag contains…. Please enjoy breakfast. The first session will begin at 9:00 a.m. in the room to your left. Thank you! If you have any questions, don't hesitate to ask any of the registration staff."
- An explanation of the registration area setup: For example: There will be five registration tables on the window side of the foyer, marked A–D; E–J; K–N; O–S; and T–Z. Name badges will be set up accordingly. There will be tables behind with bags on them to give to the attendees. A full list of attendees will be at each post. To the left of the registration table there will be a single registration table signed with on-site registration and speaker check-in. The lead registrar will be set up here.

Job Descriptions

Job descriptions for the lead registrar and on-site registration person are as follows. Each role (room monitor, etc.) should have a job description.

Lead registrar: The lead registrar is responsible for supervising the on-site registration team as well as:

- Processing new attendees who register on-site
- Making substitutions and creating new name badges
- Managing monies collected on-site for registration and ensuring that each evening monies are put in safe-keeping
- Making any necessary corrections to name badges
- Managing any on-site payments
- Answering questions that on-site registration staff may not be able to
- Making decisions about schedule changes, as required
- Working with other conference staff to manage on-site crises that may arise

On-site registration staff: Each on-site registration staff member will be responsible for welcoming attendees to the conference as well as:

- Giving each attendee the correct name badge
- Giving each attendee the correct additional tickets
- Giving each attendee a conference bag or materials
- Directing each attendee to the next step (breakfast, session, etc.)
- Answering questions about the conference and/or venue
- Sending those who haven't paid, haven't registered, have name badge changes, and so on, to the lead registrar
- Knowing where to get answers
- Knowing what to do in the case of a crisis

Training On-Site Registration Staff

The best time to fully train the staff is the night before the conference begins. Everything will be fresh for them. It's also a time to build a strong dynamic of the team. This is generally done in the on-site office. It's a time to bring in pizza, soft drinks, and upbeat music.

By now, the schedule has been designed (no longer then four- to five-hour shifts), adjusted, and finalized. Staff members have already been sent all the information they need. Tonight is the time to put the puzzle pieces together. Put the name badges in badge holders, attach lanyards, set up the badges in alphabetical order in the badge slots, add special tickets, become familiar with some of the attendees, and make up the conference bags as well as understand the pieces that are contained in them. Do a tour of the venue, including the main meeting room, any breakout room, meal function rooms, the registration area, the trade-show floor, nearby washrooms, emergency exits, and so on. Review the manual in detail. Review communications (will it be by walkie-talkies? By smartphone?). Role-play a couple of registration scenes: a typical attendee, an attendee with questions, and so on. Review "what if" scenarios. Have a flipchart or white board in the room that can be used for changes by all who use the room. Be sure to answer any and all questions from the on-site registration staff.

Supervising On-Site

Let's face it—working on-site is tiring. It's the supervisor's job to ensure that staff don't get overtired or cranky or panic in any situation. Be sure to ask staff if they are okay. Be sure they have enough breaks and lots of protein and water. If there are signs of fatigue, deal with the person one-on-one out of sight of other staff and attendees. That individual may need an extra break. Be sure to look after yourself in the same way. Continue to compliment the staff and thank them for their efforts.

POST-EVENT REPORTING

The final 10 percent of the work that needs to be done is the reporting. A historical documentation can be used in future years to ensure continued success.

The registration manager's job is to:

- Send thank-you letters and letters of reference to the on-site registration staff
- Reconcile registration
  ◦ Check the numbers of paid registrants for each category
  ◦ Prepare final registration lists for organizers
- Follow up on any unpaid registrations
- Prepare any recommendations for future conferences
  ◦ Should there be as many categories?
  ◦ Should registration open earlier?
- Prepare a list and explanation of anything that went wrong and recommendations for preparing better in following years (for example: Registration desk was overcrowded day one; next year, let's add a staff person)
- Prepare any changes to the **on-site registration manual** and training process

REGISTRATION MOBILE APPS

Technology now allows the event professional and registration managers to be in constant contact with all registrars. At the time of writing, companies have designed mobile apps for registration. From anywhere in the world, using only a smartphone and Wi-Fi, an event professional can access every function of the registration process. What this means for registrants is that should they have an error, event professionals can respond within seconds of receiving the request on their mobile phone. What this means for the organization is immediate access to numbers, dollars, the database, and much more. What's next?

What Happens When There Is No Premium Pricing for On-Site Registration?

A mid-sized regional association moves its conference every three years to locations best suited for its membership to attend. Attendance is generally in the range of 750 to 800. Prior to contracting a management company to manage the conference, the association did not offer an early bird registration fee or a premium fee for on-site registration. Historically, attendees complained in evaluations about cramped meeting rooms and not having enough food and beverage or handouts. Historically, about 10 percent (75 to 80 people) would register on-site. The association did not account for the influx of on-site registration in their design of the program. The association had very little cash flow prior to the conference: Everyone waited until the last minute to register since there was no benefit to register early.

The new management company suggested both an early bird fee and a premium on-site fee to counteract both issues. This also meant less crowding and enough food and beverage and handouts on-site.

In the first year with the new management company, 72 percent of attendees took advantage of the early bird registration and 4 people registered on-site. Evaluations from attendees were very complimentary, indicating that the early bird offer saved them money and that, for once, there was no crowding on-site. This also provided much-needed cash for the association throughout the pre-conference stages.

In the second year, the association decided to continue the early bird fee offer but decided it wasn't fair that those who make a last-minute decision to attend the conference had to pay a premium fee on-site. The management company again tried to explain the reasoning behind a premium fee but were voted down by the conference committee. The management team factored in a 5 percent on-site registration (about 40).

Here are the results of year two:

- 79 people registered on-site (a full 10 percent). Thus by not charging $100 for a premium fee, the association lost $7,900 in revenue.
- The meeting room was not large enough, and twice during the first morning there were two unscheduled breaks to bring in chairs. The venue setup had to be changed from half-rounds to theater to accommodate latecomers (who may have paid full fee and early bird, but didn't necessarily pay on-site). This disrupted the entire audience, who had to move their materials from the tables (and then had no tables!). The cost to the association was an additional $250 in labor. It could have been as high as $500, but the management team negotiated. The venue changed the room in record time: 12 minutes!
- The speakers were disrupted but kind enough to "go with the flow."
- Food and beverage were hugely impacted. As the morning wore on, it was apparent that more food had to be prepared. There was a shortage of food during the first break, and the venue banquet staff scrambled to bring out more. Attendees who came late to the break (again, not necessarily those who had registered on-site) complained about not having enough food. By lunch, the banquet staff had it pretty much under control but still ran out of food at the buffet. Registration staff was dealing with many unhappy attendees, trying to appease them and reassure them that more food would be brought out.

(Continued)

MANAGING REGISTRATION: WHAT YOU NEED TO KNOW AND WHY | CHAPTER FIVE 83

- The conference included one large workbook from a speaker. Fortunately, the management team had prepared an overage of 10 percent. The management team had to print five extra copies of a 40-page document.
- Fortunately, the host hotel had bedrooms they could commit to those who expected to get a room the day they arrived to the conference. With some negotiations, the management team was able to get these bedrooms for a $10 per night premium.
- There was a shuttle service set up from the host hotel to travel to the convention center and again one evening to the off-site gala venue. Because of the increased numbers, another bus was scheduled, increasing the cost to the association by $800.
- The biggest concern was risk management. The plenary room was at capacity, and the venue could not open the door to take over the next part of the ballroom because it was being set for a conference (that was coming in as the association was moving out). (At one point, a member of the association team told the management team "to make the room bigger"!) This also meant that all the audiovisual equipment would have to be moved and re-set.
- The registration team felt the biggest impact. One person had been designated the lead registrar; she had been working with the management team solely on registration. She was set up across the foyer. She was fully prepared—except the numbers were much higher and it seemed they everyone came in at once the first morning. She pulled another registration person off the registration line to work with her. This second person did name badges and talked to the registrants and people in line to keep them appeased as the main registrar input their registrations. The association had to pay a premium for extra registrant purchases processed at the last minute ($2.75 each, for a further expense of $220). Name badges were not checked for accuracy— though no mistakes were brought to anyone's attention—as they were not printed from the input registration. Fortunately, the registration team didn't run out of lanyards; however, the team did run out of some of the materials for the conference bags (and there wasn't a single bag to spare!)
- The main registration area was now down one staff member: she had to cope as best she could (and she did well!).

The biggest impact was on attendee satisfaction. The final evaluations spoke of not enough food, waiting in line too long, the room being too crowded, the loss of table space, etc. Many wanted to know how the conference logistics had deteriorated so much from the previous year, when it had appeared to be finally improving. Many blamed the venue.

Clearly none of this would have happened had the association again charged a premium for on-site registration. What will the association do in the future? The management company contract has ended, so it is hoped that the association now understands the impact of not having a premium price and will create one in the future. At the post-conference meeting, the management company pointed all this out to the association. The decision is now in the hands of the association.

SUMMARY

Registration is the first level of correspondence with the attendee. It needs to be smooth, contain all the information the attendee needs, and be open to further questions that the attendee may have. It is a complicated process; to ensure success, policies and procedures must strategically be designed up front, before people are invited to register. Once the pricing structure is set (and all the other details of the event or conference are known), it's important to know what information the organizers want to collect and why. Determining whether the organizers will have customized registration software or contract with a registration company is the next crucial step. Once the overview of the conference/event and the registration forms have been uploaded, the organizers can see the registrations at any time. This will help the organizers design room setups, determine food and beverage guarantees, know which sessions are more popular, determine if more marketing must be done to prompt people to register, and much more. The information gathered for dietary needs and any disabilities can be shared with the staff at the venue so they can be prepared. Name badges and data lists are also prepared from registrations; guidelines need to be written about consistency and visual impact, along with who has access to the lists.

As it gets closer to the conference/event, event professionals can begin to determine on-site policies, procedures, and staffing requirements. At a minimum, there should be a lead registrar to handle on-site registrations and supervise on-site registration staff. The event professionals can look to college- and university-conference-related programs for staffing. All staff should be briefed prior to the conference and have written materials to help them. An on-site training program must take place the night before so that staff understand the lines of communication and the procedures. After the conference, a full report must be written to be included in the conference historical documentation. At a minimum, a full reconciliation of funds collected from the various pricing opportunities must be included. Remember: 80 percent of the work is completed prior to the conference, 10 percent is done on-site, and 10 percent will take place post-conference.

Now that you have completed this chapter, you should be competent in the following Meeting and Business Event Competency Standards:

MBECS Skill 5: Manage Meeting or Event Project

Subskills	
5.03	Manage running of meeting or event

MBECS Skill 7: Develop Financial Resources

Subskills	
7.03	Manage registration process

MBECS Skill 10: Perform Administrative Tasks

Subskills	
10.01	Coordinate office administration
10.02	Manage information systems
10.03	Write reports

KEY WORDS AND TERMS

registration
attendee
planning organization
fee structure

on-site payment
registration form
privacy statement
confirmation letter

method of payment
post-event reporting
on-site registration manual

REVIEW AND DISCUSSION QUESTIONS

1. How will standardizing the registration policies and procedures help the registration team throughout the process?
2. What are the main items to include in a registration form?
3. What purposes does the registration form serve?
4. Historically, how has registration progressed over the years? What are the advantages of web-based registration?
5. What are the main items to be included in the confirmation letter?
6. What must be included in the on-site registration manual?
7. What are the effects of not having a policy for premium on-site registration?
8. Where is a good place to source on-site registration staff?
9. What is the purpose of writing a post-event registration report?
10. Why is a privacy statement required?

ABOUT THE CHAPTER CONTRIBUTOR

Sandy Biback, CMP, CMM, has been involved in the design and implementation of business events/conferences and trade shows for over 30 years through Imagination+Meeting Planners, Inc. She has been an adjunct professor of meetings and convention management at the University of Nevada, Las Vegas, and George Brown College, Toronto, Canada. She currently teaches courses in risk management, site logistics, and sponsorship in a post-graduate program at Centennial College, Toronto, Canada. She is an active member of PCMA (Professional Convention Management Association) and CanSPEP (Canadian Society of Professional Event Planners).

CHAPTER 6

Food and Beverage Production

Chapter Objectives

After completing this chapter, the reader should be able to:

- Identify different types of events and caterers
- Explain the difference between meetings, conferences, conventions, and "events"
- Differentiate between food and beverage suppliers and their capabilities
- Lay out function space
- Explain preparation and production of food for "events"
- Explain how to manage alcohol service

Producing food and beverage for meetings and events presents a smorgasbord of opportunities. Norman Radtke/fotolia

Chapter Outline

Introduction
Food and Beverage Planning
  Questions That Must Be Addressed Early When Planning and Producing the Food and Beverage
Health and Safety
Exclusive Food and Beverage Providers
  Qualified Suppliers
  Food and Beverage Capabilities

Event Setups and Layout
Décor
Staff
Food
Alcohol Service
  Types of Alcohol Service
Summary
Key Words and Terms
Review and Discussion Questions
About the Chapter Contributor

INTRODUCTION

Foods and beverages in meetings and events is one area that can accomplish many goals for their providers, from gaining the public's eye for new restaurants to helping size up the competition in a saturated market. Meeting and event venues give food and beverage providers an easy and inexpensive way to put themselves in the food spotlight, even for just one afternoon. Those entities that take the time to prepare a unique experience for the convention or event's patrons will reap the benefits of increased business through word-of-mouth marketing. How can patrons skip the impromptu pirate ship set up at the local seafood festival or pass up on homemade gelato at the Italian festival? They cannot and will not, which

Rubber Chicken Story

By

Sean Barth

As I walked into the main banquet room at the Westin for the annual Christmas party, it was unlike any other catering event I had ever been to before: it looked like China! It prompted me to reflect back on all the horrific memories of wedding parties I had gone to as a child with my parents. I remember the same question asked by every server: "Will that be chicken or beef?" or "Will that be chicken or fish?" The protein was always served with vegetables and rice. I just remember pretending to be hungry enough to not get into trouble. The chicken was eternally dry and tasteless, and the vegetables were always mushy and flavor-free. You were lucky if you had a little chicken juice on your plate to help you swallow the rice.

These are now long-forgotten memories: It has been some time since I have eaten an old, rubbery piece of chicken at a catered function. Chefs these days realize that to build repeat business, serving well-prepared, delicious food is paramount. As customers, we do not always gush over every meal, but if there is a bad entrée in among the lot, we will never forget it. Our palates are just too advanced for our own good, and the food movement we have all come to love has spoiled us.

Not only should the chefs of today be complimented, but the set designer and visionary who designed the room and theme deserve kudos, too. I remember sitting in an empty, antiseptic banquet facility. The tablecloths and napkins were the only color in the room beside the tan walls and dull carpet. The wait staff was always in their normal penguin attire, black and whites with a bow tie. Boring right? But not at this Christmas party. I felt like I was walking down a street in ancient China. The facility was decorated enough to make you take a second look: Had I traveled through a time warp? The wait staff wore traditional Chinese clothing; the walls, tables, and more were decorated in traditional Chinese fashion.

What does it take to keep people coming back? Usually just a good story. Be unique, be creative, but whatever you do, don't be afraid to think out of the box to wow your guests.

is why it is a good idea to plan a great experience for your guests, even if the event is set up in the parking lot outside a local grocer for the afternoon. These meetings and events are all about the "wow" factor: or getting people to recognize your meetings and events business and its ability to produce unique events in special locations.

Before getting too far into the chapter, it is imperative to understand a few terms that have not been defined in previous chapters.

Festival organizer – The individual or group responsible for hosting the special event or festival. Synonymous with meeting, event, and convention organizer.

Festival sponsor – The organization or entity responsible for financial support. Synonymous with meeting, event, and convention sponsor.

Food and beverage provider – Any restaurant, caterer, hotel, church, school, nonprofit, or other entity that plans to procure, produce, and sell food at a special event, festival, meeting, or convention.

Festival – A day or period set aside for celebration or feasting.

FOOD AND BEVERAGE PLANNING

It is important that the reader understand that there are differences between the entities that get involved in festival and special event food and beverage and those that get involved in more typical planned special events like corporate meetings and reunions. The latter are often handled by caterers. Thus, the event professional only deals with the "broad brush" aspects, such as theme, site, and the number of people who will attend. The rest is left to the caterer.

It is easy to see the difference between festivals and special events and meetings, conferences, and conventions. Festivals and special events are most often outdoor events to celebrate a time, an area, a heritage, a way of life, a type of food or beverage, or something else to do with the area where it is held. Meetings, conventions, and conferences are planned and held, most often, in hotel conference spaces, convention center meeting spaces, or some other enclosed area dedicated to these types of meetings. These meetings are usually planned and coordinated by someone on the hotel/conference space side and by an event professional on the other side. Festivals and special events, on the other hand, are usually organized by nonprofit organizations made up of community volunteers. This may not seem like a huge distinction, but it makes all the difference in the type of people with whom you will be engaged. While in meetings, conventions, and conferences, you may sometimes work with a nonprofessional planner, say, for a family reunion. With festivals and events, almost everyone is a volunteer. This means that the event professional needs to learn how to work closely with nonprofessional planners, people who may have never done this type of activity before. Thus, the thrust of this chapter is to provide detailed knowledge of the foods and beverages necessary to manage and supervise volunteers. This will also put the event professional in a better position to deal with and assess the quality and capability of a caterer.

Special food events and festivals draw people from all walks of life. A traditional local BBQ cook-off will draw both professional and amateur entries. This provides a great selection in food, but also requires special consideration when planning the logistics of the festival or event. It is similar to that of a hotel sales department in a large metropolitan city. The event professional has to work with different markets in different ways so that everyone can be successful.

Questions That Must Be Addressed Early When Planning and Producing the Food and Beverage

Before deciding on the food and beverage to be served at the event, it is important to consider some "contextual elements" of the meeting and event. Thus the event professional should first look at the following:

Type of Event   One of the first issues or questions that an event professional needs to deal with is the question, "Who does it benefit?" Is it an event to support the local population, such as a church festival? Is it meant to draw people in from other towns, cities, and states? In this case, it could be a festival *or* sporting event *or* convention *or* meeting. Does the entity hosting the event raise money for a charity? Is it a beer festival with food as a sideline, like a "Burgers and Brew Festival," where patrons are there for the beer yet appreciate the food? Is it an annual local event to display before patrons the culinary talents of local chefs, similar to a "Taste of New York" event that brings 40 of the city's top chefs together each November?

From a convention and meetings standpoint, you may have to ask different questions. What is the overall scope of the project? Is it to train employees? Or is the function more special, resembling a reward for a company's best salespeople? In this environment, it is important to understand the client's needs and overall goals in order to provide the best possible service/value.

Demographics of Attendees   Another question to be answered is, "Who will be attending the festival/event/convention?" Is there any historic data on past attendees? What is the age range of the attendees, and how much do they spend on an average day at this event? What is the price point for admissions? For registration? Are there sponsors?

Location   The question, "Where is the event going to be held?" must be answered early. What type of amenities will be accessible: water, electricity, sewer, and trash collection? How much space do you have to work with? The location of the meeting and event has everything to do with its success. A great deal of planning must be spent on this part of any meeting and event. Whether a festival or a planned meeting is at hand, many things have to be considered. If it is an event in the community (a park, for instance), space, utilities, and parking must be looked into. In a more traditional space, such as a hotel, location still plays a big part because of utilities. Some creative event professionals want to use nontraditional hotel spaces, which is a great idea, but a feasibility study needs to be done quickly to see if it would be possible. A major consideration for traditional meeting spaces (hotels, convention centers, etc.) is whether multiple meetings and events can be held on-site at the same time. Space must be allotted carefully so that the different meetings and events do not hinder each other. Hosting a high school cheerleading competition next to a "Sounds of Nature" lecture is probably not the best idea because of the group differences in wants, needs, and behaviors. The high school competition will have lots of people cheering, while the nature lecture probably requires a quiet space in order for attendees to fully enjoy the lecture. While these can be hosted at the same time, proximity and location must be taken into account.

Additionally, there needs to be an understanding upfront regarding who is going to provide what; regardless of whether it is a festival, special event, meeting, or convention. There is nothing worse than showing up on the day of the meeting and event and not having the proper tables to set your display on because the lines of communication got crossed, or finding that insufficient numbers of wait staff were assigned. As sustainability ventures grow, the climate of meetings and events is also changing. It is important to work closely with the meeting, event, convention, and festival organizers in order to agree on guidelines for food and beverage production. Likewise, these guidelines need to be in writing and agreed upon before committing to the event.

Space   Depending on the type of meeting, event, or festival, the organizers may provide different levels of support. Event organizers may commonly include space. Space is a limited commodity, whether your event will be held in a parking lot, a convention center hall, or a hotel ballroom. You need to be sure there is enough space to accommodate your event and its attendees and their needs. Space may account for a large portion of the cost for the event, depending on where or what it is. Space is often purchased by the meeting entity and sold again to vendors. In conventions and expositions, this is how nonprofits make a large portion of their annual operating funds; hotels and conference centers may use this as a negotiation tool. A wedding at a local hotel might receive a reduced ballroom rental fee if the hotel can gain revenue by booking a certain number of rooms for the wedding party.

If a large space is being resold as vendor space at a festival or exhibitor space in a convention center, certain sizes of allotments (usually 10 feet x 10 feet) may be sold at a set price. Space is also broken down by location. This is very important, and needs to

How Much Space?
Space Requirements for Receptions

Minimum (tight)	$5\frac{1}{2}$ to 6 square feet per person
Comfortably crowded	$7\frac{1}{2}$ square feet per person
Ample room	10+ square feet per person

Space Requirements for Tables

Rounds	60-inch round =	5-foot diameter =	Round of 8
	72-inch round =	6-foot diameter =	Round of 10
	66-inch round =	Compromise size =	Seats 8–10
Rectangle	6 feet long	30 inches wide	Banquet 6
	8 feet long	30 inches wide	Banquet 8
Schoolroom or classroom	6 or 8 feet long	18 or 24 inches wide	
Half-moon table	Half of a round table		
Serpentine	$\frac{1}{4}$ hollowed-out round table		

be addressed up front with F&B (food and beverage) providers. The location in which they are set up will predict the overall quality of the event. Often, location is dictated by services such as electricity, water, and sewage. If event organizers are providing these services, then the locations of F&B providers can be challenging. Most special events can be produced with very few set services like water and electricity, although as providers get more and more creative, their list of desired services also increases. The event organizers must also consider variety. It is usually impossible to please everyone. However, listening to the attendees' desires goes a long way toward producing an event that will be successful and stand the test of time. This could mean keeping all food and beverage in one area, similar to a mall food court; or the food and beverage could be scattered throughout the whole landscape of the event. Both raise significant issues from multiple perspectives and will be discussed later in the chapter.

Price   The price to produce the food and beverage at the festival or event may include the following:

- *Equipment* – Tents, tables, chairs, trash receptacles, recycling containers, linens, and signage for the event. Most major cooking appliances are provided by the food and beverage entity producing the event.
- *Marketing efforts* – For the set fee, the organizers may help to get the name of food provider out to the public in a number of ways.
- **Logistical support** – This may be given before, during, and after the event. Depending on the location, organizers may help unload and load the equipment, supplies, and products brought by the food and beverage providers. They may offer staff to help collect food tickets during the festival, and perhaps to help out in the production of food for the event.
- *Licenses and permits* – Depending on the jurisdiction of the event, local organizers could provide the appropriate licensing and permitting for the food and beverage providers. For example, in South Carolina, each food and beverage provider

needs a certain permit to produce food at a special event. However, each festival organizer is responsible for acquiring all the permits associated with tenting for the entire event. In this case, the event organizers would have to provide the permits for tenting, even if the F&B provider were supplying its own tents.

- *General commissary* – For events large enough, or those that have a location that is hard to get in and out of, event organizers may decide to provide a general commissary for common used goods. In addition, with sustainability in mind, event organizers may do this in order to reduce the amount of waste. Event organizers could provide and make mandatory the use of china, silverware, and so on in an effort to reduce waste.
- In some areas, event organizers have to use a certain percentage of recyclable goods in order to obtain a permit for the event. This means getting all the vendors on board to deliver goods in these sustainable packages.

The rest of the goods needed to host a successful event are the responsibility of the food and beverage provider or caterer. These can include the following:

- *Equipment* – Anything else that may be needed to procure, produce, and sell the goods. This can include normal equipment—an oven, stove, fryer, grill, or propane wok—or specialty equipment used to produce food for the event.
- *Labor* – An event is an opportunity for a company to put its best foot forward, so the importance of labor should not be overlooked! Food and beverages employees may see working at an event as a punishment. But keep in mind that a special event or festival needs to be staffed by the most outgoing employees in the establishment. Much of the guest satisfaction is derived from interacting with the staff, so only outgoing people need apply.
- *Product* – Unless it is a competition where everyone is making the same dish, food and beverage products are purchased and delivered by the food and beverage provider. This will be discussed in length in the next section of the chapter.

From the food and beverage provider's perspective, there are many things to consider when planning a special event or festival; this includes the level of service desired, the type of food served, how you are going to serve it, and so on.

The event professional must "guarantee" a certain number of diners and pay the F&B provider for that amount, regardless of how many attendees actually show up. Thus, it is critical to have an accurate count. One method is to require meeting and event attendees to obtain tickets prior to the meal. The price of the meal is included in their registration or ticket price, so they are not charged extra. However, by obtaining tickets at the beginning of the event, the professional can get a close to "real-time" count. The event professional can also negotiate a certain percentage of seats to "set over" the guarantee. The average **over-set** is 5 percent, but should be adjusted: 100 guests = 10 percent over-set; 100–1,000 guests = 5 percent over-set; over 1,000 guests = 3 percent over-set.

HEALTH AND SAFETY

Several different types of permits may be needed in order for the festival or special event to proceed without the intervention of the local authorities. These permitting processes are in place to protect both the consumer and the producer, and should not be viewed as an added hurdle. Make sure to do your homework when considering the different entities and permits you will need. Check with the local governing bodies. Familiarize yourself with the permits needed in your area, as many of these laws are being updated due to the large volume of special events being held. The various types of permits that may be needed to host or to participate as a vendor at a special event or festival are listed here:

- *Special event permit* – Most towns and cities require the hosting body to file for a special event permit. In this process, the local governing agency requests information on the event as a whole. The agency will question the timing, the location, activities, any anticipation of disruption to normal daily activities, the demographics, the signage, the layout of event, whether the event is public or not, the anticipated level of noise, parking, if alcohol is involved, and the hosting entity itself. There are even more special permits required in some states. For example, in South Carolina, additional permits are necessary if there are to be street closures, a moving parade, beer/alcohol, and live entertainment.
- *Alcohol permitting* – The state department of revenue requires a special permit to dispense and sell alcohol at an event. This may fall on one person, not the entity as a whole, as it usually entails a criminal background check to make sure that person does not have outstanding warrants or arrests. Alcohol permitting comes at a price. It usually means that local law enforcement officers must be hired, too. The number of officers needed depends on the location size and layout and number of attendees. They are there to protect the hosts as well as the attendees. They can protect money drops as well as take care of the occasional overindulger. This permit is also where you pay state and local alcohol sales tax after the event. Usually a percentage of sales is taken. In the case of a local beer festival, it was a percentage of each drinking ticket sold. Out of $54,000 in tickets sold, the tax liability was $3,400.
- *Tent and fire protection permitting* – This will be required in some states where temporary tents are being used. The fire department always has a say in the traffic flow of a special event. They need to be able to make sure that they can get their equipment in place should an emergency occur. They also have final say on the maximum number of attendees allowed and how the festival or special event is arranged.

EXCLUSIVE FOOD AND BEVERAGE PROVIDERS

Qualified Suppliers

When dealing with food and beverage suppliers, it is important to know all of the options for purchasing food and beverage. Sometimes a chain property like Hyatt has national accounts with large food and beverage providers. If this is the case, a company such as U.S. Foods could be the **exclusive provider** for that property. This means that all food and beverage items must be purchased from U.S. Foods, exclusively. In turn, the business will receive favorable terms due to the group buying power of the Hyatt brand. This could include perks like reduced costs, favorable delivery times and days, and many other buyer perks. If it is a smaller nonchain property, a series of F&B providers may be used. In this case, food and beverage providers should be screened and a list of *approved suppliers* (suppliers that the property is allowed to use) should be developed. This list makes choosing the right provider an easier task, as the suppliers have already been vetted and approved by the company. Another way to handle the purchasing function is to have suppliers that are *preferred*. These suppliers are contacted first when purchasing goods. If the items needed cannot be provided by the *preferred* supplier, the buyer works his or her way down the list to the next **preferred supplier**.

This could take on another life if a different type of location is considered. Most convention halls, outdoor sporting venues, and even some state and locally owned land have contracts with certain food and beverage suppliers. For instance, a sporting arena usually has an *exclusive* food and beverage provider with whom it works. This would be the only entity allowed to sell food at that particular venue. Outside caterers in this case are not allowed to provide food and beverage services in this venue. The situation could also be a similar for festivals, where one food and beverage provider supplies the food for all vendors at this particular festival. Even if the vendors do not usually use this F&B provider, it would be necessary in this instance. This may create friction between the F&B provider and the vendor if there is a discrepancy in the quality of products normally used and the one the company is forced to use in this instance. Further, deals can be negotiated through group purchasing and delivery charges if exclusive providers are used for outdoor, unique events. Additionally, exclusive providers can offer perks like on-site logistical help to house and cool foods. Benefits such as these can make the difference in producing a quality event.

Food and Beverage Capabilities

There are many ways in which an F&B supplier can be of service to a hospitality entity. They are indispensable allies both on- and off-site in providing good service to guests. On-site, F&B suppliers can help the kitchen prepare its menus by advising on new products or variations of products that fit the requests of the guest. They are the direct line to what is available to purchase and at what price. They are most helpful when it comes to pricing: They can offer suggestions on product quality and physically price out menu items in order to fit the price structure for an event. They also have the day-to-day knowledge of how products fare in the marketplace (whether consumers like them or not). This information can go a long way to make an F&B operation run more efficiently: It limits waste associated with bad purchases and gives the kitchen staff the support it needs to make informed product requisitions.

Off-site F&B suppliers can provide assistance in a number of ways. They can simply help with equipment by providing cooler and freezer trucks. For a large event without a traditional kitchen, it is imperative to provide cooler space to keep food from spoiling. It is one thing to serve hot dogs and burgers to 200 people. Those products can be stored in a couple of ice chests. But think about something like the Masters Golf tournament, which feeds close to 100,000 people a day. Normal facilities cannot store or produce that amount of food, so temporary facilities must be set up. One such facility is a series of refrigeration and freezer trucks that can be provided if purchasing their products.

Another function that F&B suppliers can provide is in the requisition and issuing of food. They can consult with event organizers and set up systems for food purchased by individual vendors, or they may be able to run the whole operation themselves. This can happen one of two ways:

1. The F&B supplier can assist the event organizer to design policies related to the dispersal of food and beverage on-site during the event. This can be handled in various ways depending on how F&B sales are being handled. It could be that the product is not charged for and the F&B entity pays the event back at a set rate, or the F&B entity could sell the goods and then be given a portion of their sales by the event organizers. At the Heritage Golf tournament, concessionaires are given all the products needed to serve food and beverage for each day of the tournament at no cost to them. They sell the products and then give all the money back to the Heritage Foundation. The Foundation then pays the concessionaires a set portion of their overall sales after the tournament is over.

2. The F&B supplier can set up shop at the event and conduct work as usual. F&B entities can directly purchase goods from the supplier on-site. For smaller functions, this can be done with minimal extra hands, just someone on-site and one delivery driver who can commute back and forth to the distribution center. For large entities, it could be a very large undertaking, with an entire distribution system set up and manned for the duration of the event.

The two processes described above have different positive and negatives aspects; both have security issues and control quality and security in different ways.

Food and beverage choices must be analyzed before any decisions are made. It is important to look at similar products to test for desirability. In today's food market, there are many choices; the undesirable choices must be weeded out. You must be able to systematically weed out the sections: to see what is most important in price, value, and quality. For different events, different considerations need to be thought through. For a teachers' conference, a good value is always going to be imperative. However, for a high-priced wine tasting, quality is probably going to be more important. This is why it is good to get to know the meeting and event organizers and understand their vision for the event.

Types of Food Functions

Box Lunch: This is meant to be carried away from the lodging facility for a meal in a remote location. It can be eaten on a bus on a long ride to a destination or eaten at the destination. Box lunches can also be provided to attendees at a trade show.

Breakfast Buffet: This is an assortment of foods with a variety of fruits and fruit juices, egg dishes, meats, potatoes, and breads.

Brunch: This late-morning meal includes breakfast and lunch items. A brunch can be a buffet or a plated, served meal.

Continental breakfast: This is typically a bread or pastry, juice, and coffee. It can be upgraded with the addition of sliced fruit, yogurt, and/or cold cereals. Most are self-service with limited seating. A more expensive alternative is "seated continental service."

Dinner buffet: This includes a variety of salads, vegetables, entrées, desserts, and beverages. Often meats are carved and served by attendants. Otherwise they are self-service.

Full-served breakfast: This would be plated in the kitchen and would normally include some type of egg like eggs Benedict, a meat like bacon or sausage, a potato item like hash browns, fruit, and coffee.

Full-served lunch: This is a plated lunch, usually a three-course hot meal, and often includes a salad, main course, and dessert. A one-course cold meal is sometimes provided, such as a grilled chicken Caesar salad.

Full-served dinner: This could be a three- to five-course meal, including an appetizer, soup, salad, main course, and a dessert. Food is pre-plated in the kitchen and served to each guest seated at tables (usually round but sometimes rectangular). This style of service is often referred to as American-style service.

Off-site event: This is any event held away from the host venue. It could be a reception at a famous landmark, such as the Statue of Liberty in New York, at a museum, a picnic at a local beach or park—almost anywhere.

Receptions: These are networking events with limited seating, which allow for conversation and interaction. Food is usually placed on stations around the room on tables and may be served butler style. Beverage service is always offered at these events. Light receptions might only include dry snacks and beverages and often precede a dinner. Heavy receptions would include hot and cold appetizers, perhaps an action station, and are often planned instead of a dinner.

Theme party: This is a gala event with flair. It can be a reception, buffet, or served meal. Themes can be almost anything: international, perhaps, where different stations are set up with food from different countries; or such ideas as a casino.

EVENT SETUPS AND LAYOUTS

There is an unlimited number of ways in which any room or space can be retrofitted to host an *Event,* some more common than others. This section will briefly cover the common meeting setups and then move on to some more creative event sets. Planned events like weekly sales meetings and other corporate initiatives are usually hosted in common meeting room setups. See Figure 1 for more detail.

Depending on the type of meeting and the overall purpose, one of these setups or a variation may work well. Some other ideas are slanted theater style, where the chairs are angled, or a classroom-style setup using crescent-shaped or round tables in order to give the group an opportunity to listen to the lecture but also be able to work in small groups at the same table when needed. There are many online resources where you can input the size and layout of your meeting room and see how various setups will look. Free software demos can be found at:

- Meeting Matrix
- Optimum Settings
- Room Viewer

In addition to the space and setup, many other things need to be considered in order to confidently negotiate a successful meeting. There needs to be a general idea of how much space is required for the setup—a tricky task for new caterers. Consult the charts in order to gain a grasp on how much space is needed for various setups.

When working in dedicated meeting spaces, the online tools discussed above can be a lifesaver. On the other hand, what can you do when a potential client drives you to an empty field and explains that they want to host 5,000 people for a two-day wine tasting and public event? There is not a piece of software designed that will tell you how to pull that off. Good planning and a solid understanding will help guide you through to a successful event. When catering an event of this nature, it is good to get in on the ground floor, maybe even helping with the planning of the overall event (see *Planning and Management of Meetings, Expositions, Events, and Conventions,* by Fenich, for more detail on the planning function).

FIGURE 1

Types of room set-ups/layouts.

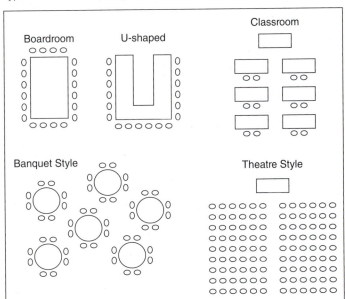

Each event will be set up differently. It really comes down to a dependency on utilities and needs. If the F&B provider needs electricity or water to create the product, then the location it is given is based on those needs. Be sure to obtain as much information about the location as possible. Have a map drawn of electricity and water outlets as well as any other pertinent information. Use this information when it comes time to sell space to vendors and food and beverage providers.

Likewise, the layout is key for indoor events. Traffic flow, safety, and overall ambiance (see Chapter 2 on managing the site) must be considered. Thinking specifically about how many and what types of people are going to attend the event is crucial. Who is the group and why are they here? Wedding parties have very different perceptions than a regularly scheduled board meeting. Wedding parties want to mingle, dance, and carry on, while attendees of a prescheduled meeting want to be comfortable and do the work they came there to do. Think about how many people will attend and how long it may take them to get through a buffet line. If it is a large group, the event professional may split the buffet into two parts so it causes less of a jam or use some action stations. Each event is different and should be planned for accordingly.

Whether an event is held inside or outside, the fire chief has the final word in the layout of a meeting and event. For large events, a visit from the fire department to check and make sure that the layout is safe is a given. For indoor events, laws govern aisle width, how many aisles you need, and the number of doors required. Outdoor events are a little different. The fire marshal will look to see if there is enough space between food and beverage provider tents in case of a fire, if there are clear lanes of traffic for emergency vehicles, and if there are clearly marked exits for patrons. Keeping these things in mind when designing the layout of an event will keep day-of-changes to a minimum.

DÉCOR

Ambiance sells the event, and consistency is king for overall success. It is not just art or just food being *sold* at an art and seafood festival, it is the experience. Having junior fishing tournaments, people in aquatic costumes, an all-seafood "Iron Chef" challenge, seafood sold at the food and beverage providers' booths, and other seafood-related activities can go a long way in contributing to the success of an event. Other seafood- and art-related activities, such as environmentally sustainable programs involved (think "Keep Our Waters Clean" programs), a petting zoo with aquatic animals for the children, live arts and crafts, and a juried art show for prizes, could help to sell the overall "art and seafood" experience.

The same can be said for indoor, hotel-like meetings and events. Long gone are the days when nice centerpieces were all that were needed. Now "the show" sells along with an upgraded level of food. Think of an Asian-themed event where the room transforms your experience and makes you think you just stepped foot in Asia. The room can be decorated like the set of a Hollywood movie, with large streetscapes and a life-sized Tibetan Bell. The waitstaff can be dressed in traditional Asian clothing, and the food aroma evokes a Thai market. To take the event to the next level, the event professional could consider offering calligraphy lessons, a mah-jongg tournament, or maybe even a traditional Japanese dance routine that everyone could watch and then learn. The idea is immersion and engagement: to take people away from what they expect and really wow them. The more time that can be dedicated to the details, the more successful the meeting and event will be.

Other examples of "wow factor" details include six-foot boats in which people prepared and served food for seafood festivals, a prison motif for a BBQ burn-off, a papier-mâché crab tent for a crab festival, a larger-than-life watermelon that people served food out of (think Oscar Meyer Weiner Mobile). These are all ideas that draw people in.

Extreme Makeover: Home Edition or How We Handled Food and Beverage While They Were Taping a TV Show While Building a House

By

Sean Barth

Where do you start when you get a phone call two weeks before Christmas and someone asks you to serve meals for eight days, 20 hours a day in someone's backyard, six weeks from now? And all the food that will be served has to be donated because there is no money to buy ANYTHING! Furthermore, it is only days before the holiday season, and many of the people who could make donations are on vacation. What is the first logical step? Do you go look at the facility? Oh yeah, there is no facility! Do you begin to plan meals? Of course, there is no kitchen. Would it be best to start looking for volunteers to prepare and serve the food? Well, there is no food! So, where do you start?

There is not one right way in which all this can be handled. And on the best day, this may seem impossible. We may need to hire Robert Irvine (oh wait, he did raise a large sum of money for the same family, over $100,000, to be exact) to help us out. The best answer? Start somewhere and move forward. Break the overly large project down into consumable portions, (ironic metaphor planned). There are a few major components to this type of a project. When broken down into small parts, it seems manageable.

First, figure out the magnitude of this type of a project. How many volunteers are we feeding each day? How many different serving areas do we need? In this case, it was one space for about 1,000 volunteers per day and a separate VIP section close to the build site where companies can purchase the space in order to help raise money for the project. Here is a breakdown of what the food and beverage coordinator put together after the event was over:

- Served 18,000 meals to volunteers over eight days. Served from 6:00 a.m. until 3:00 a.m. for eight days. Main meal services were breakfast, lunch, and dinner; although there was always something to eat.
- Worked several deals with local vendors to provide off-hour snacks (wings, pizza, sandwiches, candy, chips, and drinks) to keep the volunteers going.
- Rotated three groups a day through VIP section, both food and sponsors consisting of 18 unique F&B providers and 24 unique sponsors.
- Negotiated to have close to $2,000 in food and supplies delivered to stock the house once it was built.
- Provided 24-hour coffee, drink, and snack service both in the dining area and brought to the build site.
- Only had three dedicated employees. The rest were volunteers provided daily, with no advanced notice of who it may be or when they might show up.

This is considerably easier to look at in hindsight. The only information provided to the food project coordinator was the dedicated meal times and the

(Continued)

approximate number of volunteers per day. There was no mention of 24-hour service (although it was expected), and there were several additional things that popped up that had dramatic effects:

- Project coordinator found four vendors in two days to provide food and drink for 2,000 at the kickoff party. Coordinator found someone in less than an hour to provide coffee to the event when the conveniently nice weather took a hard turn to very cold very quickly.
- Coordinator helped orchestrate a sponsored oyster roast in a unique location for almost 100 people in less than 6 hours (found sponsor, transportation, donated food, unique location, equipment)
- Coordinator helped to put on a wrap-up party for over 400 on the last day of the build, all donated. Held it at a very unique location previously unused for events in an effort to help market this new venue.

With such a small amount of information given, sometimes it was necessary to just make decisions and ask for forgiveness if they were not the right ones. This story can go a long way to showing the reader that sometimes decisions just have to be made. It is certain that no one had ever before invaded this nice woman's backyard and served 18,000 meals out of it. Something unexpected is always going to happen, mistakes are always going to be made; however, it is the recovery that will set you apart from your competition. I think the best example of this was trying to serve coffee all day, every day. The build was in January, and there was quite a cold spell going on. It did not get above 24°C for four days. The dedicated coffee machine was hooked into an exterior water supply line, (also known as a hose). The water line was lying on the ground, so it kept freezing. It was a challenge to constantly keep changing out water lines each time a new one froze. It is the little things that make the most difference. It was a pleasure to see that we could keep the many volunteers warm with coffee and hot chocolate for just a small amount of extra work on our part.

All in all, about 60 local and national partners helped make the event a reality. The companies combined donated goods and services of more than $50,000 to make this event a reality on the F&B side. From small mom-and-pop businesses to large national accounts, the volunteers and sponsors credited with building the house for this deserving family, did so, full and happy.

STAFF

Staffing is a hard concept for new managers to grasp. While the manager may want enough staff to set up, serve, and clean up without taking too much time, the bosses will always want to see low labor cost. Is it possible to please everyone? Yes, as long as some sort of baseline numbers of staffing are used. Considerations for staffing include the type of service, number of people, location, and the skill level of the staff. More staff will be needed for a 100-person wine-paired dinner than for a 100-person continental breakfast buffet. A rule of thumb is to use one server for 30 to 40 guests for a buffet service. For more intensive types of service, the number can be adjusted to one server for every 8 to 10 guests, if meals have to be prepared tableside or if there are other labor-intensive serving routines. For every meeting and event this rule of thumb may be adjusted up or down accordingly.

Service Staff Requirements

Bar: One bartender per 100 attendees. More bartenders = better service.

Meals: Range of one server per 8 diners to one server per 40 diners. Hotel standard is one per 32. Many event professionals prefer one per 20.

Some rules of thumb:

In general

Rounds of 10: 1 server for every 2 tables

Rounds of 8: 1 server for every 5 tables

With poured wine or French service

Round of 10: 2 servers = every 3 tables

Round of 8: 1 server = every 2 tables

Buffets 1/30–40

1 server per 30–40 guests

1 runner per 100–125 guests

French or Russian service

Rounds of 8 or 10: 1 server per table

Staffing for an off-premise special event can be an even harder decision. Details, like the distance from the catering truck to the event location, come into play. How much equipment will be moved over this distance must also be considered. Nothing can make a great event start more horribly wrong than by understaffing for off-premise catering. By the time the understaffed event starts, the staff is sweating and tired and has no desire to provide the level of service that guests expect and deserve. In off-premise catering, there is not additional staff to fall back on if you plan incorrectly. It is imperative to also plan enough staff to set up and break down the event, especially for festivals and other special functions. Extra people are always needed on-site and when guests are leaving a site, so scheduling accordingly is key. It is also a good idea to put the most experienced staff on special events. It helps if the staff working the event is well versed in all F&B activities. At one moment, they could be helping to serve a guest; at another, they may be asked to help finish cooking one of the dishes being served. Having all-around good people working makes everyone's job easier. The key is to have people who are knowledgeable about the overall product and can relate that quickly to the guests.

FOOD

None of the foregoing matters if the food product delivered is not great! The type of meeting and event does not matter; for better or for worse, food is what is most often remembered. With the globalization of food and the entertainment world so entwined in food production, it is hard to be successful while producing ho-hum food products. Once again, the wow factor is critical. The bar has been raised, and the expectations of guests are considerably higher than they once were. It's no longer enough to offer a choice between bland, rubbery chicken and tough, flavorless steak. If there is not at least one wow factor, guests feel as if they have been duped into a third-rate party. It is almost as if the guests expect that Emeril himself is going to pop in and "bam" everyone's meal. Since this is not possible, it is imperative that a tremendous amount of thought be put into the food being produced.

Food prep is one key to a successful event. It can be very difficult to see the challenges that lie ahead in a preparation list. It may be thought that with enough people working together, everything can be prepared on-site on the day of the event. What if the special function seeks to serve 60,000 spectators, 54 luxury skyboxes, and 6,000 buffet style before a football game and there is no kitchen within two miles? Can food preparation be started the same day? Of course not. That is why planning and preparation are critical. For large functions, similar to the one just mentioned, a *production schedule* is paramount for the organization of the back of the house staff. This schedule gives the kitchen staff an idea of what needs to be produced on which days in order for everything to be ready by the meeting and event. Cookie trays can be made a few days out, condiments can be packaged and refrigerated, fruit can be cut a couple days out if cooled correctly, dips and other things can be prepared, and when it gets close to production time food can be par cooked and stored until it is needed.

Food preparation for off-premise events includes getting all the tools and equipment necessary for preparation, production, service, and cleanup. What food is being served and how much of it is being produced at the location of the event versus off-site comes into play. It is crucial to not only produce the food, but to do so in a manner that is safe for the consumers. Proper storage, cleaning, and sanitizing principles must be adhered to. Everything that can be done prior to getting to the site of a special event must be done. There will always be a piece of equipment someone forgot to pack or a food item that the kitchen needs, so having a fall-back option is another key to a successful event. This may mean having someone back at the restaurant or hotel to run product and equipment, or mean being familiar with the local area in order to send someone to get the missing items from local merchants. For example, some PGA golf tournaments that allow multiple caterers on-site will set up a commissary where the caterers can pick up items that they either forgot or have run out of. This type of setup is necessary when driving on- and off-site is not an option for many hours in a row. This gives caterers an opportunity to purchase their goods in a convenient location.

Equipment and production go hand in hand in delivering exciting and great-tasting food at meetings and events. For normal catering held in a hotel or convention center, the equipment available could be endless. There are always stoves, ovens, fryers, steam tables, and other pieces of equipment and tools needed to produce food. In this case, anything is possible. All the equipment at your disposal can produce an infinite number of creative dishes with sufficient time and manpower.

Food Quantity Guidelines		
Type of Reception	**Type of Eaters**	**No. Hors d'oeuvres PER Person**
2 hours or less (dinner following)	Light	3–4 pieces
	Moderate	5–7 pieces
	Heavy	8+ pieces
2 hours or less (no dinner)	Light	6–8 pieces
	Moderate	10–12 pieces
	Heavy	12+ pieces
2–3 hours (no dinner)	Light	8–10 pieces
	Moderate	10–12 pieces
	Heavy	16+ pieces

Like food preparation, production needs a plan. It is crucial to plan production just like a movie producer would plan filming a car chase. Things have to be done in a certain order for everything to fit together. If a protein is cooked too early, it could end up being dry and chewy. If one waits too long to start a risotto, it won't have time to cook and the flavors mature.

For off-premise events, what you bring with you is all that you have. This does not have to be limited in any way, as there are completely portable food production facilities, but these come at a very high price and not many can afford that luxury. Over the years, there have been many unique ideas, from gas pizza ovens on a trailer that have the ability to produce high-quality fresh pizzas on-site anywhere you can tow a trailer, to completely portable outdoor kitchen setups. This is another area where creativity counts. It is not the person with the most tools who wins; rather, the one who is the most creative rises to the top. From grills to toaster ovens and dry ice, there have been some very creative uses of equipment in the production of event food and beverage. Whatever equipment is considered, make sure it has a purpose. Space is limited, and extra product and equipment will not do anything other than slow the process down.

When the festival ends, it is time to clean up and leave. Generally, there will be a time when everyone is allowed to start packing up. At that point, large vehicles are allowed on event grounds again so that all equipment and product can be removed.

For most outside events, the organizers will request that a certain tear-down process be followed. Each process is different, and it is necessary to understand up front what is expected. Sometimes it is as simple as removing the equipment and products; however, sometimes a deeper level of commitment is necessary. Trash must be disposed of in the appropriate containers. The majority of recyclables get thrown in the trash during the cleanup process by vendors and volunteers most closely associated with the event. Take the time to follow through on the commitments of the event; make sure any recycling rules are adhered to. An event professional should leave the area better than he or she found it, and everything else should fall into place.

Types of Service in Food

Action stations: Sometimes referred to as *performance stations* or *exhibition cooking*. **Action stations** are similar to an attended buffet, except food is freshly prepared as guests wait and watch. Some common action stations include pastas, grilled meats or shrimp, omelets, crepes, sushi, flaming desserts, Caesar salad, Belgian waffles, and carved meats.

Á la carte: Guests are given a choice of two to three entrées, with a minimum of two predetermined courses served before the entrée choice.

Attended Buffet/Cafeteria: Guests are served by chefs or attendants. This is more elegant and provides better portion control.

Banquet French: Guests are seated. Platters of food are assembled in the kitchen. Servers take the platters to the tables and serve from the left, placing the food on the guest's plate using two large silver forks or one fork and one spoon. Servers must be highly trained for this type of service. The use of the forks and spoons together in one hand is a skill that must be practiced. Many hotels are now permitting the use of silver salad tongs.

Butler Service: At receptions, *butler service* refers to having hors d'oeuvres passed on trays, where the guests help themselves.

(Continued)

Cart French: Less commonly used for banquets, except for small VIP functions, this style is used in fine restaurants. Guests are seated and foods are prepared tableside using a *rechaud* (portable cooking stove) on a *gueridon*. Cold foods, such as salads, are prepared on the *gueridon* (tableside cart with wheels), *sans rechaud*. Servers plate the finished foods directly on the guest plate, which is then placed in front of the guest *from the right*. Bread, butter and salad are served from the left, while beverages are served from the right. All are removed from the right.

Combination buffet: Inexpensive items, such as salads, are presented buffet style, where guests help themselves. Expensive items, such as meats, are served by an attendant for portion control.

Hand service: Guests are seated. There is one server for every two guests. Servers wear white gloves. Foods are pre-plated. Each server carries two plates from the kitchen and stands behind the two guests assigned to him or her. At a signal from the room captain, all servings are set in front of all guests at the same time, synchronized. This procedure can be used for all courses, just the main course, or just the dessert. This is a very elegant and impressive style of service used mainly for VIP events because the added labor is expensive.

Family style/English service: Guests are seated, and large serving platters and bowls of food are placed on the dining table by the servers. Guests pass the food around the table. A host will often carve the meat. This is an expensive style of service. Surpluses must be built in.

Plated/American-style service: Guests are seated and served food that has been pre-portioned and plated in the kitchen. *Food is served from the left of the guest*. The meat or entrée is placed directly in front of the guest at the six o'clock position. *Beverages are served from the right of the guest. When the guest has finished, both plates and glassware are removed from the right.*

American Service is the most functional, common, economical, controllable, and efficient type of service. It usually has a server to guest ratio of 1:20 or 1:30, depending on the level of the hotel.

Preset: Some foods are already on the table when guests arrive. The most common items to preset are water, butter, bread, and appetizer and/or salad. At luncheons, where time is of the essence, the dessert is often preset as well. These are all cold items that hold up well.

Reception: Light foods are served buffet style or are passed on trays by servers (**butler service**). Guests usually stand and serve themselves and do not sit down to eat. A reception is often referred to as a "walk and talk." Plates can add as much as one-third to food cost because people often select more items or larger portions; however, plates should always be included with reception food service. Control can be managed by selecting appropriately sized plates. Some receptions serve only finger food (food eaten with the fingers), while others offer fork food (food that requires a fork to eat).

Russian service: (1) Banquet Russian: The food is fully prepared in the kitchen. All courses are served either from platters or an *Escoffier* dish. Tureens are used for soup and special bowls for salad. The server places the proper plate in front of the seated guest. After the plates are placed, the server returns with a tray of food and, moving counterclockwise around the table, serves

(Continued)

the food from the guest's left with the right hand. With this style of service, the server controls the amount served to each guest. (2) Restaurant Russian: Guests are seated. Foods are cooked tableside on a *rechaud* that is on a *gueridon*. Servers place the food on platters (usually silver), and then guests serve themselves. Service is *from the left*.

Waiter parade: In an elegant touch, white-gloved servers march into the room and parade around the perimeter carrying food on trays, often to attention-getting music and dramatic lighting. This is especially effective with a flaming baked Alaska dessert parade. The room lighting is dimmed, and a row of flaming trays carried by the waiters slowly encircles the room. When the entire room is encircled, the music stops and service starts. Guests are usually applauding at this point. (Flaming dishes should never be brought close to a guest. In this case, after the parade, the dessert would be brought to a side area, where it would be sliced and served.)

Mixing service styles: You can change service styles within the meal. The whole meal does not have to conform to one type of service. For example, you can have your appetizer preset, have the salads "Frenched" (dressing added after salads are placed on table), the main course served American, and have a dessert buffet.

ALCOHOL SERVICE

Alcohol is part of many meetings and events. Where and how alcohol is served is key in keeping the event and its consumers safe. First, consider the alcohol's role in the event; is it merely part of the event (as in a wedding where alcohol is served, but hopefully not the main attraction), or is it the main attraction (as in a Craft Beer Festival where everyone is there specifically for the beer)? Answering that simple question makes all the difference in how alcohol should be handled.

Regardless of alcohol's role, there should always be training involved. It is the responsibility of the event professional to ascertain that all servers of alcohol have proper training and are old enough to legally serve alcohol. In a hotel or catered event, it may be assumed that servers are trained. Never assume. Check with the service provider to be sure. At festivals and special events such as staff festivals, craft beer festivals, and wine festivals where large quantities of alcohol are served, the volunteers may or may not have had experience selling or serving. Training staff in proper service techniques and to recognize the signs of overindulgence is paramount. In some states, alcohol training is mandatory for anyone who serves alcohol. One of the two nationally recognized alcohol awareness programs may be too much training for someone who only does this one weekend a year, but if you have staff in your hotels and catering companies who always serve alcohol, then it is imperative that they receive one of the certifications. The two recognized certifications are:

- Servesafe Alcohol: www.servesafe.com
- Tips Training: www.gettips.com

Whether the event is on-site in a hotel where the liquor license is held, or it is in the middle of a field, when serving alcohol, the law does not care. Local, state, and federal laws that cover the sale and service of alcohol must be adhered to. Regardless of the function, the drinking age is always the same in the United States: 21. Some states may even mandate how long alcohol can be served at a special function. Other municipalities will use different tactics to cut down on the amount of time alcohol may be served. They can pressure event organizers into condensed hours of service, urge organizers to provide alternate forms of transportation for those who may have overindulged, or scare prospective organizers with the threat of increased law enforcement presence. All these things assure the same thing though, that attendees go home happy and SAFE!

Alcohol laws vary by state, county, and sometimes township. For example, there are several counties in Texas where you can imbibe freely but just a couple of blocks down the road you have to purchase a "membership" to legally consume alcohol. Some towns control the consumption of liquor in different ways than beer or wine by limiting quantities or heavy taxation. The event professional must become familiar with the laws in each new locale so there is never a problem. Ignorance does not exonerate an event professional. Some things to learn are:

- The hours of service and continual service for special functions
  ○ How late can drinks be served at a hotel wedding?
  ○ If it is a special event, how many consecutive hours can alcohol be served?
  ○ How early does serving at sporting events have to stop? Often well in advance of the conclusion of the sporting event? Is it before the third quarter of a football game, or the seventh inning of baseball?
- Where drinks can be consumed
  ○ Are there open container laws?
  ○ Does there need to be fencing around the event if alcohol is served to contain the crowd, and can alcohol only be consumed behind that fence?
  ○ Whether certain locations are banned from alcohol consumption
    ○ A wedding at an NCAA football stadium where alcohol is usually banned
    ○ Family reunions at public parks
- The monitoring policies
  ○ Does a security team have to be employed if alcohol is made available to attendees?
  ○ Must tickets be provided in order to limit the amount of alcohol served?
- Who can provide alcohol
  ○ Does it have to be someone who holds a liquor license, either temporary or permanent (on or off premise)?
  ○ Can attendees bring their own alcohol?
    ○ Think public music festival in the park versus a concert held in a coliseum.
    ○ If they can, is it limited in any way? Can it be in glass or other materials? Can a keg be brought in by attendees?
  ○ Can vendors also provide alcohol, or just event organizers?
  ○ Can the bride and groom bring bottles of wine from their first vacation together and serve them to guests at a wedding?
- Are there any unique liquor laws in that city, county, and state?

Once these things are considered, a plan can be created to ensure proper and safe service of alcohol to the guests.

Categories of Alcohol

Well brands: These are sometimes called "house liquors." It is less expensive liquor, such as Kentucky Gentleman Bourbon. Well brands are served when someone does not "call" a specific brand.

Call brands: These are priced in the midrange and are generally asked for by name, such as Smirnoff Vodka or Jim Beam Bourbon.

Premium brands: These are high-quality, expensive liquors, such as Kettle One Vodka, Grey Goose Vodka, Crown Royal, Chivas Regal, or Tanqueray Gin.

Number of Drinks per Bottle (assumes 1.5 ounce shots)				
Number of Drinks per Bottle				
		1 ounce	$1\frac{1}{4}$ ounce	$1\frac{1}{2}$ ounce
Liter	33.8 ounces	33	27	22
5th—750 ml	25.3 ounces	25	20	16

Types of Alcohol Service

There are a few different ways in which alcohol can be served in usual catering settings. For weddings, rehearsals, corporate Christmas parties, and other such events usually held in hotel ballrooms, the following three service types can be used:

- Cash bar: Everyone pays for his or her own drink individually.
- Host bar: The host of the event picks up the bill at the end of the function.
- Tickets: A set number of tickets is given to each guest for alcoholic beverages—this strategy attempts to limit the amount of alcohol served to any individual guest.

These three types of service all have their advantages and disadvantages. Cash bars do not prevent anyone from overconsuming and can be a bit cumbersome for large crowds, but they make a large amount of money for the hotel or caterer. Tickets only prevent someone from overdoing it if no one else gives them extra tickets. Furthermore, tickets are also an easy way to handle alcohol tastings. For a set admission price, a predetermined number of tickets are given to each attendee to try different wines or beers. Once they use their tickets, they have to purchase more. When "over drinkers" have to purchase their tickets in one specific location in order to use them for tastings, it adds an extra level of security. A host bar, while very gracious, can be very costly, and people tend to overconsume at a higher rate because they are not paying for each drink. These three methods can often times be combined. Conventions or weddings can offer a host bar for a certain time period at the beginning of the event and then change over to a cash bar sometime later evening. A cash bar can be set up to serve liquor at a beer tasting for those who do not enjoy beer.

This chapter has so far addressed the nuances of alcohol service and setup. When it is time to implement the service of alcohol, there are a few things to keep in mind:

Location: It is important to think about the placement of the beverages at both weddings and other indoor functions as well as at outdoor festivals. For indoor events, a good rule is to keep beverage service away from food service if possible in order to keep the overcrowding of one area to a minimum. For outdoor events, it has more to do with whether alcohol is the main theme of the event (beer festival), or supplemental to what is going on (Italian heritage festival), or just there as a bonus. As stated with regard to food earlier in the chapter, alcohol can either be arranged altogether with food and vendors or be separate. One main thing to remember about the location of alcohol service is to make sure it is somewhere you can control.

Equipment: This could be as simple as some ice chests and a six-foot table or could entail an elaborate set-up. It really depends on the event. For indoor events, regular bar setups are common. A checklist can be developed for the common things that are needed, including alcohol, mixers, glassware, service wear, garnishes, storage, and a bartender. A number of outdoor festivals will use the same type of bar setup if beer, wine, and liquor are being served from the same place. Over the years, different service types have been used. A popular service type for beer service is the portable beer trailer. This is a one-stop shop for draft beers: It holds and cools kegs and has exterior taps for serving a variety of beers.

Service: For indoor events, many types of service can be used, from cocktail service, where you have staff walk around with trays of drinks, to table service, where patrons are served at their tables. Having servers pass drinks on trays is good if the event has a signature drink. If the event calls for something more elaborate, similar to fine wine service, the staff must be trained for those settings. Wine service itself takes a highly skilled or practiced individual with some training and lots of practice. Putting untrained individuals in these settings will leave guests unhappy and staff feeling less than confident. For outdoor events, the main type of service is counter service, where guests order drinks at a table or bar where they are served directly. For some larger outdoor sporting events, servers are employed to make the distribution of drinks easier for the guests.

Staff: The staff needs to be trained in the types of alcohol service that are provided to guests. It is also important that servers get certified to serve alcohol so that they can recognize the adverse effects of alcohol and slow or stop service to people when necessary. Staff members also need to have some general alcohol knowledge. As consumers become more acquainted with alcohol, they are more inquisitive. As more and more alcohol is produced in smaller quantities in more locations, guests are becoming more inquisitive about local flavors and characteristics, especially with craft beers, locally produced wines, and small-batch single-barrel liquors. Having someone on staff who can answer these questions helps the guests interact and showcases the local flavors.

Storage: The location of the storage should be close and accessible for all events. The only other requirement for storage is that it is safe and can be locked. If it is a large enough event, one person should be in charge of issuing all alcohol. Reducing the number of people who have access decreases the number of mishaps that can occur around alcohol service.

SUMMARY

Food and beverage is a critical element in many meetings and events. F&B can play a crucial role in delivering the wow factor. F&B can be produced by caterers, hotel staff, or volunteers. Regardless of who produces the F&B, it is critical that the event professional be knowledgeable about all its aspects. It is not enough to "let the caterer do it." Even if an experienced caterer is utilized for a meeting and event, the event professional needs to have adequate knowledge of F&B planning and production. The wants and needs of attendees must be paramount in producing F&B functions.

The objective of this chapter is to provide the event professional with an overview of F&B production and logistics; not to provide details on how to be a server or how to be a chef. There are other chapters in this book series on the subject of F&B, including Chapter 10, "Food and Beverage," in *Meetings, Expositions, Events, and Conventions: An Introduction to the Industry* as well as Chapter 10, "Food and Beverage Planning," in *Planning and Management of Meetings, Expositions, Events, and Conventions.* Further, entire books have

been dedicated to providing this information, such as *A Meeting Planner's Guide to Catered Events, On-Premise Catering: Hotels, Convention & Conference Centers, and Clubs, Catering Operations and Sales,* and more. The event professional should seek them out.

Now that you have completed this chapter, you should be competent in the following Meeting and Business Event Competency Standards:

MBECS Skill 18: Coordinate Food and Beverage Services

Subskills		Skills (standards)
H 18.01	Determine (implement) food and beverage service requirements	
H 18.02	Select (develop) menus	
H 18.03	Plan (implement) service style(s)	
H 18.04	Select food and beverage provider(s)	
H 18.05	Manage alcohol service	

KEY WORDS AND TERMS

festival organizer	general commissary	action stations
festival sponsor	over-set	American Service
festival	exclusive provider	butler service
logistical support	preferred supplier	

REVIEW AND DISCUSSION QUESTIONS

1. What are the two recommended training programs for servers of alcohol?
2. List 10 different types or examples of food and beverage providers.
3. Is it an acceptable practice to "let the caterer do it?" Why? Why not?
4. What are some of the unique challenges of doing F&B outdoors?
5. Are the laws governing the sale and distribution of alcohol the same across the country? Across the region? Explain.
6. What is the rule of thumb regarding the number of servers to use for an event? Buffet? Seated?
7. What happened at the Extreme Home Makeover described in this chapter?
8. What types of "permits" apply to F&B at events?
9. Explain the different ways alcohol can be served at a meeting and event.

ABOUT THE CHAPTER CONTRIBUTOR

Sean Barth, PhD, is an assistant professor in the Department of Hospitality Management at the University of South Carolina Beaufort (USCB). His academic interests include building the club-management program at USCB and recruiting and placing students in positions of responsibility in the hospitality industry, primarily in the Lowcountry of South Carolina and in nearby Savannah, Georgia. Dr. Barth has extensive experience in the hospitality industry. As assistant general manager of a Hawthorne Suites property in Lubbock, Texas, he created the menu, designed the layout, and trained employees to work the breakfast shift and social hour in a new, 82-room, all-suite hotel. In 2003, as catering manager at fine-dining establishment Skyview of Texas Tech, he managed weekly catering operations and occasional dinner service.

CHAPTER 7

Management of Human Resources

Chapter Objectives

Upon completion of this chapter, the reader should be able to:

- Describe the functions of human resources management and the legal environment for business
- Illustrate vital human resources legal concepts
- Determine workforce requirements for meetings, events, and conventions
- Develop workforce policies and procedures for meetings, events, and conventions
- Follow an established training plan
- Monitor a human resources plan
- Manage teams

Human resources are an important piece of the puzzle in producing meetings and events. S.John/fotolia

Chapter Outline

THE HUMAN RESOURCES MANAGEMENT FUNCTIONS AND LEGAL ENVIRONMENT FOR BUSINESS

The Human Resources Management Functions

Human resources management (HRM) functions include recruiting, selecting, training, evaluating, compensating, and developing employees. These management functions also include attending to employees' labor relations, health, safety, and fairness concerns. HRM is a crucial element in the attainment of any organization's goals. An effective event professional must know how to plan. Human resource planning is the process of projecting workforce needs and the preparation for the movement of people in and out of an organization or any of its departments as needed.

The HRM plans must be part of the organization's strategic plan. The goals of the organization should be established with critical consideration of the availability of the workforce (both internal and external) needed to accomplish the goals. The function of HRM also includes the ability to determine the number of employees and qualifications needed to accomplish the organization's goals at the lowest possible cost to the organization. Hence, the event professional in HRM must be able to hire the best-qualified person for a job without discrimination in regard to race, color, sex, religion, disability, or national origin. As a result, event professionals must be very familiar with the necessary federal legislations and prepared to uphold the legal and regulatory environment of business.

The Legal Environment

Labor unions and government legislations influence HRM planning and practices. Labor unions were created to support employees' interests in the organization. A union represents its members (employees) in issues pertaining to adequate wages, proper hours, and the legal and regulatory environment of business. Government legislation, on the other hand, provides the workforce with laws to regulate employers' actions and make the working environment conducive to the labor force. Figure 1 lists laws (acts) that significantly affect HRM practices.

The major legal and regulatory issues involving the management of Meeting, Expositions, Events and Conventions (MEEC) employees are the (1) Civil Rights Act, (2) Fair Labor Standard Acts, (3) Equal Pay Act, (4) Occupational Safety and Health Act, (5) Privacy Act, (6) Age Discrimination in Employment Act, (7) Family and Medical Leave Act, and (8) some current issues such as sexual harassment and the glass-ceiling initiatives. While these are from the United States, their content applies around the world.

FIGURE 1

Date	Act	Focus of Act
1866	Civil Rights Act	Outlaws discrimination based on race
1931	Davis-Bacon Act	Demands paying current wage rates
1935	Wagner Act	Legalizes unions
1938	Fair Labor Standard Acts	Restricts children's employment; requires record keeping, minimum wage payment, and overtime pay
1947	Taft-Hartley Act	Balances the empowerment of unions
1959	Landrum-Griffin Act	Demands financial disclosure for unions
1963	Equal Pay Act	Demands equal pay for equal jobs regardless of gender
1964	Title VII of the Civil Rights Acts (14th Amendment)	Prohibits discrimination on the basis of race, color, religion, sex, and national origin—the protected groups
1967	Age Discrimination in Employment Act	Forbids age discrimination in hiring (and includes age in the protected group above)
1970	Occupational Safety and Health Act	Requires workers protection from workplace hazards
1973	Vocational Rehabilitation Act	Affirmative action program reaffirms nondiscrimination against minorities, women, and persons with disability
1974	Privacy Act	Authorizes employees to assess personnel files
1974	Employee Retirement Income and Security Act	Offers protection of employee retirement funds
1976	Health Maintenance Organization Act	Compels the use of alternative health insurance coverage
1978	Pregnancy Discrimination Act	Amends Title VII of the Civil Rights Acts to include the consideration of pregnancy, childbirth, or related medical issues
1978	Mandatory Retirement Act	Raises retirement age from 65 to 70 years
1986	Immigration Reform and Control Act	Requires verification of citizenship or legal status to work in the United States
1988	Employment Polygraph Protection Act	Forbids the use of polygraphs in most HRM practices
1988	Worker Adjustment and Retaining Act	Demands employers to inform employees of impending layoffs
1989	Plant Closing Bill	Requires employers to give notice to affected employees in advance
1990	American with Disabilities Act	Forbids discrimination against those with disability
1990	Immigration Act	Increases levels of immigration to United States
1991	Civil Rights Act (Amended)	Provides protection and remedies for victims of discrimination and harassment including government employees
1993	Family and Medical Leave Act	Allows employees to take up to 12 weeks unpaid leave for family matters
1994	Uniformed Service Employment Rights Act	Forbids discrimination against those who take off work to perform their military service obligation
1996	Health Insurance Portability and Accountability Act	Permits employees to transfer their coverage of existing illness to new employer's insurance plan
1996	Illegal Immigration Reform and Immigrant Responsibility Act	Places limitations on persons who remain in the United States longer than their visa permits
2002	Sarbanes-Oxley Act	Requires proper financial record keeping for public companies

The Civil Rights Act

Title VII of the Civil Rights Act of 1964 prohibits organization with 15 or more employees from discrimination in (1) hiring, (2) compensation, and (3) terms, conditions, or privileges of employment based on race, religion, color, sex, and national origin. Listed below are some of the features of this Act:

- Hiring criteria must be relevant to the job description and specialization.
- The **Equal Employment Opportunity Commission (EEOC)** was granted enforcement power as the arm of the federal government to handle employment discrimination cases.
- Organizations cannot treat employees differently simply based on their race, color, religion, sex, national origin, age, or disability status.
- "Affirmative action" requires employers to hire appropriate rate of minorities to correct past prejudice and imbalance.
- It is illegal to participate in an employment-related activity that inappropriately excludes a protected group even though it might seem nondiscriminatory.
- Organizations were urged to refrain from *adverse (disparate) impact,* which occurs when there is a greater rejection rate in employment for a protected group (those protected under discrimination laws) than for the majority group.
- Organizations were also urged to refrain from *adverse (disparate) treatment,* which occurs when members of a protected group are treated unfairly (rejected or discriminated against) than other employees.
- Grant protection and remedies were given for victims of discrimination and harassment, including government employees.
- The Civil Rights Act of 1991 returns the burden of proof to the employer; reinforces the illegality of making hiring, firing, or promotion decisions on the basis of race, ethnicity, sex, or religion; and permits women and religious minorities to seek punitive damages in intentional discriminatory claims.

The Fair Labor Standard Acts and Equal Pay Act

- Restricts children's employment and requires record keeping, minimum wage payment, and overtime pay.
- Laws relating to compensation define the 40-hour work week.
- Requires overtime pay to hourly employee working over 40 hours per week.
- Requires employers to pay at least the minimum wage and protect employee investments in pensions.
- Requires employers to provide the same pay for men and women doing equal work.

The Age Discrimination in Employment Act

- Forbids age discrimination in hiring (includes age in the protected group).
- Protects those age 40 and older from age discrimination.
- Eradicates mandatory retirement and the illogical substitute of older workers with younger workers.

The Occupational Safety and Health Act

- Requires workers protection from workplace hazards.
- The basic premise of these laws is that the employer is obligated to provide each employee with an environment that is free from hazards that are likely to cause death or serious injury.

TABLE 1 What You Can and Cannot Ask of an Applicant

Can Ask	Cannot Ask	Potential Basis for Legal Action
• Are you over 18 years of age? • If hired, can you provide a work permit if you're under 18?	• Do not ask questions that will identify the specific age (40 years or more) of the applicant.	Age Discrimination in Employment Act
	• Do not ask any question about the applicants' religion or holidays related to religious affiliation. • Do you go to a church or mosque? • Are you Catholic, Protestant, Jewish, or Atheist?	Civil Rights Act (discrimination on the basis of religion)
	• Do not ask jokingly or otherwise any question related to applicants' complexion, color, or race.	Civil Rights Act (discrimination on the basis of race)
• If you are not a U.S. citizen, do you have the legal authority to work in the United States? • If hired, could you submit proof of legal authority to work in the United States? • How many languages can you read, write, or speak fluently?	• Are you a citizen of the United States? • Are you, your parents, or spouse a naturalized or native-born U.S. citizen? • When did you, your parents, or spouse acquire U.S. citizenship? • When did you arrive in the United States or port of entry? • How long have you been a resident? • What nationality is your spouse or parents? • What is your national origin or descent?	Civil Rights Act (discrimination on the basis of national origin)
• Do you have any physical constraint that may affect your ability to perform the job?	• Do you have any physical disabilities?	Americans with Disabilities Act

- Grants a compliance officer the authority to enter a facility to determine adherence to standards.
- Demands employer compliance with OSHA to post safety posters and fulfill record-keeping requirements.
- Demands that employers have an employee trained and certified in first aid at all times.
- Requires commercial buildings to have the following:
  ✓ Accessibility to fire extinguishers that are ready for use
  ✓ Guards on floor openings, balcony storage areas, and receiving docks
  ✓ Adequate handrails and stairs
  ✓ Properly maintained ladders
  ✓ Proper guards and electrical grounding for foodservice equipment
  ✓ Lighted passageways, clear of obstructions
  ✓ Readily available first-aid supplies and instructions
  ✓ Proper use of extension cords
  ✓ Emergency action procedures spelled out in the employee manual and during training sessions

The Privacy Act

- Forbids employers from invading employees' privacy unless there is a strong suspicion that employees are acting inappropriately.
- Employers cannot do the following unless there is a strong suspicion that grants a warrant: (1) monitor telephone communications, (2) search an employee's workspace and handbag, and (3) conduct drug testing unless it is directly related to the job.

The Americans with Disabilities Act (ADA)

- Prohibits private companies and all public service organizations from discrimination against those with disability.
- Extends protection of Vocational Rehabilitation Act to most forms of disability status (including AIDS and other contagious diseases).
- Calls for companies to make reasonable accommodations for qualified applicants and employees.
- Countries other than the United States may or may not have similar legislation.

The Family and Medical Leave Act

- Employees in organizations employing 50 or more workers can take up to 12 weeks unpaid leave each year for childbirth, adoption, or illness/illness of a family member.
- Employees must have worked for their employers for at least one year and for 1,250 hours over the previous 12 months, and there must be at least 50 employees within a 75-mile radius of work location.
- Employees must provide 30 days' advance notice prior to the medical leave.
- Countries other than the United States may or may not have similar legislation.

Current Issues

U.S. government agencies such as the Equal Employment Opportunity Commission (EEOC) and the Office of Federal Contract Compliance Programs (OFCCP) are working hard to enhance and enforce equal employment opportunity laws. Currently, employers of various organizations take issues such as sexual harassment and the glass ceiling very seriously due to the insurgence of lawsuits by the employees.

Sexual harassment includes unnecessary sexual advances, requests for sexual favors, and other verbal and physical conduct of a sexual nature that affect an individual's employment.

Sexual harassment can occur via verbal or physical conduct toward an individual. Listed below are some forms of sexual harassment:

- The creation of an intimidating, offensive, or hostile environment.
- Unnecessary and/or unwelcome sexual advances that interfere with an individual's work.
- Unnecessary and/or unwelcome sexual advances or hostile working environment that adversely affects employee's employment opportunities.

An organization can be held responsible for the sexual harassment actions of its customers, employees, and, in most cases, managers. In fact, the victims may not necessarily have suffered substantial mental distress or negative job repercussions to win a legal action. The best way to prevent a sexual harassment suit in any organization is to educate employees about the issue of sexual harassment and discourage the occurrence of such behavior in the organization. In addition, employers must keep documentation of all sexual harassment–related education, reported incidents and the corrective action taken against such incidents.

The **glass ceiling** is another major current issue attracting the attention of OFCCP. This is the unprofessed barricade existing in some organizations that hinders the promotion of women and minorities to higher (executive) positions in the workplace. Due to glass ceilings, diversity—including the representation of women and minorities and the advantages that come with it—is missing in many organizations.

OFCCP recommended the following initiatives to help curtail the incidence of glass ceiling:

- Organizations are urged to promote career development programs for women and minorities.
- OFCCP auditors monitor government contractors to ensure that they provide the necessary training and development programs to the affected group.
- OFCCP may sue to ensure that organizations are taking necessary actions.

DETERMINING WORKFORCE REQUIREMENT IN MEETINGS, EVENTS, AND CONVENTIONS

Methods of Finding Employees

There are many ways employers or event professionals can recruit people for work. However, before posting any advertisement for employment, the recruiter must determine the workforce that is needed in the organization. In many organizations, the HRM can depend on environmental trends such as economic factors, political issues, and technological changes. However, an event professional who is planning a special or specific event must be able to anticipate and make provisions for the human resources needed to cover the event. The objective of any recruiter (employer or event professional) in need of employees is to hire the appropriate number of qualified, effective people. Therefore, the recruiter must be able to implement good human resource planning, forecast the number of employees needed, and conduct an analysis of job tasks and functions.

Human Resources Planning

Human resources planning is the process by which an organization ensures the following:

- It has the right number and kinds of people at the right place and time.
- It hires individuals who are capable of efficiently and effectively doing what they are hired to do in order to help the organization achieve its goals.

Monitoring the Human Resource Plan

A human resource plan, as described above, should not be taken for granted. Event professionals or management should invest enough time and appropriate leadership for human resources planning. The initiation of the plan should include the following:

- Undertake performance evaluations
- Conduct exit interviews
- Evaluate staff turnover and reasons for leaving
- Adjust human resources plan to address current trends and issues
- Review and update job specifications and job descriptions

Forecasting the Number of Employees Needed

A human resources inventory can be developed in order to determine the number of employees needed by an organization or by an event professional for a special or specific event. The human resource inventory can be created to predict future estimates of people needed for every required job as well as the specific skills, knowledge, and abilities needed to do the job.

In MEEC planning, predicting the future estimates of people needed for an event depends on the size and scope of the event. The bigger the event, the more people who are needed. Similarly, the more complex, elaborate, or elegant the event is, the higher the skill levels, knowledge, and abilities of the employees that are needed to do the job.

Job Analysis

Job analysis is the process of exploring the activities of a job. It requires a systematic approach to studying the duties and responsibilities of the job as well as the knowledge and skills needed for performing the job. There are different methods of conducting job analysis, including observation, individual interview, group interview, structured questionnaire, technical conference, and diary (record keeping of daily activities). Regardless of the method used, the most important task is to gather enough information. Job analysts are often encouraged to use a combination of methods for best results. A good job analysis will produce a job description, job specifications, and a job evaluation (as defined below).

Job Description   A **job description** is a written statement of job activities, tasks, or expectations for what will be done in that specific position. This includes how and why the job is done and under what conditions. Some common features of a job description include a format that consists of a title, duties or tasks, responsibilities, distinguishing characteristics of the job, authority (supervisor), and environmental conditions. A job description is a great recruiting document. It is used to describe the job to potential applicants, to guide new employees, and to serve as a quasi-evaluation or evaluation tool for employees.

Job Specifications   **Job specifications** are a list of the minimum acceptable qualifications for the job, including skills, traits, personal qualities, and the background needed to do the job effectively and efficiently. Job specifications are a great selection document. Employees who meet the essential qualifications or who are most qualified for the position are usually selected for the job.

Job Evaluation   A **job evaluation** is used to specify the relative value of each job in the organization, to assess the performances of employees, and to design an equitable compensation program for the organization's workers. A job evaluation is commonly known as a performance appraisal tool. Knowing and understanding job analysis and the products of the analysis is one thing—having the ability to hire the appropriate group of employees for an organization or special event is another.

MEETINGS, EVENTS, AND CONVENTIONS EMPLOYEE/HUMAN RESOURCES NEED ANALYSIS

Budgeted Staff Needed

In MEEC planning, the type and number of employees needed for a particular event depends on the size and quality of the meeting/event. The bigger the event, the more people you need for the event; the higher the quality of the event, the higher the level of employees' skills needed. Before a recruiter or event professional should start the recruitment process, he or she should be aware of the event's budget. The number of paid employees for the event should be based on the budgeted cost of labor. For example, if an event cost $100,000 to produce, and 10% is budgeted for the labor costs, then the total labor cost, including management staff, should not exceed $10,000 (10% of $100,000 = $10,000). Of this amount, it is common for 20% to be used for supervision. Therefore, the recruiter or event professional must ensure that the number and quality of the employees, including the management staff, does not exceed the budget. However, if more employees are needed for the event, the recruiter or event professional should consider the use of volunteers.

Volunteers

The use of volunteers is a common phenomenon in event production. Volunteers are available in most parts of the world, but you have to be able to find them. There are many organizations whose major goal is to connect volunteers to their end users. Examples of these organizations include:

1. Work Exchange Team
2. Volunteers of America
3. Volunteering England
4. Your local destination marketing organization (DMO) or conventions and visitors bureau (CVB) could also provide volunteer resources as needed.

Each of the above organizations specializes in providing the number and quality of volunteers needed for a specified event or for work that needs to be done. Other splendid sources of volunteers include schools, churches, professional organizations, and nonprofit organizations. Volunteers are unpaid employees and it is not that easy to recruit unpaid employees. Bearing the above in mind, recruiters or event professionals in need of volunteers should plan in advance to actively recruit volunteers. Some of the major advantages of using volunteers include wage and benefit cost savings to the organization. Plus, the organization can always replace volunteers as needed. However, some major disadvantages of using volunteers include the following: good volunteers may not have a commitment to the organization, volunteers cannot be fired, and retraining volunteers as needed may not be cost- or time-effective. It is essential for the event professional's staff to be well trained before recruiting volunteers. Well-trained employees will portray a positive impression about the organization and its culture, which the volunteers will then follow. A recruiter or event professional who intends to use volunteers should consider establishing a volunteer program. When establishing a volunteer program for meetings, events, and conventions, the following questions should be considered:

1. Why do we need volunteers?
2. What will the volunteers do (what is the level of skill needed)?
3. Where will the volunteers be needed in order to balance paid staff time at work?
4. How long will volunteers be needed?
5. When and where can we recruit volunteers?

In addition to these questions, event professionals should ensure that the volunteer program is included in the event's budget. The recruiters and event professionals must be mindful of the volunteer expenses associated with training, supervising, and recognizing volunteers. If recruiting staff or volunteers seems like a daunting task that could prevent you from focusing on other aspects of the event, the recruiter or event professional might consider the use of outside contractors.

Outside Contractors

An organization or person who is not employed by the event professional but provides products or services for meetings/events during the actual event or show is an outside contractor. In some cases, the facility where the event is taking place could provide contractors or their employees as part of the contract for using their facility. Some of the advantages of using outside contractors include wage and benefit savings, the ability to focus on other aspects of the event, and the fact that the recruiter or event professional will not have to worry about the volatility of the supply and demand of specialized skills needed for any particular event. However, one major disadvantage of outside contractors is the potential legal liability that could arise in case of an accident. So, recruiters or event professionals must ensure that each outside contractor working at the event provide an adequate insurance certificate. In some cases, the certificate of insurance might not be enough to prevent the event professional from being sued. In addition to the certificate of insurance, the event professional should consider implementing crisis and risk management plans to help ensure the safety and security of the attendees. There are many types of outside contractors. Some are called specialty service contractors; others are called general service contractors.

Specialty Service Contractor   A **specialty service contractor (SSC)** is an organization or person hired by the event professional to perform a specific task during the actual event or show. Some examples of SSC tasks are as follows:

- Catering
- Cleaning services
- Furniture
- Photography
- Drayage & freight
- Audiovisual
- Communications/computer station
- Labor planning & supervision
- Utilities (e.g., power supply, water supply)
- Models/hostesses
- Floral
- Security
- Consulting
- Lighting
- Postal/package services
- Translators
- Business services
- Spokespersons
- Carpeting

General Service Contractor   A **general service contractor (GSC)** is an organization hired by the event professional to perform multiple tasks during the actual event or show. A GSC can do any combination of SSC tasks, including the following:

- Hiring and managing labor
- Trucks/freight movement in and out of the facility
- Storage management
- Installing and dismantling
- Developing a service manual for the event
- Developing and hanging signage and banners
- Providing booths and furniture

It is obvious that event professionals have different ways to get help for their events. However, the recruiter or event professional must be diligent about identifying and acquiring the type of help needed. It is not uncommon for event professionals to use a combination of budgeted staff, volunteers, and outside contractors. However, during the human resource planning for a specific event, the recruiter or event professional should clearly outline the number of (1) required employees, (2) contracted employees, and (3) the services to be outsourced. The recruiter or event professional should also be prepared to select recruitment techniques and methods, establish a compensation plan (salary, hourly rate, and benefits as needed), and develop a workforce diversity plan.

Recruitment

Once an event professional identifies the human resource needs for the planned event, he or she can start the **recruitment** process. The goal of the recruitment process is to provide information through a job description and specialization that will attract qualified candidates and deter unqualified jobseekers from applying. Some of the recruiting sources include internal and external search sources as follows (see Table 2):

TABLE 2	
Recruiting Sources for Internal Search	**Recruiting Sources for External Search**
• Directly inform employees (face-to-face or e-mail) • Vacancy notices on bulletin boards • Employee newsletters • Employees' special handouts • Other means of employee public notice	• Internet advertising • Newspaper advertising • Employee referral program • Trade/professional association advertising • Career fair

Selection

The review of applications and **selection** of the best candidates follows the recruitment process. This process should be based on a set of guidelines that will permit the unbiased comparison of an applicant's skills as well as his or her knowledge and ability to do the desired job. The main goal of the selection process is to choose the applicant who is most qualified for the job.

The steps in the selection process vary from one organization to another and from one level to another within the organization. For example, the selection process for a dining room server may consist of an application screening, reference check, interview, and hiring decision. On the other hand, the selection process for a unit manager may consist of an application screening, background and reference check, interview, physical examination, and hiring decision. Although the selection process varies from one organization to another, it requires that all workers be given equal employment opportunity without discrimination.

Orientation

After recruitment and selection, the next step in the hiring process is the **orientation**. The importance of a proper orientation cannot be overemphasized. This is the first opportunity for an organization to be formally introduced to new employees. This is the best time for new employees to become familiar with an organization's policies and procedures. (For more details on orientation, see the following chapter on training and supervision.)

DEVELOPING WORKFORCE POLICIES AND PROCEDURES FOR MEETINGS, EVENTS, AND CONVENTIONS

Designing Policies and Procedures

It is very important for event professionals to ensure that new employees (staff and/or volunteers) experience a positive first impression of the organization. So, in addition to proper orientation, employee policies and procedures should be in place before recruitment. The purpose of the policies and procedures is to provide the employees with some basic and acceptable direction toward the attainment of the organization's goals. When designing employee policies and procedures for meetings, events, and conventions, the following should be considered:

- The mission, vision, and goals of the organization (including employees' roles)
- The need for formal employee meetings or other means of communicating and team building
- Job description, qualification, and employee evaluation process for each position
- Reimbursement policy for out-of-pocket employee spending on behalf of the organization

- Reimbursement approval process
- The need for committees, the type of committees needed, communication style, and structure and tasks of the committees

Dealing with Volunteers

In addition to the above policies and procedural considerations, the following should also be considered for volunteer program purposes:

- The development of a volunteer policies and procedure manual (including legal and liability issues)
- Development of appointment policies for staff and procedures for orienting, training, and supervising volunteers
- A record-keeping system for volunteers' activities and time spent at work
- The need for a common station for volunteers
- The need for a volunteer uniform
- All-staff awareness of how to respond to volunteer or potential volunteer questions

Supervision

Special care should be taken to recognize potential supervisors. In some cases, employees are hired to supervise other employees; in other cases, supervisors are appointed as needed. The event professional is encouraged to have a trained staff member (a paid employee) as a supervisor. However, depending on the size of the event and the number of staff needed, volunteers might be needed to supervise volunteers. Regardless of who the supervisor is, it is essential for that person to be aware of his/her leadership styles and the perception of his/her subordinates. Two mental exercises or activities that help determine leadership style are *True Colors* and the *Myers Briggs Test.* The supervisor's perception of his or her own leadership styles should agree with that of his/her subordinates. This will help the supervisors make appropriate decisions that enhance the organization's performance.

Performance Review (Evaluation)

A performance review or evaluation is the appraisal of an employee's performance in relation to his or her job description during a given period of time. The employee evaluation is a very critical aspect of the workforce in that it can directly affect the employee's morale at work. Hence, performance standards should be based on the job analysis and job description in regard to the organization's goals. When designing evaluation policies and procedures, event professionals should consider the following questions:

- Who should evaluate whose performance?
- What format should be used for the evaluation?
- When should the evaluation be carried out?
- How should the results of the evaluation be used?

The evaluation should be job related, objective, bias-free, and fair. It should be conducted by trained appraisers (supervisors) at established periods. The event professional or appraiser should bear in mind that the purpose of an evaluation is to provide the employee with feedback on how well he or she has done and to identify employees' strengths, weaknesses, and room for improvement. Supervisors could use evaluations to set employees objectives, development plans, future job assignments, and/or compensation. Therefore, after each evaluation, it is very important for the appraiser to discuss the evaluation with the employee and keep all the necessary evaluation's documents (records) for legal purposes.

Sources of Information for Performance Reviews   Various sources of information are used for putting together performance reviews. Some appraisers gather information from personal observation, oral reports, written reports, and/or statistical reports. However the information is gathered, the most important thing is for it to be genuine and documentable.

Challenges of Performance Reviews   Appraisers and event professionals should be prepared for the potential difficulties that might arise during the discussion of the review with subordinates. In some cases, the discussion is very emotional and leads to conflicts between the subordinate and the organization or appraiser. This often occurs when the employee disagrees with the appraiser's performance review. In order to prevent or minimize this, the organization's policies and procedures should be very clear about the appraisal process, and the appraisers should be well trained. (For more information on performance reviews, see the next chapter.)

Conflict Resolution

At times, conflict is inevitable. Hence, it is essential for the event professional to have policies and procedures in place to handle potential conflicts among the employees or attendees, and/or between the attendees and employees. **Conflict** is a disagreement that results in an antagonistic or hostile relationship between two parties. Conflicts commonly occur in a team or organization. However, the organization should be prepared to resolve conflict before it becomes destructive. One cause of conflict is the competition for scarce resources, such as valuable information, needed supplies, and money.

Conflict also occurs when employees are frustrated about unclear responsibilities, bad leadership, the lack of an effective medium of communication, or the pursuit of a divergent goal. For example, in an organization with unclear responsibilities and no effective medium of communication, there may be employee disagreement about who is responsible for specific duties or who is entitled to a particular resource. Event professionals should anticipate the source of potential conflicts in their organization and establish policies and procedures to curtail them.

Suggestions for a Conflict Resolution Process for Employees

1. Separate the employees from the situation and give them time to calm down.
2. Focus on the problem, not the person. Start by complimenting the employee about something or put forth a positive statement about the employee to further calm down the situation.
3. Communicate with the employees calmly but assertively, and *not* aggressively. Do not place blame.
4. Focus on the issue, *not* your position about the issue.
5. Listen to both parties, if necessary, without forcing either party to comply. However, strive to develop common agreement or let them agree to disagree.
6. Focus on what is best for the organization. Find areas of agreement instead of areas of disagreement.
7. Refrain from a situation where one party must win and one must lose. Strive for a win–win resolution.

(Continued)

Suggestions for a Conflict Resolution Process for Guests/Attendees

1. Acknowledge the guest/attendee.
2. Carefully listen to the guest's concerns or problem.
3. Remain calm and listen without interrupting the guest/attendee.
4. If needed, ask questions that will help resolve the issue.
5. Empathize with the guest.
6. Focus on what is best for the organization.
7. Make sure the resolution is pleasing to the guests/attendees.

The above suggestions can be successful if implemented appropriately. However, depending on the situation and the parties in conflict, the supervisor in charge of conflict resolution might want to modify the suggestions as needed.

Event professionals have to be very careful and never jump to conclusions or make conjectures about the situation, guests, attendees, or employees during conflict resolution. Supervisors in charge of conflict resolution should be well trained and ready to listen without interrupting any of the parties involved in the conflict. If needed, it is okay to ask for more information for clearer understanding of the reason for the conflict. However, never cut off employees or guest/attendee when they are talking. At the end of each conflict resolution episode, it is highly encouraged to thank the person or parties for listening.

Employee Discipline

Discipline is an action against an employee who fails to follow the policies or rules of an organization. The main purpose of employee discipline is to encourage employees to behave according to the rules and regulations of the organization. It is very important for an organization or the event professional to have disciplinary policies and procedures in place. Listed below are steps that could be taken in a disciplinary procedure:

- Verbal warning (unrecorded in employee's personnel file)
- Verbal warning (recorded in employee's personnel file)
- Written warning (documented, signed, and included in the employee's personnel file)
- Suspension (documented, signed, and included in the employee's personnel file)
- Dismissal (documented and included in the employee's personnel file)

Disciplinary action steps vary from one organization to another. They also vary on the basis of the employee's offense. An employee who is caught stealing might be dismissed immediately without any warning or suspension; another employee might be given a verbal warning for not wearing a proper uniform. Regardless of the type of disciplinary action taken, the employer should document the disciplinary action with a disciplinary action form (see Figure 2 for an example of a disciplinary action form) for legal and record-keeping purposes.

The event professional or the employer should strive for a disciplinary process that is fair and effective in curtailing unwanted behavior. In order to achieve that process, the employer must ensure that the organization's policies and procedures are clear. When designing a disciplinary policies and procedures, the following should be considered:

- The rules and regulations should address all the possible bad habits (see Figure 3) that will not be tolerated and the penalties that are meted out with each offense.

FIGURE 2 Disciplinary Action Form.

Disciplinary Action Form

Date: _____   Employee Name: _____

Department: _____

Disciplinary Action:

Verbal (unrecorded) ___ Verbal (recorded) ___ Written ___ Suspension ___ Dismissal ___

Purpose of Disciplinary Action:

_____

_____

_____

_____

_____

Supervisor Signature: _____ Date: _____

Employee Signature: _____ Date: _____

Note: *Even if the disciplinary action is a verbal warning, the completion of this form will serve as documentation of the disciplinary action taken and for record-keeping purposes.*

FIGURE 3 Job-Related Bad Habits of Disciplinary Consequences.

Attendance Issues	Work-Related Bad Habits
• Tardiness • Late from break • Unexcused absence • Leaving without permission	• Dishonesty at work • The use of offensive language • Unauthorized possession of firearms at work • Violent at work/intentional destruction of organizational property • Falsification of employment document • Stealing at work • Failure to follow policies and procedure • Sexual harassment • Fighting at work • Insubordination • Not following safety rules • Coming to work intoxicated • Poor work quality • Refusing to report accidents
Appearance Issues • Improper uniform • No nametag • Dirty clothing	
Outside Issues • Working for a competing organization • Out of work criminal activities • Unauthorized strike	

- Some of these rules and regulations could be provided to the employees during orientation, in the employee handbook, and the organization's website.
- The employer must be consistent with the type of disciplinary action taken against a specific bad habit.
- The extent or severity of the disciplinary action should vary depending on the severity of the bad habit and the number of times it was committed.
- An organized disciplinary appeals process may help in guaranteeing a fair disciplinary process.

- No disciplinary action should be taken against any employee without fair and adequate investigation, evidence of bad habit, and the protection of the employee's due process.
- The disciplinary action should exemplify a corrective action rather than punishment.
- The disciplinary action should be progressive (from verbal warning to dismissal).

Dismissal is the most severe disciplinary action an employer can take against an employee. Dismissal refers to an involuntary termination of an employee from an organization due to one or more **gross misconducts**. Figure 4 shows a checklist of gross misconducts that could lead to a dismissal. Due to the severity of dismissal, employers or event professionals should take special care to ensure that all the necessary documentation of the employee's misconduct are kept and secured for record-keeping and legal purposes.

Termination-at-Will

Termination-at-will refers to the dismissal of an employee by an employer or the resignation of an employee from an organization at-will for any reason. The legal rationale is that the employer hired the employee at-will and can thus discharge the employee at-will. This doctrine is often altered if (1) there is a written employment contract and (2) if the employee is working out of a union hall. Even though termination-at-will is well recognized in many places, employers must still endeavor to keep adequate records of the event leading to termination because currently many dismissed employees "at-will" are taking their cases to court as a wrongful discharge.

Wrongful discharge refers to an inappropriate dismissal of an employee because it violates the law or the employment contract. Employers or event professionals

FIGURE 4 Gross Misconduct Checklist.

Employers who dismiss employees for gross misconduct might not be obligated to pay any benefits to these employees under the COBRA legislation in the U.S. benefits. "Gross misconduct" was not spelled out clearly by Congress when it was written into COBRA. Hence, the following checklist provides clues of what gross misconduct comprises.
- Was anyone physically harmed? How badly?
- Has the employee violated the same rule several times before?
- Did the employee realize the seriousness of his or her actions?
- Will the employee be denied unemployment benefits based on the conduct?
- Did the conduct seriously harm the business of the employer?
- Was work severely disrupted?
- Were other employees significantly affected?
- Was the employer exposed to bad publicity that would greatly harm its business?
- Was the employer's reputation severely damaged?
- Will the employer lose significant business or otherwise suffer economic harm because of the misconduct?
- Will the employer be heavily fined because of the misconduct?
- Could the employer lose its business license because of the employee's misconduct?
- Has the harm to the employer already occurred?
- Will the employee lose any license needed to work for the employer (e.g. driver's license)?
- Was there criminal activity involved?
- Was it a felony?
- Does it involve harm to a person?
- Was fraud involved?
- Was any safety statue violated?
- Was any civil statute violated?
- Was the conduct purposeful?
- Was the conduct on duty?
- Is the policy that was violated well known to the employees?
- Does the conduct justify immediate termination?
- Has the employer immediately fired other employees who did something similar?
- Did the employee have an opportunity to explain the conduct prior to the determination that it was gross misconduct?

should refrain from wrongful discharge in order to prevent unnecessary legal liabilities. However, employees could be dismissed appropriately via grounds for dismissal. Some of the grounds for dismissal include job-related bad habits, gross misconducts (see Figure 4), and lack of adequate qualifications.

Sick Leave

Sick leave refers to employees' payable time off due to illness. Some employers can afford to grant full pay to their employees for sick leave for up to 12 working days per year, while others may grant sick leave without pay. Event professionals or the management should consider instituting sick leave policies and procedures that will follow the legal environment and discourage employees from using sick leave as additional vacation time.

Communicate Policies and Procedures to Staff

Regardless of who is supervising, the importance of management's communication with the employees cannot be overemphasized. The management should be mindful and diligent about the use of the following communication channels with subordinates: e-mail, Facebook, Twitter, word of mouth, newsletters, blogging, and other forms of social media. In addition, the management should consider using the organization's website (if possible) to make information available to all subordinates, including volunteers. Volunteers' orientation materials, policies and procedures, training manual, and schedules may be posted online for easy accessibility purposes.

Monitor Implementation of Policies and Procedures

Developing workforce policies and procedures is one thing; the ability to monitor the implementation of the policies and procedures is another. Event professionals and/or management should establish a system that will inspire employees to follow the organization's policies and procedures. The following should be considered:

- Make sure that all employees understand what is required of them; training and communication policies and procedures must be clearly stated.
- Motivate employees by recognizing or rewarding those who adhere to the organization's policies and procedures in spite of difficult challenges.
- Implement valuable employee development programs that will challenge employees to be responsible for their personal improvement.
- Establish good recruitment, selection, orientation, training, evaluation, and disciplinary policies and procedures that will help develop more responsible and disciplined employees.

In addition to the above, event professionals and/or management must also keep a scorecard of employees' performance and adherence to their organization's policies and procedures. The scorecard should be reflected in the employees' periodic performance evaluations.

FOLLOWING ESTABLISHED TRAINING PLANS

Training Goals

It is very important for the training and development programs of the organization to help maximize employees' performance efficiency and excellence. The goal of these programs should be the enhancement of employees' performance qualities for optimum productive capacity and revenue or profit maximization. Hence, when training new employees, it is very imperative to assess current skills and abilities of the employees and volunteers, determine gap analysis, review the human resources budget for the organization and any site-specific training, consider how the employees will be evaluated, and whether outsourcing is needed. (For more information on training, see the following chapter.)

Volunteer Tasks

When considering enlisting the aid of volunteers, think of the current skills and abilities of the staff and their gap analysis (where help is mostly needed). Consider, too, what volunteers could do to help the event professionals manage their employees in order to maximize profit. There is no good excuse for having employees work overtime when there are volunteers looking for something to do. Hence, event professionals or management should consider using volunteers for the following tasks, if needed:

- **Moderator**: In educational conferences, introduces the speakers and ensures that the speakers and attendees' needs during the presentations are met.
- **Registration assistant**: Greets, answers questions, and distributes the registration packet to attendees.
- **Moderator coordinator**: Ensures that all moderators are assigned to the appropriate rooms at the right time. Might also be responsible for training moderators (as needed).
- **Hospitality coordinator**: Coordinates the provision of hospitality for VIPs, speakers, and, in some cases, volunteers.
- Meetings, events, expositions, or conventions **evaluation coordinator**: Coordinates the meeting's evaluation data collection.

The event professional or management should be very mindful of the importance of volunteers and treat them with utmost respect. Failure to respect volunteers undervalues the services and financial savings they bring to the table, which could backfire against the organization.

Outsource When Needed

In some cases, event professionals or management may decide to outsource some of the labor. This is an opportunity for an organization to focus on what it does best and outsource activities that are not part of its core competencies. For example, the International Council on Hotel, Restaurant, and Institutional Education (ICHRIE) knows the value of outsourcing the organization's annual summer conference. This approach has proven to be more cost-effective for ICHRIE. Regardless of the tasks that an event professional or management intend to outsource, it is very important to consider the following in the agreement:

- *Service description:* Ensure that the service to be provided is well described, including the timeline/time frames and the performance expectation of the tasks to be carried out.
- *Outsourcer's obligation:* Ensure that the responsibilities of the outsourcer are very clear, including the number of employees needed for different aspects of the events. The employees or volunteers' shift, start, and end time should be clearly delineated in the agreement as needed.
- *Payment:* Ensure that the payment plan is clear and well documented, including who is responsible for additional service contracts such as catering, flora, audiovisual, and carpeting.

The event professionals or management should be aware of the importance of monitoring the quality of work of the outsource provider. The goal is to ensure that the tasks carried out by the outsource provider satisfy the needs of the organization.

MANAGING TEAMS

Creating a Team Environment

Event professionals and/or management should attempt to build teams within the organization that strive for a common goal or position the employees to work as a team. Team building aims to bring employees together to work amicably toward the attainment of the organization's goal. To be successful in this endeavor, employees must trust one another, be open-minded, agree to disagree, and accept the final decisions of the team. The focus of team building is to help employees work together cohesively.

An effective team-building process should include:

- Adequate communication of the purpose of the team
- Understanding the strengths and weaknesses of each member of the team
- Development of interpersonal relationships
- Obvious goal(s) and objectives for the team
- Clear and precise roles of each member of the team
- Established behavioral norms
- Team performance reviews

Adequate Communication of the Purpose of the Team   An effective level of communication will keep team members abreast of what is going on in the organization. Event professionals and/or management should be aware of the different types of communication channels available to them and use one or a combination to reach each member of the team. Adequate communication within a team can lead to a more productive team, with fewer interpersonal conflicts.

Understanding the Strengths and Weaknesses of Each Member of the Team   A preliminary evaluation of each team member may be necessary in order to learn the following:

- Expertise: Which task is appropriate for each team member?
- Knowledge: Does the team member have enough knowledge to carry out the task?
- Skills: Does the team member have the necessary skills to perform the task?
- Abilities: Does the team member have other abilities?
- Attitudes: Does the team member have a likeable manner? Is he/she fit for his/her role in the organization?

Development of Interpersonal Relationships   The importance of interpersonal relationships in team building cannot be stressed enough. Interpersonal relationships require a level of maturity among team members so that they can work together in a manner that will curtail conflicts and/or resolve conflicts. A team with good interpersonal relationships pulls together to attain the team's goals, even if some members disagree with one another.

Obvious Goal(s) and Objectives for the Team   It is imperative for each team member to know the goal(s) and objectives of the organization/team. The following (acronym **SMART**) should be clear and obvious to each team member:

- Specific: Are the specifics of the goal(s) and objectives clear to each member? Can the team handle the assigned task?
- Measurable: Is the accomplishment of the goal(s) and objectives measurable?
- Achievable: Are the goal(s) and objectives realistic and achievable?
- Relevant: Are the goal(s) and objectives relevant to the purpose of the team?
- Time frame: When should the task be accomplished?

Clear and Precise Roles for Each Member of the Team   It is essential for each member of the team to know his/her role and how it impacts the overall goal(s) and objectives of the team. Event professionals and/or management should ensure that each member of the team is actively involved in accomplishing what is assigned to him/her. Supervisors should be aware of the possibilities of freeloaders and discourage such behavior.

Established Behavioral Norms   The importance of team standards or set of behavioral norms cannot be overemphasized. The team should have a set of behavioral norms that each member must adhere to as a team. These standards or behavioral norms could be based on the existing standards of the organization, developed by the team, or based on the combination of the existing standards plus the standards developed by the team. The team supervisor should be very aware of the team's established behavioral norms and ensure that they are followed. The team supervisor or management should also ensure that the team's established behavioral norms support the purpose of the team.

Team Performance Reviews   Reviews are an evaluation of a team's performance in relation to its goals and objectives. **Team performance reviews** are an essential part of team building; they educate the team leader about the level of cohesiveness within the team and how they work well together to attain the goals and objectives of the team. The team's performance reviews should be based on goals and objectives of the team and other effective team-building characteristics. When designing a team performance review, event professionals should consider the following questions:

- Who should appraise the team?
- What format should be used for the appraisal?
- When should the appraisal be carried out?
- How should the results of the appraisal be utilized?

The event professional or appraiser should keep in mind that the purpose of the team appraisal is to provide the team with comments on how good it has done and identify the team's strengths, weaknesses, and room for improvement. The result of the team performance review could be used to reorganize the team, realign the team's purpose, develop a team enhancement plan, adjust future job assignments for each member of the team, and help determine the type of recognition, reward, or compensation for the team.

SUMMARY

Management of human resources includes the process of recruiting, selecting, orienting, training/developing, and evaluating for the purpose of attaining the goal and objectives of an organization. Many laws have been passed to enhance the function of the management of human resources. However, the major legal and regulatory issues involving the management of meeting, events and conventions employees are the: (1) Civil Rights Act, (2) Fair Labor Standard Acts, (3) Equal Pay Act, (4) Occupational Safety and Health Act, (5) Privacy Act, (6) Age Discrimination in Employment Act, (7) Family and Medical Leave Act, and (8) additional current issues such as sexual harassment and glass-ceiling initiatives.

Human resources planning is the process by which an organization ensures that it has the right number and kinds of people at the right place and time; they are capable of efficiently and effectively doing what they are hired to do in order to help the organization achieve its goals.

Some characteristics of an effective team-building process include the following: (1) adequate communication of the purpose of the team, (2) an understanding of the strengths and weaknesses of each member of the team, (3) the development of interpersonal relationships, (4) obvious goal(s) and objectives for the team, (5) clear and precise roles of each member of the team, (6) established behavioral norms, and (7) team performance reviews.

Now that you have completed this chapter, you should be competent in the following Meeting and Business Event Competency Standards:

MBECS Skill 11: Manage Human Resource Plan

Sub Skills		Skills
11.01	Determine workforce requirements	
11.02	Establish workforce policies and procedures	
11.03	Monitor human resources plan	

MBECS Skill 12: Acquire Staff and Volunteers

Sub Skills		Skills
12.01	Develop selection criteria	
12.02	Recruit staff and volunteers	
12.03	Interview candidates	
12.04	Select best candidates and offer positions	

MBECS Skill 14: Manage Workforce Relations

Sub Skills		Skills
14.01	Supervise staff and volunteers	
14.03	Manage teams	
14.04	Evaluate Staff	
14.05	Process terminations and resignations	

KEY WORDS AND TERMS

Equal Employment Opportunity Commission (EEOC)
sexual harassment
glass ceiling
human resources planning
job analysis
job description
job specifications
job evaluation

specialty service contractor (SSC)
general service contractor (GSC)
recruitment
selection
orientation
conflict
discipline
dismissal
gross misconducts

termination-at-will
moderator
registration assistant
moderator coordinator
hospitality coordinator
evaluation coordinator
team performance reviews

REVIEW AND DISCUSSION QUESTIONS

1. List five major legal and regulatory issues (acts) involving the management of meetings, events, and convention organizations. Why should event professionals or management be concerned about these acts?
2. Why should a recruiter not ask jokingly (or otherwise) any question related to an applicant's complexion, color, or race?
3. How can event professionals or management control labor costs through human resources planning?
4. Discuss five factors that should be considered when designing employee policies and procedures for meetings, events, and conventions.
5. Discuss what an event professional or management could do to strive for a disciplinary process that is fair and effective in curtailing unwanted behavior.
6. Describe some of the characteristics of a good staff (employees and volunteers) training program.
7. When might event professionals or management consider outsourcing?
8. Describe seven characteristics of an effective team-building process.

ABOUT THE CHAPTER CONTRIBUTOR

Godwin-Charles Ogbeide, PhD, MBA, is a faculty member in the Department of Food, Human Nutrition, and Hospitality Management at the University of Arkansas Fayetteville. He is an active member of the Professional Convention Management Association (PCMA) and the International Council on Hotel, Restaurant, and Institutional Education (I-CHRIE). His teaching/ research interests are in the areas of meetings, events, and convention management, and strategic management and leadership development in the hospitality industry. Ogbeide is an award-winning professor with over 25 years of experience in the hospitality industry, a member of I-CHRIE Strategic Committee, a board member of ICHRIE, and a member of PCMA Faculty Task Force.

Training and Supervision

CHAPTER 8

All personnel involved in producing a meeting/event require training—especially food servers. djordjevla/fotolia

Chapter Objectives

Upon completion of this chapter, the reader should be able to understand:

- The main types of employee training
- An assessment of training needs
- Training program design and implementation
- The duties and expectations of a supervisor
- The motivation of full-time employees vs. volunteers
- Employee performance evaluations
- Processing terminations, separations, and resignations

Chapter Outline

INTRODUCTION

The purpose of this chapter is to provide an overview of training and supervision as applied to both full-time employees and volunteers. With respect to training, an emphasis is placed upon how to assess training needs and how to conduct training programs. Some of the more critical aspects of supervision are also given special emphasis.

PROVIDING TRAINING

Training is used by organizations to influence employee behaviors to be consistent with the mission of the organization. Training can be classified as pre-service training, in-service training, and developmental training.

The orientation of a new employee or volunteer to the workplace by the supervisor is called **pre-service training**. This orientation is generally the first job-related training that he or she receives upon entering the organization.

Orientation

The orientation of a new employee or **volunteer** typically includes an explanation of the organizational structure, normal work hours, benefits, dress code (or uniform) requirements, expense accounts, and emergency/evacuation procedures in the workplace. An explanation of the organizational structure should, if possible, include reference to the informal structure as well as the formal structure (i.e., the organization chart and the chain of command). The orientation to the informal structure should be designed to provide the employee with the kinds of information, skills, and attitudes known to facilitate effective performance in the work environment and known ways of overcoming obstacles to task completion. A pre-service orientation should also convey the mission of the organization, its future vision, and any written policies and procedures that he or she will be expected to follow.

Orientation of new employees or volunteers should also include making them feel welcome. Introductions of colleagues and co-workers should be done at a time and in a way that will minimize disruptions of their work, so that they can meet and greet the new person in the most positive manner. Attention to small details, such as where and how to request office supplies, will also help make the newcomer feel welcome.

Introductions to co-workers may also provide an opportunity to delegate some specific aspects of the orientation to them. For example, cash control procedures and the use of required forms for planning and carrying out events could be taught by a person knowledgeable in these areas. An appointment could be made with one of these employees to explain such forms and procedures to the new hire at a specific future date and time. More technical kinds of instruction, such as the use of smartphones and other communications devices, may also be delegated to fellow employees, especially if this is not to be made part of future in-service training.

It is important to remember that the orientation of a new employee or volunteer forms an important first impression of the organization and can affect his or her long-term attitude. If conducted properly, this initial orientation to the workplace will make the newcomer feel like an important addition to the team of colleagues with whom he or she will be working. Indications of whether this has been achieved are sometimes revealed by the questions that the new hires ask at the conclusion of the orientation. They should be encouraged to ask questions at the end, particularly if they didn't ask any questions while the orientation was taking place.

Training

A training program should be designed to foster the following:

- Proper job description and responsibilities; the timeline/time frames for the duties to be carried out (on a periodic basis).
- Clearly introduce supervisor or team leader to trainees to foster positive decision-making authority and accountability. Knowing the supervisors or team leaders also will help the staff know whom to call regarding questions and concerns.
- Provide employees and volunteers with a thorough job description and procedures as a reference or personal guide.
- Give trainees a brief introduction to the meeting, event, exposition, or convention they will be working in order to understand the attendees, event schedule, and what to expect.
- Distribute the meeting, event, exposition, or convention risk management and crisis management plans and procedures.
- Clearly delineate the start and end time of work shifts.

In-Service Training

In-service training is usually conducted for one of two reasons: 1) to update and expand upon the initial orientation, and 2) to teach employees and volunteers how to use new technology and equipment.

Updating/Expanding Initial Training   Information covered in the initial employee or volunteer orientation needs to be repeated and updated over time. Employees and volunteers may not recall all of the information given to them during their initial orientation. The initial orientation may also have been deficient in some respects. Organizational policies and procedures may change over time. Furthermore, the future vision of the organization may change as a result of ongoing strategic planning efforts. Training is thus necessary to bring employees up-to-date with respect to current organizational culture and direction.

Training for Use of New Technology and Equipment   Increasingly rapid advancements in technology require an ongoing technology training program. As new types of computer hardware and software are developed and acquired, it is essential to train employees in their proper use. These training programs should usually be conducted annually—and more often when necessary.

Developmental Training

The goal of **developmental training** is to enable employees at all levels in the organization to realize their potential for personal growth and achievement. This training improves the chances of advancement for employees with potential for moving up in the organization. Leadership training is one example; it usually does not include volunteers, interns, and others who are not permanent employees of the organization.

Developmental Training Needs   Developmental training needs must be assessed subjectively by a supervisor. Employees with potential for advancement in the organization may be identified in annual performance reviews or by observation of their superior task performance. Investment in developmental training is usually only justifiable for full-time employees and not for volunteers or interns, with the possible exception of interns slated for future full-time employment. Another criterion for selecting employees for developmental training is the future vision and strategic plan of the organization. Particular employees may show promise for fitting into the organization's future. Developmental training is often very specialized in nature and may be best contracted to outside training firms rather than conducted in-house. For example, leadership training courses may be contracted out to a consulting industrial psychologist or his or her training firm.

Assessing Other Training Needs

Training needs should be assessed in terms of both the tasks to be completed in the organization and the employees and volunteers who conduct those tasks. The need for in-service training is sometimes indicated by a gap between the desired level and the actual level of task performance. Acquisition of new technology to be used for new or different tasks usually requires employee training for optimum task performance. Other reasons for poor task performance are not so obvious, and some type of systematic **needs assessment** is necessary to identify these other training needs.

Needs Assessment   An assessment of training needs can be conducted at different levels of detail, depending upon the time and resources available. At a minimum, observation and conversations with employees should be conducted where problems in task performance are thought to exist. For example, it may quickly become apparent from observation that a lack of understanding is the reason that the time-saving features of a new photocopy machine and its interface with employee computers are not being fully used.

More comprehensive methods of needs assessment are necessary to identify the full range of training needs that may exist. A survey questionnaire administered to all employees and volunteers is one of the best ways to conduct a comprehensive assessment of training needs. However, such surveys are only as good as the questions asked and must be designed and conducted by persons skilled in survey research methods. For example, confidentiality of survey responses is usually an important survey requirement. If confidentiality is promised and the promise is not kept, this may reduce the reliability and comprehensiveness of survey results. For best results, a needs assessment survey should be contracted out to a firm or a university that specializes in this type of needs assessment. This can be expensive in terms of both time and money.

An alternative to the survey method of needs assessment is the focus group. A focus group involves only a small number of employees and/or volunteers, usually no more than 10 to 15 people, who are intensively interviewed for up to two hours in a private room. A highly skilled "moderator" is in charge of the focus group and implements a questioning strategy designed to bring to light problems in task performance that might benefit by in-service training. Like the survey method, a focus group should be conducted by a skilled person (a person known as a "moderator" in the jargon of focus group research). Contracting for focus group needs assessments is usually not as expensive, and results can usually be achieved faster than with the survey method. However, it is usually not as comprehensive as the survey method because of the small number of people involved, and the quality of results achieved depends upon selecting the most knowledgeable employees as focus group participants.

Analysis of Needs Assessment Results   The different training needs identified by the needs assessment should be analyzed to determine whether a training program is really necessary for each of them. Upon close inspection, it may be determined that some of these needs can be met by on-the-job training. Unfamiliarity with a new copy machine could be one example. As long as one or more employees understands how to use the machine, he or she could be asked to teach colleagues on an informal basis. A "snowball" effect could ensue, with new learners teaching others until everyone in the organization understands the workings of the new machine. This is an example of continuing the practice of delegating some technical training to fellow employees in the process of new employee orientation.

Other areas identified by a needs assessment may apply to only older employees, because these *needs* are already common knowledge to younger employees. Text messaging on cell phones is an example of this. Many older employees do not use text messaging but can be encouraged to learn how (by themselves) in order to become current with state-of-the-art communication practices. It would be a waste of training resources to conduct a formal training program for this communication skill when all but the oldest employees in the organization already have it.

After this process of elimination, the decision can be made to develop in-service training programs. In addition to training programs that are deemed necessary after a needs assessment, the company should research and review training programs used in similar organizations, particularly training involving technology. This may include new program delivery, such as webinars, as well as new content and objectives.

Writing Training Objectives

Training objectives must be written for each in-service training program that is to be designed and delivered. Objectives give direction to a training program and provide a means for assessing its effectiveness. They should be written in terms of the expected change in behavior of the employees or volunteers being trained. They should also be measurable, so that it can be determined whether the objectives have been achieved or to what degree they have been achieved. Ideally, one should be able to answer the question of whether an objective has been achieved with a yes or no response or by stating the degree of achievement as a quantitative percentage (50 percent achieved, for example). Objectives should also be stated with respect to a given time frame. For most training programs, this is normally the day and time that the program ends. However, a later date may be an appropriate time to assess the achievement of training objectives, especially when the trainees are expected to apply their new knowledge after the conclusion of the training. *Train the trainer* programs are an example of this, where those who are trained are expected to become trainers and train others. Those who complete such a program, but who do not conduct any subsequent training themselves by a deadline date of perhaps one year later, would be judged not to have achieved a principal program objective.

Training Program Design

The subject of a training program is usually dictated by the topics emerging from the needs assessment and subsequent training objectives. One entire training program is usually required to address one particular training need, and, at times, a training program may be designed to address only one objective of a particular training need. The length of the training program is, in turn, determined by the scope of the training need or objective(s) being addressed. The length of a training program usually ranges from a half day or less to one or more full days.

A location for the training must be selected at the same time that the day and time(s) for the training program are chosen. It may be somewhere within the workplace or at an off-site location. The latter usually provides more privacy and enables both the trainer(s) and the training participants to enjoy an optimum learning environment. It is important to have a training room large enough to comfortably accommodate the number of people being trained. A list of registered training participants by age and gender should be consulted at this point. Good lighting and temperature control are essential requirements for the training room as well as comfortable seating and nearby restroom facilities.

The equipment that will be needed for the training program should also be considered in conjunction with selection of the training room. The room should either have built-in audiovisual and computer equipment or adequate wiring and wireless access for such equipment. Other necessary nontechnical equipment should also be identified or purchased at this time, including items such as flip charts, a white/black board, magic markers, and paper products for use in training activities. Specialized computer training software may also be required by the training facilitator.

Who is to conduct the training is an important consideration. Entire training programs may be contracted out, but if so, they still usually require some adaptation to specific training topics and objectives. If trainer expertise is available in-house and/or if there is no budget for contracting with a professional training firm, decisions must be made as to who will be in charge of conducting the training and, for large training programs, who will be his or her co-facilitators.

In general terms, the structure of the training program content follows the design of any good presentation and includes an introduction, a main body of content, and a conclusion. However, the similarity ends there. Because training programs are designed for adult learners, they must be designed for adult styles of learning. This means relating to real-world experience as much as possible and minimizing the standard didactic student–teacher classroom format. For training programs that last a full day or more, the first hour deserves the most attention in program design.

Conducting a Training Session

All good training programs begin with introductions keyed to a printed roster of participants' names and, if possible, contact information so that participants can follow up and network with each other after the conclusion of the program. The person in charge of the training program should begin the introductions by giving a detailed description of his or her own background and contact information, modeling the kind of open communication that participants can then emulate. One of the best ways to break down communication barriers and start the program on a positive note is with an icebreaker. An icebreaker allows participants to get to know one another in an entertaining way. There are many sources for icebreakers, but the best approach is to select one and then modify it so as to relate to the objectives of the training program.

A printed agenda should be distributed and reviewed after the icebreaker and introductions. This lets participants know what "road map" the training program will follow. At this point, it is useful to ask participants what they expect to get out of the training program. If participants express objectives that are not included in the program agenda, it is best to be flexible and make modifications to accommodate them.

The introductory portion of the program should end with basic information on the location of the rest rooms, emergency exit locations, and basic rules such as the need to turn off all cell phones—including the facilitator's phone. This illustrates the point that the facilitator is more than just an instructor: He or she must follow the rules, too. The message? *We are all in this together*.

The method of delivery is a major consideration for the main body of content of the training program. Adult learners do not respond well to straight lecture presentations. Although short periods of lecture are sometimes necessary for delivering highly technical information, various other forms of delivery should also be used, avoiding hour-long periods of lecture whenever possible. The delivery can include other methods of instruction such as discussion, role playing, and case studies. A large literature exists for many lesser-known methods of instruction, with the main principle usually being to engage the training participants in some way rather than having them be passive consumers of classroom lecture material.

It is also important to schedule an adequate number of breaks during a training day, with coffee and/or other refreshments, if possible. The training program should consist of a series of content sessions that build upon one another and are interspersed with a liberal number of breaks and adequate times for meals. Provision of the noon meal is recommended to help ensure that all participants come back after lunch to attend the afternoon sessions.

The day before the training begins, a pilot test should be conducted of the training facilities and of the times required for delivery of the training modules. If problems are to occur, it is better to identify and correct them in advance rather than have a day of training get off to a bad start due to some unexpected glitch.

As part of a training program for volunteers for the annual Richmond Folk Festival, the company that organizes it called *Venture Richmond* includes one important module entitled, "Basic On-Site Safety." It is organized around the following sequential steps:

1. <u>Be Alert</u>
   - Watch for a variety of inappropriate patron behaviors and first aid needs.
   - Stay calm and accurately report incidents.

2. <u>Take Appropriate Action</u>
   - Know how to reach festival personnel and report an emergency.
   - Know when and how to take care of matters yourself.

3. <u>Listen for Further Instructions</u>
   - Do not leave a lost child or someone in need until help arrives.

4. <u>Evacuation Procedures</u>
   - All staff and volunteers will be notified via radios. Announcements will also be made from festival stages.
   - Encourage people to move to the free-flowing exits in a safe and orderly fashion. Guests will be looking for you to stay calm and offer clear direction.

A half hour or more should be devoted to closure at the end of the training session. This should include participants filling out a written course evaluation form as well as a discussion of whether the course met the expectations of the trainees. It should also provide participants with the contact information of all those attending (if this was not included in the roster handed out at the beginning of the program). Another strong component for closure is to give each participant a chance to tell one way in which she or he will put some of what was learned in training to use in the workplace by some future date. Sometimes participants are asked to write a reminder letter to themselves, which the facilitator sends to them at a later date. A final gesture of good will is for the facilitator to shake the hands of all participants as they leave, thanking them for their attendance.

SUPERVISION

Supervision of employees takes place at all levels of administration in an organization and is largely a leadership function. Supervision is referred to as executive leadership at the top levels of the administrative hierarchy. This is because the chief executive officer supervises other executives at a subordinate level in the hierarchy. At the level of administration concerned with front-line employees and volunteers, the **supervisor** is charged with carrying out the directions and policies dictated by his or her superiors.

The Leadership Function

The supervisor does this through effective **leadership** of his or her frontline employees or volunteers, those people who actually perform the necessary tasks to get the work done. The supervisor may sometimes do some of the work him- or herself in order to model high standards of performance. The supervisor must effectively communicate the expectations, roles, and responsibilities of his or her team members. He or she must encourage them to work as a team and to accept the diversity of fellow team members as a strength rather than a weakness or a source of conflict.

It is the job of the supervisor to encourage effective communication, to delegate tasks and responsibilities, to set goals for the work team(s), and to monitor team progress toward those goals. The supervisor must also monitor the performance of individual team members and provide regular feedback on their job performance. When providing feedback, the supervisor can be most effective by assuming a counseling role. This means treating unacceptable performance as a problem to be overcome and offering to work with the employee to resolve the problem.

In the leadership role, the supervisor should coach and mentor his or her workers. This is usually done by meeting with each one of them on a periodic basis, getting to know them and breaking down the barrier of fear that employees usually have of the power that the supervisor has over them. The supervisor should attempt to build trust, so that employees will not be afraid to come forward when they have a problem. However, with respect to conflicts with other employees, he or she should encourage employees to attempt to resolve the issue through face-to-face communication before coming to the supervisor with such problems. (For more information, see Chapter 7.)

Motivation of Staff and Volunteers

Employees expect clear directions from their supervisor for work that must be done. Basic communication is therefore a necessary part of employee **motivation**. One cannot expect either paid employees or volunteers to be motivated to work if they do not know what they are supposed to do. An example of this is an annual two-day fall festival in a large city on the East Coast of the United States that depends mainly upon volunteers to set up and staff the event. This festival takes place on a Friday and Saturday, but requires three days to decorate the venue and prepare for the event. Most of this preparatory work takes place on Thursday, a day when the most volunteer help is needed. A common complaint from some volunteers on this day every year is that they are not told what to do, which frustrates them and causes some to leave early while there is still much work to do.

The way in which a supervisor communicates with staff and volunteers is also an important aspect of employee motivation. Giving work orders to employees and expecting them to be obeyed by virtue of the power that the supervisor has to impose negative sanctions often creates a reluctant and fearful type of employee motivation. It works as long as the supervisor is present, but can result in disgruntled employees and work slowdowns after the supervisor leaves the scene. This is commonly referred to as an *authoritarian* style of supervisory leadership. This is in contrast to *democratic* and *charismatic* leadership styles, which can motivate employees to follow a supervisor's directions out of respect and desire to do what he or she says must be done, rather than out of fear.

Motivational Needs and Expectations   Workers have needs and expectations that a supervisor should attempt to identify and satisfy in order to prevent work slowdowns and to motivate increased productivity. Basic worker expectations include a safe, clean work environment and fair treatment by their supervisor. Equal pay or other compensation for equal work is an important part of the fairness expectation. When these expectations are not met, workers usually become dissatisfied and work slowdowns can result. Volunteers at the East Coast festival referred to above are each given a certain number of food and drink tickets as compensation for three-hour shifts of work during this Friday and Saturday event. Each year there are a few volunteers who, for some reason, do not receive their food and drink tickets. This causes obvious dissatisfaction. When this happens, the chairman of the event immediately gives these person(s) their expected share of tickets. This usually satisfies these volunteers, and they complete their volunteer shift with no further complaints.

Although it is necessary to meet the expectations of employees, as in the above case, just meeting them does not necessarily motivate them to do more and better work. To motivate employees, it is necessary to satisfy other needs beyond the basic expectations of the workplace. Other needs include positive recognition from their supervisor for doing a good job, freedom from oversupervision (micromanagement), and for paid employees, the possibility for personal growth and future advancement in the organization. Lack of recognition by their supervisor for work well done is an obstacle to employee gratification. Public recognition of work well done, if only a pat on the back, is a motivator. As a rule, supervisors should praise both paid employees and volunteers in public and only tell them of their shortcomings in private.

An effective way that a supervisor can motivate a team of employees is to describe in general terms the work task(s) they are expected to complete, but to ask them to decide the specific details of how they will conduct the assigned work. This usually results in some innovative work procedures that may be more efficient than if the supervisor were to dictate the exact way in which to do things. The opportunity to decide *how* the work is to be completed is a self-motivator, because it makes employees proud of *how* they have done the job in addition to being proud of *what* they have done. An example of this in the previous case of the East Coast festival is the assembly of a series of wooden display booths (chalets) during the festival's setup days. A team of volunteers is assigned to the assembly of a particular chalet, but is not told now to complete this task—other than to inform them that the ends of the wooden pieces are alphabetically coded so that matching letters indicate where any two pieces must be joined by bolts or screws. This task of chalet assembly seems to be accomplished faster each year, despite the fact that the volunteers on these teams are usually not the same persons from year to year.

Although the freedom to make decisions on how to complete work is a strong motivator, additional guidance and training are sometimes needed by volunteers. Volunteers should be matched to jobs for which they have necessary skills. One job in the set-up of the East Coast festival referred to in the above examples is the construction of a wooden stage at one end of the dance floor. This usually requires at least one or more volunteers with carpenter skills. A dozen prefabricated modules are kept in storage from year to year for the stage assembly, and one or more of these wooden modules must usually be repaired before they are all joined together to form the level floor of the stage at a height of approximately four feet above the dance floor. These repairs, as well as the repair or construction of several sets of stairs connecting the dance floor to the floor of the stage, are usually assigned to one or more volunteers with previous carpentry experience. The skilled volunteers then give guidance to others on the team with no such experience, who are taught how to safely assist those with the carpentry skills.

Motivating Volunteers Special consideration must be given to motivating volunteers, so as to have them return to volunteer another time. After the conclusion of an event, it is particularly important to celebrate the contributions of volunteers. A thank you letter should be mailed to all volunteers, with an invitation to a special awards ceremony. An awards ceremony does much to consolidate a loyal cadre of volunteers who will return to work on similar festivals or events in the future. Every volunteer there can be publicly presented with a certificate honoring their contribution to the event. The certificate should have their name printed on it and be signed by the chairman of the festival. Some volunteers who provide exceptional service to the event may be presented with a special gift. There may also be volunteers with coordinator roles who should be given similar recognition. There also may be groups of volunteers representing different constituencies or geographic regions. If so, a special award can be presented to the group of volunteers who contributed the most to the festival or event.

Maintaining communications with past volunteers can help maintain their loyalty and also encourage them to volunteer again in the future. A volunteer newsletter is one such communication device, which can be sent either electronically or by regular mail. A computer list-serve is another useful method to keep volunteers informed. Similarly, a blog to which volunteers are encouraged to contribute their thoughts and experiences is another useful communication tool. A website may also be established for a large festival or event, with links to the site provided to every volunteer.

Evaluating Staff and Volunteers Full time employees and volunteers should both be evaluated based on the expectations that their supervisor has of them. For full time employees, the supervisor's year-end performance expectations are usually based upon the employee's job description, as well as performance objectives agreed upon at the beginning of each year and any other responsibilities assigned during the year. Volunteers may not be evaluated annually due to the shorter duration of their tenure.

For them, evaluation may consist of only a rating of their performance at the end of their stint as a volunteer, together with the supervisor's decision on whether or not they would be welcomed back as volunteers at another time.

Effective evaluation of employees and volunteers provides feedback to those evaluated, as well as providing important decision criteria for supervisors. Positive evaluations can be very motivating to employees, while shortcomings identified in performance evaluations often point up the need for employee training to enable them to reach their goals. Thus, the supervisor's decisions on future training needs can be an important outcome of staff and volunteer evaluations.

Supervisors should keep good records on employees, including summaries of any critical incidents during the employment period. These records can be used at the performance review session to document either positive or negative aspects of employee behavior. Different kinds of rating scales may also be used to quantify employee performance and capabilities, and this information can be retained in the employee's personnel file for future reference.

Conducting a Performance Review   The performance review should be conducted as a face-to-face sit down meeting between the supervisor and the employee. The supervisor should begin by telling the employee the purpose of the meeting. (S)he should always begin the meeting on a positive note by making reference to *strengths* exhibited by his/her performance during the employment period to which the evaluation review pertains. (S)he may then bring up *shortcomings* of the employee in one of several different ways. One common method of addressing the shortcomings is called the "tell and sell" approach. With this method, the supervisor *tells* the employee what (s)he believes are his/her shortcomings, and then proceeds to *sell* the employee on what the supervisor believes are ways to improve his/her performance. A second method is called the "tell and listen" approach. With this method, the supervisor tells the employee what (s)he believes are his/her shortcomings, and listens to reasons that the employee gives for the shortcomings. The employee is then asked to identify ways to deal with his/her shortcomings, and some type of negotiated agreement ensues on how the employee will strive to improve.

A third method is called the "problem solving" approach. With this method the supervisor tells the employee the perceived shortcomings and then asks the employee to discuss each one with the supervisor, as a problem to be solved. The first step in doing this is to define the problem, which can often include taking into account the employee's personal life situation. The next step is to analyze the problem with the employee and together come up with alternative solutions. Agreement is then reached on which alternative to select as a means to resolve the problem underlying the particular shortcoming discussed. Of the three methods, the problem solving method is usually superior to the first two methods, because the employee is treated as an equal and works together with the supervisor to find optimal ways to strive to improve. Because the employee has input to the agreed-upon solution to the problem, (s)he is self-motivated to implement the solution rather than only paying "lip service" to it at the time of the performance appraisal.

Terminations, Separations, and Resignations

Terminations, separations, and resignations are related actions, which all result in the employee leaving the organization, either for some designated period of time or permanently (for more information, see Chapter 7). Terminations are the most serious actions, and result in the employee permanently leaving the organization. Some common reasons for termination include failure to enforce an important organizational policy, insubordination, intoxication, immorality, and lack of ethical integrity (e.g. theft, extortion, assault).

Terminations often represent a failure on the part of both the employee and the supervisor. Common failures by the supervisor include initially hiring the wrong person for the job, and/or not providing sufficient training after hiring a person known to be deficient in some areas. A common failure on the part of a supervisor at the time of termination is not following proper procedure prior to discharging an employee. Proper procedure usually involves attempting lesser disciplinary actions prior to outright discharge of the employee. Among the more common lesser disciplinary actions are the following: verbal reprimand, written reprimand, demotion, and suspension. Verbal reprimands are usually considered adequate disciplinary action for minor violations of organizational policies. Written reprimands are also used for minor policy violations, but are placed in the employee's personnel file upon notification of the employee. A written reprimand is usually removed from the personnel file after a certain period of time during which the employee displays satisfactory behavior relative to the reason for reprimand. Demotion and/or suspension are more serious disciplinary actions, which can be used for more serious infractions, or as a *next* step following verbal and/or written reprimands for lesser infractions that do not result in the desired corrected behavior on the part of the employee. Demotion is the moving of an employee from one position to another in the organization that provides less pay and/or status. Suspension is the temporary separation of an employee from the organization without pay. The length of time of the suspension depends upon the severity of the infraction. Legal proceedings often take place during a suspension, and, in cases where the employee is judged innocent of the presumed infraction, (s)he is reinstated and reimbursed for the pay forgone during the period of the suspension. Termination of employment usually follows a period of suspension, during which an investigation is conducted to substantiate the employee's presumed infraction.

Separation of an employee from the organization may occur for a variety of reasons, most of which are not related to disciplinary actions. The most common form of nondisciplinary separation is called a *layoff* or *furlough*. This is a separation from the organization, without pay, for an undetermined period of time. It is usually a necessary personnel action caused by lack of work, or, more commonly, the need to reduce expenses resulting from budget cuts. The term *furlough* usually refers to a *relatively* short period of separation. For example, state employees may all be told that they will be *furloughed* for one work week at the end of the fiscal year to make up for an unexpected state budget shortfall.

Resignations are voluntary terminations from the organization usually initiated by the employee. Retirement is the most common form of resignation; it is usually initiated by an employee when he or she voluntarily ends his service to the organization because of reaching minimum retirement age. It is illegal for most public sector employers, and private sector employers with 20 or more full-time employees, to force an employee to retire at a *mandatory* retirement age, as long as the employee can still effectively do his or her job.

An employer may offer *voluntary* resignation to an employee in lieu of forced termination for some presumed infraction. This can benefit both the employer and the employee. The employer can avoid the time and effort required for an investigation to substantiate the presumed infraction justifying termination, and the possibility that the employee could prevail upon contesting termination. For the employee, a resignation may appear better on his or her long-term record of employment than a termination.

Documentation and Security Considerations   It is important to maintain written documentation of employee terminations, separations, and resignations. Copies of required documentation should be shared with superiors; having employees sign off on documentation signifies their approval of these actions. Reasons for resignations should be documented by written notes gathered during an exit interview.

Security considerations for departing employees should include acquiring their keys and deactivating their access codes for locked facilities. Computers and other equipment used by employees while they were on the job should also be turned in and inventoried by the supervisor, with corresponding identification tags and serial numbers recorded as part of the departure documentation. In cases of a hostile departure, the supervisor should walk the departing employee to the door or gate to the premises at the end of the last day of work in order to minimize the possibility of theft. Police or security guard presence may also be advisable in such cases.

Follow-up actions by the supervisor after the permanent departure of an employee should include formally notifying the people with whom the employee interacted on a periodic basis while on the job. These include external customers and suppliers, internal payroll and support staff, and workplace colleagues.

SUMMARY

Training and supervision are related and both subsegments of human resources. Supervision includes the orientation of new employees to the workplace, which is the first type of training that employees receive. In-service training expands upon training received in the initial job orientation. It also fulfills additional training needs identified by formal needs assessments and by supervisory observation. Developmental training helps prepare full-time employees for advancement opportunities in the organization.

Supervision for festivals, events, meetings, and conventions involves the effective leadership and motivation of both full-time employees and volunteers to ensure that they complete the tasks assigned to them. The effective supervisor does this in a manner consistent with the directions and policies dictated by his or her superiors. Motivating volunteers requires special consideration by the supervisor. Volunteers require clear training and work assignments as well as frequent feedback from their supervisor. They also need to be thanked in a variety of ways, including a letter and/or certificate of volunteer service. The supervisor should "celebrate" the contributions of volunteers with some type of awards celebration, at which time formal presentations of awards can be made to top performers.

Other important duties of the supervisor include employee performance evaluations and the processing of employee terminations, separations, and resignations. When conducted from a problem-solving perspective, employee performance evaluations can have rewarding outcomes for both the employee and the supervisor. Employee terminations are sometimes necessary, but, when possible, should be preceded by lesser disciplinary actions. Written documentation is essential for all actions regarding terminations, separations, and resignations. Security considerations are also essential, particularly in the case of hostile terminations.

Now that you have completed this chapter, you should be competent in the following Meeting and Business Event Competency Standards:

MBECS Skill 13: Train Staff and Volunteers

Subskills		
13.01	Provide Orientation	
13.02	Provide Training	

MBECS Skill 14: Manage Workforce Relations

Subskills		
14.01	Supervise staff and volunteers	
14.02	Motivate staff and volunteers	
14.04	Evaluate staff and volunteers	
14.05	Process terminations and separations	

KEY WORDS AND TERMS

training	needs assessment	termination
pre-service training	supervision	separation
volunteer	supervisor	resignation
in service training	leadership	
developmental training	motivation	

REVIEW AND DISCUSSION QUESTIONS

1. Identify the three basic types of employee training.
2. How are training needs assessed? Is there more than one way to do this?
3. What are the characteristics of well-written training objectives?
4. Name some of the important considerations in training program design.
5. Describe how to conduct a training session.
6. Describe how to provide closure at the end of a training session.
7. Describe the ways in which needs and expectations are key to employee motivation.
8. How are volunteers motivated to return another time?
9. Describe the alternative approaches to employee performance reviews.
10. Discuss the process of terminating an employee.

ABOUT THE CHAPTER CONTRIBUTOR

Allan S. Mills is an associate professor in the L. Douglas Wilder School of Government and Public Affairs at Virginia Commonwealth University in Richmond, Virginia. Prior to his entry into academia, Mills developed an interest in the hospitality industry through his management of a wholesale institutional food distributing company. He began his academic career at the University of California, Davis, where he was mainly responsible for teaching administration and research methods courses. He moved from there to Texas A & M University, where he became interested in the broad field of tourism, in addition to hospitality, by teaching graduate research methods and advising graduate students on research applications for tourism research projects. He has been teaching both undergraduate and graduate tourism classes at Virginia Commonwealth University for the past 25 years.

CHAPTER 9

Optimizing Speakers, Entertainment, and Performers

Learning Objectives

Upon completion of this chapter, the reader should be able to:

- Determine meeting/convention/event requirements for speakers, entertainers, and performers (SEPs)
- Develop selection criteria for SEPs
- Design an effective environment for SEPs
- Select SEPs
- Secure Contracts

Pyrotechnics can be entertaining, yet dangerous. circotasu/fotolia

Chapter Outline

MEETING/CONVENTION/EVENT REQUIREMENTS FOR SPEAKERS, ENTERTAINMENT, AND PERFORMERS (SEPs)

Most meetings and events will require the use of speakers, entertainers, or performers (SEPs). The purpose of SEPs can be to motivate, educate, and/or entertain attendees, depending on the goals and objectives of the meeting or event. These may include performing artists, celebrities, professional or amateur speakers, musicians, politicians, civic leaders, and other entities that may increase interest in an event and drive attendance as well as direct attendee traffic flow.

The selection of SEPs will be determined by the goals and objectives of the event. The difference between a corporate event and an event where people may pay a registration fee to attend will impact the choice of SEPs. For example, one of the largest trade shows in the United States, the Specialty Equipment Manufacturers Association (SEMA), has had celebrity NASCAR racer Jeff Gordon appear to build awareness and interest in the show. At other times, SEPs are brought in for their relevance to the meetings' objective. For example, Microsoft Chief Executive Officer Steve Ballmer speaks at the company's annual shareholder meetings.

SEPs may serve to kick off a morning general session or provide entertainment during a lunch, a banquet, galas, and receptions. Trade shows often use SEPs to lure attendees to visit otherwise low-traffic areas. By strategically placing speaker stages and performance areas, attendee traffic flow can be "redirected" and provide for greater exposure to areas that are not so heavily visited. Furthermore, speakers are featured in workshops and other educational sessions. Webcasts and webinars are other forums where SEPs are often required. SEPs for a general or keynote session should energize your attendees and set the tone for the event, whereas those for an educational session may be used to create a more serious learning environment. A multiday program could require numerous types of SEPs in order to meet its overall objective. Appropriate scheduling of SEPs is vital to the success of any meeting or event. For example, holding a general session with a famous keynote speaker and a trade show opening at the same time could sabotage the success of the event. Likewise, scheduling popular two similar SEPs at the same time could result in a cannibalization of the program and frustrate attendees.

SELECTION AND USE OF SEPs

The selection of SEPs should be guided by the goals and objectives of the event as well as the image and purpose of the organization. Financial considerations and social responsibility also come into play. An example of not considering the image and purpose of the organization occurred when the U.S. federal government's General Services Agency (GSA) was internationally criticized for hosting a lavish event at a Las Vegas hotel during the peak of the economic downturn of 2010. Over $800,000 was spent for a meeting of 350 agency employees, including a $75,000 team building exercise in which participants assembled bicycles. The U.S. inspector general's report stated that GSA spending on conference planning was excessive, wasteful, and in some cases impermissible. This brought international media attention to the agency, hurting not only its reputation but the events industry as a whole.

Types of SEPs

Different SEPs are appropriate for different situations. There are a variety of resources available to the event professional.

Speakers Bureau   A **speakers bureau** is a professional broker who helps find SEPs that match the objectives and budgets of events. For example, *Leading Authorities* is a speakers bureau that represents top business, leadership, political, and motivational speakers. Its roster includes keynote speakers such as former prime ministers, former members of Congress, CEOs of multinational companies, prominent journalists, and renowned policy experts. Other speakers bureaus include the *National Speakers Association, Executive Motivational Speakers Bureau, and Premiere Speakers*, among many others. The *Premiere Speakers* website lists a wide range of topics covered by its SEPs, including motivation, politics, health and wellness, and personal growth. The International Association of Speakers Bureaus (IASB) website provides a speaker bureau locator. Speaker fees can range from a few thousand to well over $100,000 per 30- to 90-minute appearance. Travel fees, special concessions (such as food and beverage provided on-site), and special needs typically incur additional costs.

Actors' Unions and Agents   The event professional may consider hiring a well-known celebrity through an actors' union such as the Screen Actors Guild (SAG) or the Actors' Equity Association. An agent can relieve you of the responsibility of dealing directly with SEPs.

Local Experts   A convenient and often inexpensive or free source of speakers includes local dignitaries or industry leaders. This will reduce transportation and lodging costs. The local convention and visitors bureau/DMO or chamber of commerce will be able to assist the event professional in locating appropriate people.

Faculty   Informed and trained speakers can be found at many colleges and universities. Many faculty members conduct research in specialized areas and are often excited to share their knowledge. The compensation for faculty speakers can be very reasonable and may only involve costs of travel and lodging.

Corporations   Many corporations are becoming sources for guest speakers on topics ranging from service standards to team building. For example, as one of North America's most successful airlines, *WestJet* is often approached by organizations to speak on its expertise. Speakers can be hired through the WestJet website. Another well-known corporation with executives in high demand for speaking engagement is *Zappos.com*. In some cases, companies will offer these speakers at no cost for the purposes of goodwill and publicity; or, they may charge fees to cover costs.

Organization Members   An important source of speakers for annual meetings or conventions that hold numerous workshops can be found within an organization itself. Whether it is a nonprofit professional association or a corporation, there are sure to be leaders who could speak on topics of interest to attendees. In the professional world, members of an organization typically prefer peer-to-peer learning because they can relate to the experience and knowledge of the speaker. The speaker will most likely have in-depth knowledge of the organization due to their personal experience as a member.

A common method of gaining member input is to send out a call for papers, a call for topics, or a request for proposal (RFP) to the membership. Individuals may self-select to speak on a topic or may suggest other appropriate speakers. This process is not only an efficient and effective way of identifying appropriate SEPs, but it also engages membership in the selection process. Speaker RFPs are typically distributed well in advance of the event to ensure compliance with selection criteria as well the ability to contract with and promote the SEPs. This in turn helps promote the event. (For more detailed information, see Chapter 13 on public relations.)

Volunteer Speakers   In contrast with the more expensive option of paid speakers, many organizations rely heavily on **volunteer speakers** (typically not professional). For example, the Professional Convention Management Association (PCMA) typically hosts over 90 educational sessions during its three-day annual meeting. Hiring professional (paid) speakers for such an event could be cost prohibitive to the association. Instead, the bulk of the presenters are members of the association.

The benefits of using volunteer speakers include:

- Reduced expenses, as the speaker may be paying for his or her own transportation and lodging
- A connection to the organization or industry may increase their credibility
- An awareness of current industry topics
- Increased attendance at sessions, if speakers are popular industry leaders

However, using volunteer speakers can be problematic and may negatively impact the image of the organization. Potential challenges include:

- The speaker may have industry knowledge but lack effective presentation skills.
- The speaker may not adequately prepare for the presentation.
- The speaker may not follow the speaker guidelines provided.
- The speaker may use the session as a platform for self-promotion.

The Needs of SEPs

Well in advance of the event, the needs of SEPs should be determined to ensure that they are able to effectively perform in the selected venue. This is especially true in unique venues that may not be fully equipped to handle special requirements, such as staging, utilities, and audiovisual support. For example, a celebrity chef demonstration may require the use of natural gas and running water. **Indoor pyrotechnics** require extensive discussions with the fire marshal and venue management to comply with local fire codes and liability insurance and to ensure attendee safety.

Additionally, other advance considerations include:

- Transportation
- Lodging
- Security
- Special dietary needs
- Additional insurance
- Hold-harmless riders
- Protocol
- Background checks

Selection Criteria

It is imperative that the event professional fully understand the attendees' **demographics** and **psychographics** prior to contracting with an SEP. Demographics represent factors such as age, education, ethnicity, and income. Psychographics include psychological variables such as values, attitudes, and opinions. One challenge today is that multiple generations with different demographics and psychographics attend the same events. For example, selecting a hip-hop band for a gala may be inappropriate and offensive to older attendees, whereas a classical music quartet may turn off some younger attendees. SEPs that are not appealing or appropriate may result in attendees leaving the event, or not attending at all. This can impact everything from food and beverage guarantees to their loyalty to the organization.

Selection criteria are often developed by a committee, and the SEPs are chosen by consensus. In other cases, the decision may hinge on the opinions of the CEO, board of directors, or event sponsors.

Things to consider:

- The event's main objective
- Input from stakeholders and attendees
- The type of event it is (association, corporate, charity, sport, concert, social, political, recognition ceremony, etc.)
- Who the potential attendees are
- Budget constraints
- Indirect costs such as technical, labor, facility, and setup charges
- Legal implications
- Duration
- Location and venue
- Season/weather
- Schedule/timeline
- Duration of program
- Compensation/benefits
- License issues
- Sponsorship fit with SEPs
- Potential for media coverage
- How to maximize marketing efforts

A comprehensive checklist of things to consider prior to contracting an SEP is found in Appendix 1, at the end of the chapter.

SEP Performance

Because hiring SEPs can be extremely expensive and crucial to the success of an event, it is imperative that the event professional actually view a live performance or at a minimum a digital video recording of the SEP prior to contracting his or her services. This can be obtained upon request through the speakers bureau, talent broker, or the SEPs themselves. Many SEPs have an online presence through their representatives or their own YouTube channels. In addition, obtain and check the references from other organizations that have hired the SEPs.

Sponsorships

Most organizations rely heavily on sponsorships to pay for SEPs. The cost of a major celebrity for a one-hour general session can run well over $100,000. Sponsors are often required to offset such costs and to keep registration prices low. They can be organizations or individuals who support the event (or portion thereof) through financial means, service, or trade. For example, a radio station may provide free on-air advertising in exchange for exposure at the event. In some cases, this will be a single sponsor who typically receives significant marketing exposure for their sponsorship. This includes a website presence, print ads, signage, inclusion in program, podium time, speaking opportunities, and overall brand exposure.

Sponsors may heavily influence the selection of SEPs. Many organizations offer tiered sponsorship levels to make participation in the event more accessible. The amount paid will impact the type and amount of exposure and benefits received (see Table 1). The $5,000 sponsor today could be a $50,000 sponsor tomorrow. In order to achieve the desired long-term relationships with sponsors, event professionals must proactively assist them in making the most of their sponsorship. Moreover, it is vital

TABLE 1 XYZ 2012 Annual Conference

Sponsorship Levels and Recognition

Supporting Sponsor $5,000–$9,999
- Supporting Sponsor recognition on signage in one high-traffic area (inclusion) at conference
- Logo and hyperlink featured on the XYZ conference website
- Logo displayed on jumbo screens before the general session

Silver Sponsor: $10,000–$39,999
- Silver Sponsor recognition on signage in one high-traffic area (inclusion) at conference
- Logo and hyperlink featured on the XYZ conference website
- Logo displayed on jumbo screen before the general session

Gold Sponsor: $40,000–$69,999
- Gold Sponsor recognition on signage in one high-traffic area (inclusion) at conference
- Logo and hyperlink featured on the XYZ conference website
- Logo displayed before general session on jumbo screens
- Signage honoring Gold Sponsors at EXPO booths
- Conference bag insert (sponsor is responsible for printing and shipping)

Platinum Partner: $70,000 and up
- Platinum Partner recognition on signage in one high-traffic area (inclusion)
- Platinum Partner recognition on the XYZ conference web page
- Featured Platinum Partner recognition in the XYZ preliminary and final conference program
- Platinum Partner recognition on stage at the general sessions
- Plaque honoring Platinum Partners displayed at their EXPO booths
- Conference bag insert (sponsor is responsible for printing and shipping)
- VIP photo shoot with XYZ leadership and award recipients
- Preliminary conference mailing List
- Post conference mailing list

that the objectives of the meeting or organization are in line with those of the sponsors. For example, no matter how much funding may be offered, having a youth-oriented event sponsored by a tobacco company anywhere in the world would likely be considered inappropriate by attendees and members and potentially cost the organization its reputation.

DESIGNING AN EFFECTIVE ENVIRONMENT FOR SEPs

Adult Learning Environment

Both volunteer and professional SEPs will benefit by being provided with an effective learning environment. This applies to the attendees as well. Whether the event is in a conference center specifically designed to host training or educational sessions or is a multipurpose meeting space in a hotel or convention center, the physical comfort and layout of the room will have an impact on the success of the event. Knowing the requirements of the SEP prior to signing facility contracts is imperative. Performers must have the space to perform. You can't have a stilt walker entertain guests if the ceilings are low.

The first consideration is the objective of the event. Select event space that will support the outcomes expected. In most cases, the event professional will be looking for space many months before the actual event. If the event professional makes a poor selection in meeting space, the venue cannot be changed if other groups have already contracted the alternative space. Requiring a larger room at the last minute may also incur additional fees. Another important consideration is how that space is utilized. There are a variety of room sets available (e.g., school room, theatre, hollow square, conference style) and each has its own benefits and challenges. The room set can dictate the relationship between SEPs and the attendees. For example, if a hollow square setup is selected and there are 100 people in attendance, then there will be a large empty space in the middle of the room, and it is doubtful that the attendees will be able to see and hear the SEP or each other.

Other physical requirements are the size and type of tables. Again, selection is dictated by the objectives of the event. There are numerous choices available (see Table 2). It is imperative that the attendees' comfort be considered. Cramming 12 people around a 60" round table makes for a poor dining experience. If attendees have laptops, meeting materials, food items, and so on, it is best to opt for a wider table. In addition, most hotels and convention centers use standard-sized banquet chairs, which are rarely comfortable for long periods of time.

Temperature is another consideration. Make sure the room temperature is between 70 and 74 degrees. Nothing puts an audience to sleep faster than a warm room, especially after they have eaten a meal. It is generally better to err on the side of the room being too cool rather than too hot. The ambient temperature of the room will probably rise due to the body temperature of the attendees. Good air circulation is also important.

Of course, the general attractiveness and cleanliness of the room or event space have an impact on the event. Dirty carpets, windows, and walls; poor lighting; and odors from kitchens or service areas all detract from the learning environment.

Performance Environment

When designing a performance environment, the planner must consider not only the ability of the SEP to effectively and safely perform or speak in the space, but also the overall experience and engagement of the audience. Such considerations are often impacted by demographics and include sight lines, sound, lighting, special effects, legalities, safety, sense of security, and audience comfort (e.g., seating, temperature, fresh air). If the audience is not engaged, the purpose of contracting an SEP may be defeated; however, if the participants are not or do not feel safe, the organization/event may lose its credibility.

TABLE 2 Table Specifications

Type	Size	Uses
Rounds*	60"	Banquets, roundtable discussions for 8 to 10 people (18 to 30" wide)
	72"	Banquets, roundtable discussions for 10 to 12 people (18 to 30" wide)
		*May only use half the table if space is needed for workspace
Cocktail Rounds	15 to 30"	Receptions, cocktail parties; height varies 36 to 50"; tall chairs or barstools may be used as well
Rectangle	6"	Workshops, reception areas for 2 people
	8"	Workshops, reception areas for 3 people
Novelty*	Varies	Food or product displays, refreshment breaks
		*Serpentine or half moon (for example)

Sight Lines

A large audience eagerly awaited the cooking demonstration that was part of the Canada Day festivities in Trafalgar Square, London. Famous chefs were flown in from Canada and given all the tools they needed to prepare Nova Scotia lobster. Unfortunately, the majority of the audience was unable to see anything but the chef's upper body due to poor sight lines from the seating area. A simple solution such as an overhead mirror or TV monitors would have made the event a success rather than frustrate the audience and chefs alike.

Décor

Décor can be vital to the success of an event, especially themed ones. Décor includes lighting, decorated balloons, event centerpieces, floral design, foam props, balloon sculptures, fabric draping, and the use of plants, linens, and tableware. Everything from color scheme to texture must be considered to ensure that the decor is not only effective but memorable. However, depending on the objective of the event, décor can either enhance or detract from its success. For example, too much emphasis on décor may distract the audience and take away from the impact of the keynote speaker. On the other hand, a fire breather performing in a classroom environment would not be as entertaining or enchanting as he or she would be performing poolside, at night. Cross-cultural awareness is also key: color, religion, feng shui, and even superstitions can be crucial. In the end, décor will largely be dictated by budget constraints. The cost of decorative items and labor must be taken into account. For example, a large corporate event in Honolulu featured a jungle theme décor consisting of vines strung throughout the ballroom. Although the cost of the vines was minimal, the labor was intensive and had a significant impact on the budget. Oversight of the décor may result in negative implications for both the event professional and the host organization.

Off-Site and Challenging Environments

Ancillary activities—such as cocktail receptions and **off-premise** happenings— are the main drivers for event attendance. Unique venues and experiences beyond what could be provided at a typical hotel or convention center create memories that stay with attendees long after the event. For example, the International Association of Exhibitions and Events (AIMEE) hosted an interactive reception at the Georgia Aquarium in Atlanta for its annual meeting, with marine animals, entertainment, regional delicacies, and VIP tours. Entertainers and performers included a popular local band, stilt walkers, aerialists, and expert speakers on marine biology. As another example, the Professional Convention Management Association (PCMA) held its 2013 annual convention in Orlando. One off-site evening took place at SeaWorld, featuring Shamus as the top entertainer.

The use of SEPs off-site has become increasingly common; it is often a very convenient and cost-effective way of enhancing a meeting or event. In some instances, a **keynote** speaker is irreplaceable. If he or she misses a flight and cannot make it to the venue, it can be vital to the success of a meeting or event. This is especially true with speakers. Rather than requiring a speaker to travel, many planners arrange a live feed broadcast at the event. If the speaker customizes the message, it can be a very effective way of engaging the audience. It is vital that planners check feed connections and make sure the SEPs are ready to begin on cue. Otherwise, the loss of audience engagement is imminent, and the objectives of the meeting may not be met.

Featuring SEPs in an off-site performance, where both the SEP and audience must travel to the location, can add much more complexity to the checklists of event professionals. The potential risks and additional costs often involved in off-site locations cannot be emphasized enough. The planner must ensure that he or she has full access to all the resources needed on-site, particularly in remote locations. This includes safe and easy access to event site, electricity, toilet facilities, shelter, emergency medical equipment and supplies, in addition to the standard audiovisual requirements. A full **walk-through** of the location should occur one to days in advance of the event so that provisions can be made if necessary. Finally, off-site venue details should be fully disclosed to SEPs prior to signing the contract, to ensure they are comfortable, willing, and able to effectively perform in such an environment. This is especially true with challenging environments where SEPs may be required, such as floating stages, private islands, farm fields, rooftop performances, and even jumping from airplanes.

Security

Security not only involves the physical protection of SEPs and attendees, but also situations requiring confidentiality, such as corporate secrets and **intellectual property**. Man power—such as bodyguards, registration attendants, and room monitors to check entry credentials—is needed. Because of corporate spying, mobile technology may need to be monitored or restricted, depending on the content and objective of the event. The use of Twitter and YouTube can positively impact an event through exposure, but can be detrimental to a company during a confidential meeting.

Protocol

Protocol cannot be generalized across groups: it is specific to each individual organization's procedures. These procedures are established by policy, which can differ significantly among organizations. Therefore, assuming that all stakeholders and event professionals understand an organization's protocol may result in embarrassment, failure, and international incident, in some cases. It is vital to gain an "insider's" knowledge of protocol to ensure overall success.

Safety/Insurance
Fire Walkers Burned

Nearly two-dozen self-improvement buffs were injured during a "fire walk" experience on the first night of a four-day seminar with renowned self-help guru Tony Robbins. Many of the injured reported second- or third-degree burns on the soles of their feet after they walked across eight-foot beds of burning coals that were heated to about 2,000 degrees. Some 6,000 attendees paid between $600 and $2,000 each to attend the seminar; it included motivational talks and exercises like fire walking, which are designed to help people overcome their anxieties (or, as one attendee said, "it's a metaphor for facing your fears."). A spokesman for the event organizer said the firm has been safely providing this experience for more than three decades.

Secure Contracts

Once the SEP has been identified, there are three steps in the contracting process: the offer, negotiations, and mutual acceptance.

1. **Offer** Once you have decided on a particular SEP and checked his or her references, you must write an offer letter. This document outlines the appropriate considerations that may be included in the binding contract. An offer letter can be considered a binding contract if signed by both parties. However, since this is typically the beginning of the negotiation process, considerations often change through numerous counteroffers.

2. **Negotiation** Negotiation is the process by which an event professional and a venue representative (or other supplier) reach an agreement on the terms and conditions that will govern their relationship before, during, and after a meeting, convention, exposition, or event. The goal of negotiation is to create a mutually beneficial relationship between the SEP and the event professional. In some cases negotiation is not possible: The price is the price. This is especially the case when dealing with high-profile SEPs or their representatives. However, if negotiation is an option, the following principles should be considered.

   Principles of Negotiation
   - Have well-defined expectations of SEPs.
   - Know your bottom line. How far are you willing to negotiate?
   - Have a clear understanding of flexibility (including scheduling and compensation)
   - Understand the negotiating style of the other party (i.e., some negotiators "play hardball," while others approach the process in a more congenial manner).
   - Do not divulge all possible considerations at the start of the negotiations (additional concessions may be required to reignite stalled discussions).
   - Ensure clear and well-documented communication.
   - Archive all communication in case of legal issues or misunderstandings.

   SEP fees are often where the decision to hire or not is made. However, the cost of hiring SEPs may go well beyond performance or speaking fees. For example, many SEPs may demand first-class air travel or five-star hotel accommodations. Such factors quickly drive up the initial cost of the speaking or performance fee.

   Considerations for Negotiating Fees
   Although negotiating a flat fee covering all expenses (including travel, housing, etc.) would be most desirable for the meeting/event sponsor, this is not always possible. In such cases, the following negotiating points may be considered:

   - Suggest a reduced fee if no travel is required.
   - Offer SEPs the ability to sell products such as books, DVDs, training materials, and so on, at the event.
   - Provide free event registration.
   - Offer additional nights or VIP treatment at the host hotel.
   - Offer free or reduced price for brand exposure, such as a trade show booth or advertising.
   - Use the SEP for more than one event.
   - Provide spouse or guest accommodations.
   - Award a percentage of sales of recorded presentation or performance of SEP.
   - Offer an association with high-profile events, attendees, or other SEPs.

3. **Mutual Acceptance** Once negotiations are completed and all parties have reached an agreement, a legally binding contract is created. Since contracts cover

far more than compensation, it is vital to have all SEPs (paid and volunteer) sign contracts. The first rule of contracting is to put everything in writing and have all authorized parties sign. However, in many cases, it is desirable to have legal counsel review the contract before it is signed. When contracting with SEPs or their representatives (such as a speakers bureau or agent), the following should be considered and outlined in both the offer letter and final contract:

- Compensation (amount and payment schedule).
- Expenses covered (e.g., hotel, transportation, food).
- Performer or speaker guidelines and expectations.
- Time, date, location, and duration of performance.
- Audiovisual needs or restrictions (i.e., speaker must provide laptop).
- Submission due dates (e.g., for SEP bios, photographs, video clips for website promotion, handouts, and special requests).
- Termination and liability.
- Considerations for amending the contract.
- Ramifications for breach of contract (liquidated and/or actual damages).
- Methods of dispute resolution (arbitration, mediation, or litigation).
- **Cancellation clauses** and penalties.
- Intellectual property rights (e.g., ownership, distribution, use, or sale of recordings and photographs of SEP).
- Risk management (security and safety precautions).
- **Confidentiality agreement.**

Monitoring Contracts

Some events may have more than 100 SEPs, and therefore more than 100 separate contracts. Furthermore, contracts may be written up to one year in advance, so it is imperative to stay in communication with contracted SEPs or their representatives to ensure that the contract terms are still viable. For example, if a volunteer speaker for a breakout session is ill, it may be desirable to cancel the session with no further recourse. However, if the SEP is a keynote speaker who cancels at the last minute, damages are likely to occur and legal recourse may be required.

Speaker Guidelines

Speaker guidelines outline everything an SEP should know to perform/present in the most effective manner for a particular audience. These guidelines impact an SEP's knowledge of the organization, the goals and objectives of the event, and the demographics and psychographics of the attendees. The guidelines are especially important to volunteer and paid speakers who present at educational sessions. They provide the framework for speakers as they prepare their presentations and outline limitations such as duration, content (topic and level), and self-promotion. They create measurable objectives (one of the SMART objectives) and reiterate contract terms of what will and will not be provided to speakers. In some cases, the speaker is required to sign a form stating that he or she has read and will comply with the speaker guidelines. The financial and time commitment of attending a three-day event can be extreme. There is only so much time in a day, with the average attendee only able to attend five to six sessions a day. The relevance of content is key to a speaker's success. Attendees who feel that a session did not meet their expectations or the stated objectives of the session may become disgruntled with both the speaker and the organization, potentially resulting in long-term damage to their relationship as members. Entertainers and performers must understand their audience and be prepared to perform appropriately to maximize entertainment and minimize the possibility of boring or offending the audience.

Guidelines

The International Association of Exhibitions and Events (IAEE) provided this helpful information for SEPs to review as they develop their presentation for the Midyear Meeting.

The IAEE Audience

- Show managers seeking additional, new, and practical cutting-edge skills to enhance their industry knowledge
- All industry professionals looking for new ideas and fresh approaches on how to conduct business
- Marketing managers and sales managers seeking a base of knowledge in the industry they represent
- Industry suppliers, including hotel personnel, who seek a complete overview and understanding of the show development process

Your Challenge

As a speaker/moderator or panelist for IAEE's Midyear Meeting, your challenge is to address the topic(s) related to the interests and needs of associate members; association, consumer, and independent show organizers; and exhibit managers.

Attendee Priorities

Attendees have high expectations and come to learn. Their top priorities are:

- "Nuts and bolts" information that they can put to work in their programs immediately
- An interactive learning environment in which they "learn by doing"

Speaker Registration

All speakers will need to register online. Speakers receive complimentary registration to the event for the day of their presentation. You will be provided with a complimentary code to use when registering upon receipt of your signed speaker agreement. Please DO NOT register until you have received this code.

Housing and Travel

Please visit the Hotel and Travel page on IAEE's Midyear Meeting website to secure hotel accommodations. It will be your responsibility to make arrangements with the hotel of your choice.

Speaker Introductions

All speakers are required to submit a 50- to 75-word description of their professional accomplishments as they relate to the topic.

IAEE staff members will be responsible for the introductions of the speakers/moderators. Moderators will introduce the other panel members. IAEE will provide these to you as submitted by the panelists. Please remember to keep this portion of the presentation brief.

Room Setup

To encourage interactivity during the sessions, the standard set for the session rooms will be crescent rounds.

(Continued)

Audio/Visual Equipment

IAEE provides the following in each session room:

- Laptop computer for PowerPoint presentation
- Data projector/screen for PowerPoint presentation
- Lavalier microphone per presenter
- One handheld mike for each session
- One wireless mouse/remote per session for multimedia presentations

Please complete and submit your Special Audio/Visual Request Form if any special arrangements need to be made.

Presenter Materials

A visual presentation is mandatory to accommodate the visual learner. The visual should be in the form of a PowerPoint. A PowerPoint template is provided; your presentation will need to be entered into this template. You are not allowed to sell during your presentation, and no company logos are permitted in the presentation. Click the PowerPoint Presentation link in the menu to access the PowerPoint Template.

In our effort to remain eco-friendly, IAEE will NOT provide printed copies of takeaways on-site.

Noncommercial Nature of IAEE's Seminars

To maintain the educational integrity of the conference program, presenters are advised not to use their session(s) as a platform for the promotion of their products and services, or for monetary gain.

IAEE provides a unique forum for professionals to have an open dialogue and creative exchange of ideas free from commercial content. Your cooperation with this is greatly appreciated.

Session Evaluations

At the conclusion of the course, please ask participants to complete and submit the session evaluation by adding a slide at the end of the PowerPoint presentation and a note at the end of your script. Each presenter will receive feedback from his/her session.

Note: One common comment made in past evaluations is that the session description does not match the content presented. Attendees expect printed session descriptions to match the content that you deliver. Please be sure that you are comfortable with the session description included with your speaker agreement.

On-Site Checklists

The following are frameworks for elements that should be part of checklists pertaining to different aspects of on-site production.

Technical

- Make sure you have covered all equipment needs (lectern, podium, stage, microphone(s), projection screens, computers, lighting, video, and sound equipment).
- Ensure computer compatibility.

- Befriend the on-site technician in case you need him or her in an emergency.
- Check all microphones and sound levels well in advance of the speaking engagement or performance.
- Ensure that speakers or room monitors are able to deal with simple technical situations, such as dimming the lights or changing volume levels.
- Check sight lines to the stage or podium to make sure that the audience can see the SEP from all angles, and that potentially distracting factors (such as backlight or glare from a window) will not interfere with the message or performance.

Care and Handling of Speakers

The following are frameworks for elements that should be part of checklists pertaining to different aspects of handling speakers.

Arrival and Check-In

- Ensure that the SEP has a 24-hour contact number for the planner or assigned host in case of emergency changes or questions before, during, and after the event.
- Secure the cell phone number of SEPs.
- Be specific with transportation logistics.
- Will the SEP be picked up? Who do they need to meet? What time, and where?
- If SEPs are responsible for getting to the venue on their own, do they have clear directions?
- Upon arrival at venue, where do they check in?
- Provide a **welcome packet** including: a welcome letter from the event professional, contact information for the event organizer/assigned host, a rehearsal schedule (if appropriate), an event badge, a map of the facility showing the SEP's specific presentation location, the location of a speaker ready room, a copy of the room setup, a list of local attractions, invitations/tickets to ancillary events, and a gentle reminder stipulating what charges the host organization will cover (including food and beverage, spa, recreation, and retail).
- An in-room amenity is a special touch: Provide flowers, a fruit basket, or a bottle of wine as a gesture of appreciation.

Presentation or Performance

- Speakers should be asked to arrive a minimum of 15 minutes prior to their presentation; however, entertainers and performers may require much more time for setup.
- **Speaker ready room** (green room): Provide a location for SEPs to rest, mentally prepare, check A/V equipment, review their presentation, enjoy light refreshments, and/or mingle with other SEPs or meeting sponsor.
- If possible, assign a host who will meet the SEP in the speaker ready room, take care of any additional needs, and escort him or her to their presentation location.
- An A/V technician will need sufficient time to wire the SEP with mike for sound or recording purposes.
- Have water available at the podium.
- The SEP should be introduced to the **room monitor** prior to the performance.
- A room monitor's responsibilities may include: checking entrance credentials, scanning badges, distributing materials, introducing the SEP to the audience, conveying emergency precautions, alerting the SEP of time constraints, passing the microphone to attendees during Q&A, and/or collecting speaker evaluations.

A room monitor should know who to contact in case of an emergency such as loss of power, computer crash, or illness.

- A certificate of appreciation or small memento may be presented to the speaker at the conclusion of the presentation.

Follow-Up

- Shortly after the event, send a thank-you letter to the SEP.
- If evaluations were collected (and they should be), it is customary to send the results to the SEP so he or she can improve his or her performance or presentation. These evaluations will also impact the organization's decision of whether to contract with the SEP in the future.

Cancellation   The worst-case scenario is a last-minute cancellation by the SEP. This is not uncommon in large events with multiple sessions. It is vital to have a contingency plan that may include substituting speakers or refunding fees to attendees. Using social media such as Twitter or Facebook can expedite communication to alert attendees in case of a cancellation or meeting room change.

Technology and the Presenter   In addition to promoting the appearance of the SEP, including those who are unable to attend in person, and informing attendees of last-minute changes, there are many technologies that can be applied to enhance the attendee experience and the effectiveness of the presenter. Technology has the potential to increase the attendees' **return-on-investment (ROI)** and satisfaction with the event. For example, Facebook groups can be used to engage potential attendees and start discussions well before the live presentation. These both assist the presenter in preparing what the attendees want to hear and enable attendee networking to start in advance of the event. Prior to the event, interviews with invited speakers can be posted on YouTube to generate interest. During the event, live streaming of popular sessions enables the participation of members who were not able to physically attend and increases interest for the remainder of the event. No matter if they are present or not, it is vital to keep the membership engaged. Following the event, recordings of successful sessions or a summary video may be distributed as a promotional item to increase attendance at the current and following events and meetings. Furthermore, such online groups can keep the discussion going long after the meeting is over, increasing the perceived value of participating in the event. Another example of technology's impact on speaker engagements is the projection or use of live Twitter feeds during the presentation. A caveat is that a filter—such as time delay, editing, and content monitoring—should be employed to avoid potentially embarrassing, offensive, or disruptive tweets. A variety of wireless devices can be employed to engage attendees and instantly poll the audience. This technology provides the presenter with feedback about audience understanding and/or agreement and keeps the audience focused due to the interactive nature of the presentation. Services provided by companies such as polleverywhere.com offer an audience response system based on texting from any mobile device. The services range from free to several thousands of dollars, depending on the number of participants.

Handouts   Speaker audiences appreciate handouts summarizing the content of the presentation. Handouts can be used as a guide to follow the presentation and for note-taking purposes. However, the distribution of paper handouts at events is on the decline. In effort to be "green" and save money, this information is often provided via email, web-link, USB drive, or CD prior to the event. Kiosks with the handouts saved in digital format may be placed in high-traffic areas so that attendees can download handouts directly to their laptop or smartphone. In order to ensure attendee satisfaction, handouts (whether in paper form or digital) must be thorough and clear. Handouts should have the ability to stand on their own, as attendees will often have a plethora of information thrown at them during an event and likely forget much of it. Handouts can serve as "takeaways" to be shared by the attendee with others; this may help validate the need for the person to attend the event.

SUMMARY

Speakers, entertainment and performers (SEPs) may serve to motivate, educate, and/or entertain attendees, depending on the goals and objectives of the meeting or event. There are a variety of SEP sources available to event professionals, including speakers bureaus, actors' unions and agents, local experts, faculty, corporations, and members of the host organization. SEPs may be paid or unpaid: There are benefits and challenges associated with each. Although there are many considerations in the selection of SEPs, the initial focus should be the ability to support the goals of the organization and their appeal to the attendees. Sponsorships are a common way to finance events and SEPs. Sponsors often have significant influence in the selection process. It is also important to consider the learning and/or performance environment to insure the maximum return on investment. Once the SEP has been identified, the contracting process begins, consisting of an offer, negotiations, and mutual acceptance. Speaker guidelines provided by the host organization should convey everything an SEP should know in order to perform/present in the most effective manner for a particular audience.

Now that you have completed this chapter, you should be competent in the following Meeting and Business Event Competency Standards:

MBECS Skill 17: Engage Speakers and Performers

Subskills		Skills (standards)
17.01	Determine meeting or event requirements for speakers and performers	
17.02	Develop selection criteria	
17.03	Select candidates	
17.04	Secure contracts and communicate expectations	

KEY WORDS AND TERMS

speakers bureau
volunteer speaker
indoor pyrotechnics
demographics
psychographics
ancillary

off-premise
keynote
walk-through
intellectual property
protocol
cancellation clause

confidentiality agreement
welcome packet
speaker ready room
room monitor
return-on-investment (ROI)

REVIEW AND DISCUSSION QUESTIONS

1. Why are SEPs important for events?
2. How would you select the most appropriate SEPs for a particular event?
3. Where can SEPs be found?
4. What are the pros and cons of using of volunteer rather than paid speakers?
5. Why should all SEPs (paid and unpaid) be required to sign contracts?
6. Why is it important to provide SEPs with guidelines prior to the event?
7. Aside from any compensation, what should be included in a contract with an SEP?
8. How can the costs of SEPs be reduced?
9. What should be done prior to contracting with SEPs?
10. What must be considered when designing environments for an SEP's presentation?
11. What needs to be considered prior to accepting a sponsor?
12. How can the use of technology with SEPs positively and negatively impact ROI?
13. Aside from what is mentioned in this chapter, how can technology add to an SEP's presentation?

ABOUT THE CHAPTER CONTRIBUTORS

Curtis Love, PhD, CHE, is an associate professor and executive director of the graduate studies program at the William F. Harrah College of Hotel Administration, University of Nevada, Las Vegas. His teaching and research concentrations are in the areas of meetings, conventions, trade shows, and destination marketing.

Orie Berezan, PhD, is a customer satisfaction and loyalty professional. Berezan has over two decades of direct hospitality management experience in global markets such as Canada, Japan, and Mexico with brands such as Intrawest, Playground, Four Seasons, and Duetto (www.duettoresearch.com). Berezan has taught event management at the University of Nevada, Las Vegas, and currently instructs management-related courses at the California State University. He has published numerous academic papers, studies, and monographs.

APPENDIX 1

What are the goals and objectives of the meeting/event?

- ☐ Appearance
- ☐ Autograph
- ☐ Banquet
- ☐ Breakout Session
- ☐ Celebration
- ☐ Classroom
- ☐ Contest
- ☐ Dinner Program
- ☐ Educational Session
- ☐ Event
- ☐ Fair
- ☐ Graduation Ceremony
- ☐ Honors Program
- ☐ Influential
- ☐ Keynote
- ☐ Luncheon Program
- ☐ Meeting
- ☐ Networking
- ☐ Occasion
- ☐ Political
- ☐ Product Endorsement
- ☐ Reception
- ☐ Reunion
- ☐ Sales Rally
- ☐ Shopping Mall Draw
- ☐ Sports
- ☐ Theatrical
- ☐ Training
- ☐ Wrap Party

- ☐ Association Gathering
- ☐ Award Presentations
- ☐ Board Meeting
- ☐ Cabaret Theme
- ☐ Ceremony
- ☐ Conference
- ☐ Convention
- ☐ Draw in New Members
- ☐ Entertainment
- ☐ Exposition
- ☐ Fund-Raiser
- ☐ Group Consulting Session
- ☐ Hosting Concert
- ☐ Interactive Program
- ☐ Lecture
- ☐ Mall
- ☐ Motivational
- ☐ New Product Introduction
- ☐ Panel
- ☐ Praise Membership
- ☐ Promotion
- ☐ Retreat
- ☐ Roast
- ☐ Seminar
- ☐ Special Event
- ☐ Spousal Program
- ☐ Trade Show
- ☐ Workshop

Other: _____

What type of speaker does the organization need to achieve those goals and objectives?

Notable, Star, Dignitary, Prophet, Famous Person, Intellectual, Luminary, Impersonator, Philosopher, Sage, and Teacher

- ☐ Actor
- ☐ Architect
- ☐ Astronaut
- ☐ Author
- ☐ Business Leader
- ☐ Comedian

- ☐ Ambassador
- ☐ Artist
- ☐ Attorney
- ☐ Broadcast Media
- ☐ Character Portrayals
- ☐ Composer

- ☐ Dancer
- ☐ Economist
- ☐ Emcee
- ☐ Entertainment
- ☐ Futurist
- ☐ Health
- ☐ Host
- ☐ Inspirational
- ☐ International Affairs
- ☐ Inventor
- ☐ Judge
- ☐ Leaders
- ☐ Marketing
- ☐ Mayor
- ☐ Military Leader
- ☐ Movie
- ☐ News
- ☐ Photographer
- ☐ Political Leader
- ☐ Professional
- ☐ Radio
- ☐ Scientist
- ☐ Talent
- ☐ Television Personality
- ☐ Vocalist

- ☐ Doctor
- ☐ Editor and Publisher
- ☐ Entertainer
- ☐ Financial
- ☐ Governor
- ☐ Headline—News
- ☐ Humorist
- ☐ Insurance
- ☐ International Statesmen
- ☐ Journalist
- ☐ Keynote
- ☐ Look-a-Like
- ☐ Master of Ceremonies (M/C)
- ☐ Member of Parliament
- ☐ Motivational
- ☐ National Issues
- ☐ Officers
- ☐ Physician
- ☐ Prime Minister
- ☐ Professor
- ☐ Sales
- ☐ Sports
- ☐ Technology
- ☐ Theater

Other: _____

What is the goal in selecting a particular category?

- ☐ Communication
- ☐ Conflict Management
- ☐ Delegation
- ☐ Listening
- ☐ Memory
- ☐ Organizational
- ☐ Presentation
- ☐ Reading
- ☐ Speaking
- ☐ Telephone

- ☐ Computer
- ☐ Critical Thinking
- ☐ Interpersonal
- ☐ Management
- ☐ Negotiation
- ☐ Planning
- ☐ Persuasion
- ☐ Sales
- ☐ Supervisory

Other: _____

Is ethnicity a factor in your event?

- ☐ Asian/Pacific Islander
- ☐ Arabic

- ☐ African-Americans
- ☐ Armenian

☐ British   ☐ Bulgarian
☐ Chinese   ☐ Czechoslovakian
☐ Danish   ☐ Dutch
☐ Estonian   ☐ Ethiopian
☐ Finnish   ☐ French
☐ German   ☐ Greek
☐ Hindu   ☐ Hungarian
☐ Icelandic   ☐ Indian
☐ Irish   ☐ Italian
☐ Japanese   ☐ Jewish
☐ Korean   ☐ Latvian
☐ Lithuanian   ☐ Manx
☐ Norwegian   ☐ Polish
☐ Portuguese   ☐ Russian
☐ Scottish   ☐ Spanish
☐ Swedish   ☐ Swiss
☐ Thai   ☐ Turkish
☐ Ukrainian   ☐ Vietnamese
☐ Welsh   ☐ Yugoslavian

Other: _____

Speakers with Disabilities

☐ Visually Impaired   ☐ Healing Impaired
☐ Amputee   ☐ Cerebral Palsy
☐ Wheelchair user   ☐ Walking Impairment
☐ Little People   ☐ Developmentally Disabled

Who makes the final decision on the program?

☐ Administrator   ☐ CEO
☐ Committee Member   ☐ Finance Director
☐ Human Resource Director   ☐ Manager
☐ Marketing Director   ☐ Meeting Planner
☐ Owner   ☐ Program Director
☐ Public Relations Director   ☐ Sales Director
☐ Special Events Coordinator

Other: _____

Is there a budget for the following categories?

☐ Audio Cassette Tapes   ☐ Books
☐ Entertainers   ☐ Handouts
☐ Historian/Video, Audio   ☐ Hotel
☐ Meals   ☐ Sound System

☐ Speakers   ☐ Transportation (Ground/Air)

☐ Videotapes

Other: _____

What are the needs of the organization and the needs of the speaker or entertainer?

☐ Agenda: Outline of Your Upcoming Program

☐ Autographing: Will attendees request autographs of your guest?

☐ Audio Requirements   ☐ Biography of Your Company (Other)

☐ Camera-Ready Flyer   ☐ Cassette Demo

☐ Contact Person Prior to Meeting

☐ Contract (Agreement)   ☐ Distance from the Airport

☐ Exit Directions   ☐ Fee Schedule

☐ Food/Beverage (Special Diet Requirements/Schedule)

☐ Handouts   ☐ Host

☐ Hotel

☐ Introduction Sheet (Name and Title of Introducer)

☐ Liaison   ☐ List of Key Personnel

☐ List of Other Speakers/Entertainers on the Program

☐ Marketing Kit   ☐ Map

☐ Media Requirements   ☐ Media Sheet

☐ Objective of Meeting

☐ Permission and Arrangements for Back-of-Room Sales

☐ Permission for Audio   ☐ Permission for video tapping

☐ Photo Opportunity   ☐ Press Kit

☐ Profile of Your Organization   ☐ Program

☐ Reprints of News Releases   ☐ Schedule/Time in Front of Group

☐ Size of Group   ☐ Theme for Meeting

☐ Timekeeper

☐ Time Zone: Eastern, Mountain, Pacific, etc.

☐ Title of Speaker's Talk

☐ Travel Policy for Land and Air: Arrangements, Requirements, Arrival, Departure

☐ Video

Other: _____

What are the event professional's requirements?

☐ Agreement (contract[s])   ☐ Article Reprints

☐ Audio Cassette Demo   ☐ Audio/Visual Needs

☐ Bio Sheet   ☐ Camera-Ready Flyer

☐ Fee Schedule   ☐ Food/Beverage

☐ Handouts   ☐ Hotel

☐ Introductory Sheet   ☐ Marketing Kit

☐ Media Kit   ☐ Name of Speaker(s)' Program(s)

☐ Permission and Arrangements for Back-of-Room Sales

☐ Permission from Speaker or Entertainer to Audiotape Program
☐ Permission from Speaker or Entertainer to Videotape Program
☐ Photo Opportunity ☐ Press Kit
☐ Title of Speaker(s)' Program(s)
☐ Travel Policy/Land and Air ☐ Videotape Demo

Other: _____

What support materials are expected from the event professional?

☐ Audio/Visual equipment ☐ Banners
☐ Blackboard/Chalk ☐ Blank Tapes
☐ Chair ☐ Clock
☐ Computer: Hardware ☐ Computer: Software
☐ Dance Floor ☐ Decorations
☐ Drapes, Background ☐ Easels
☐ Flipchart/Markers ☐ Grease Board/Markers
☐ Head Table ☐ High Chair
☐ Interpretation ☐ Laser Pointer
☐ Lavalier (Clip-On) Wireless Microphone
☐ LCD Projector/Screen ☐ Lighting
☐ Lighting/Spots ☐ Markers
☐ Microphone ☐ Music/Sound
☐ Overhead Projector/Screen ☐ Platform
☐ Podium ☐ Podium Mike
☐ Power ☐ Projector
☐ Raised Platform ☐ Remote Mouse
☐ Screen ☐ Slide Projector, 35mm
☐ Slide Projector/Screen ☐ Stand
☐ Speaker Audio System ☐ Speakerphone
☐ Stage ☐ Stand
☐ Stool ☐ Table
☐ Video/Monitor ☐ Video Player (VCR)
☐ Video Projector

Other: _____

What is the organization's policy regarding back-of-the-room sales?

☐ Permission for Back-of-the-Room Sales: ○ Yes. ○ No.
☐ Audios ☐ Books
☐ CDs ☐ Consulting
☐ Educational Videos ☐ Manuals
☐ Newsletters ☐ Software Programs
☐ Seminars ☐ Training Materials
☐ T Shirts/Hats ☐ Videos

Other: _____

CHAPTER 10

Getting People from Here to There and Back Again

Learning Objectives

After completing this chapter, the reader should be able to:

- Understand the role of crowd management in meeting and event planning
- Identify elements in a site inspection that are part of a crowd management plan
- Develop an event design/layout to assist in crowd management
- Recognize common entrance/exit protocols
- Identify the role of security in a crowd management plan, including the various types of security

Managing and moving large crowds is part of MEEC production. Ints Vikmanis/fotolia

Chapter Outline

Introduction
Defining Crowd Management
    Site Inspections
    Event Design/Layout
    Signage
    Security

Other Considerations
    Crowd Control
Summary
Key Words and Terms
Review and Discussion Questions
About the Chapter Contributor

INTRODUCTION

"Concertgoers crushed against stage"; "People trampled underfoot during rush to get out of burning nightclub"; "Parade watcher run over by float." These are real news headlines that resulted from poor crowd-management techniques. Not only do they cause injuries and loss of life, but they also negatively affect the image and reputation of the events industry. Event professionals have an obligation to create a safe and secure environment for attendees; a large part of this can be accomplished through thoughtful and thorough crowd-management techniques. Although there is no such thing as a risk-free environment, thinking and acting proactively can greatly diminish the consequences of unwanted and dangerous events. This also ensures that there are procedures in place to deal with a **crisis** if, and when, it happens.

"They Arrested the Attendees"

The theme of the awards event was *Prohibition*. It included a reception, dinner, and dancing. The reception was held in a room decorated as a speakeasy from the Prohibition era and included bars in each of the four corners, with drinks served in teacups and saucers. There was a dance floor at one end of the room, a space for photos to be taken just inside the door, and "cigarette girls" who circulated throughout, offering attendees *swag*. The reception was scheduled to last for 1.5 hours, followed by dinner and the awards ceremony, and dancing to end the evening.

As the reception was nearing its end, the doors suddenly burst open. "Police" stormed in, arresting the more than 300 guests. The lawbreakers were taken through corridors, with more police lining the way. Event and venue staff dressed as police and prison guards stayed in character, telling attendees they were being taken to jail and pointing in the direction they were to move. Signage on the wall also indicated the way to jail. Police officers led the attendees, indicating stairs and turns, keeping attendees moving in an orderly fashion. They were led into a large ballroom that was decorated as prison yard. Spotlights shone around the room and occasional sirens went off, signaling a jailbreak. Guards greeted attendees and showed them where the dining tables, stage, and exits were.

This story illustrates one of the most creative ways to effectively move a large crowd from one location to another. It was entertaining and maintained the theme of the evening. It also involved an incredible amount of communication and collaboration between event and venue staff.

A lot of emphasis has been placed on managing crises and emergencies. These are rare instances that receive a lot of media attention because they are dramatic and sensational. It is far more common to have to deal with an irate attendee who has been waiting in line "forever" or is frustrated because he or she got lost trying to find the event. Make no mistake: These common crowd issues are more likely to happen and create a negative impression on attendees than a stampede.

This chapter begins with an overview of crowd management, followed by considerations that apply to all event types, including site inspections, event design/layout, signage, entrance/exit protocols, and security. It concludes with other considerations that are covered in other chapters, but are connected to crowd management.

DEFINING CROWD MANAGEMENT

The crowd is part of an event; without a crowd, the event would not occur. The size of the crowd can affect the perception of the quality of the event—small crowds can be perceived as the event being boring (think of yourself: do you go into a bar or club that has almost no patrons?). Some events (concerts, parades, and festivals) rely on large crowds to add to the quality of the attendees' experience. That being said, the perception of being crowded (not having enough space to enjoy the event activities) is individually determined, making it difficult for event professionals to obtain an "optimal" crowd that is acceptable for all attendees. Instead, the event professional uses a crowd-management plan to influence the attendee's perception.

Crowd management employs techniques to ensure the safe and secure movement of people prior to, during, and after an event. It includes credentialing, ticketing, queuing, flow, evacuation, and exiting. Although crowd management is a very large job, event professionals do not undertake it alone. Security professionals, off-duty and on-duty police officers, EMTs, and city officials are some of the resources that event professionals should consult in order to develop and implement effective and efficient crowd-management techniques.

In order to understand crowd management, one must understand the various terms that are generally associated with it. The expressions "crowd management" and "**crowd control**" are usually used interchangeably. However, they are not the same: Crowd management refers to the processes and steps taken in order to safely and efficiently move attendees into, through, and out of an event. Crowd control is a series of actions taken when a crowd becomes, or shows signs of becoming, disorderly and/or dangerous. Crowd control is a critical part of a thorough crowd-management plan.

The first step in developing a crowd-management plan is to know the event goals, or what the client wishes to accomplish by holding the event. The event goals provide the event professional with a framework for all aspects of an event. There are generally three to five goals; they are stated in broad terms that are easily understood and measurable. The goals are the touchstone used for all decision making in the event process. For example, if an event has a goal to provide an interactive environment for attendees, a crowd-management plan that includes barricades will be counterproductive to the event's success.

The second step in crowd management is to know the event attendees: Who are they? Why are they here? This can be as simple as demographics (age, gender, profession), or slightly more complex psychographic information (lifestyle, interests, motivations). Having information about the attendees is vital to developing an effective crowd-management plan. For example, if the event attendees have mobility issues, the event professional knows that he or she must have larger entrances/exits.

Each event is different; however, some crowd-management considerations are standard to all events. These include site inspections, event design/layout, signage, communication, security, entrance/exit protocols, and transportation. (You have read about some of these in earlier chapters.)

Site Inspections

In order to develop an effective crowd-management plan, an event professional must first understand the event site. This can usually be accomplished by conducting a site inspection. Site inspections should include emergency exits, room capacity, obstructions, and accessibility. Site inspection checklists and reports will allow everyone involved in the event to have a full understanding of the dimensions and restrictions of an event location. Pictures and precise measurements should be taken to ensure comprehensive documentation.

There are numerous lists and many articles written about site inspections (i.e., APEX, Meeting and Business Event Competency Standards) that can help event professionals evaluate and choose a site. A site inspection checklist must be developed and conducted with the event goals in mind to ensure selection of a site that is the best fit for the event. In terms of crowd management, specific elements that need to be considered include accessibility, ingress and egress, capacity, security, and emergency/crisis/evacuation plans.

An event site must be easily accessible; all event stakeholders must be able to enter, exit, and move throughout the site. In the United States, accessibility issues are covered by the **Americans with Disabilities Act (ADA)** of 1992, specifically Title III.

Exceptions to ADA requirements include private clubs, religious buildings, or historic properties: The event professional must be sure to check the level of compliance for his or her event. A note of caution: Not all countries have accessibility legislation. For example, the ADA is only applicable in the United States. Canada does not have formal accessibility legislation, but tends to follow the U.S. requirements, and Germany has legislation called the Act on Equal Opportunities for Disability Persons, which was passed in 2002.

People and materials move in and out of the event site through the **ingress** and **egress**. This can include loading docks, elevators, access to back-of-house areas, and the room(s) being used for the event. It is necessary to know the locations of egress/ingress areas in relation to the event site, the times they are available for use, restrictions, and fees. This allows an event professional to determine the resources needed to transport event materials from the trucks to the event site. Larger venues can have freight elevators and guest elevators. Freight elevators tend to be slightly larger and have padded walls; they are usually located in the back-of-house areas and will allow transport of event materials more easily. Back-of-house areas can be used to move event materials without having to worry about maneuvering through venue guests. These areas tend to be larger. Event rooms can have multiple doors, sometimes including doors from back-of-house areas. It is necessary to know the number, location, and dimensions of these doors, as well as the manner in which they open. These considerations are important in order to facilitate the movement of the event materials needed to create the event environment as well as moving attendees into and out of the event site efficiently. These considerations are also important in case of an **emergency**, as they can be used to quickly evacuate an event.

Capacity relates to ingress and egress. In the United States and Canada, capacity is determined by fire department in compliance with fire code restrictions. Keep in mind that capacity is the maximum number of people that the space can accommodate, but it does not include any event materials. Convention/conference centers and hotel space usually have listings of capacity based on room setup. In addition, *Meeting Professionals International* sells a tool called the "Arranger." This is a slide ruler that allows a planner to know the maximum number of people that a space (inside or outside) can accommodate based on several different room setups. Not only is this necessary to determine if the site is appropriate for the event, but it helps in designing the event layout to facilitate flow.

Most event locations have some form of **security** in place, ranging from cameras, motion lights, location staff, or a third-party security firm. Again, different types of events require different levels of security. For example, a business meeting likely requires rooms that lock and security cameras in order to protect any materials, and usually relies on the event staff to ensure that only event attendees access the space. On the other hand, a political event requires significant security, including security personnel and barricades. A festival can also require different levels of security personnel, from staff security to a police presence, depending on the size of the festival.

The final element that is important to crowd management during a site inspection is the location's plan to deal with an emergency/crisis. Surprisingly, there are a large number of venues that do not have emergency plans. There are other venues that have an **evacuation plan** to deal with a specific emergency, like an earthquake or flooding. Most states in the United States have some form of emergency preparedness plan, which can be found through the state government websites. Event professionals must know the emergency plans for the location where the event will be held so that it can be coordinated with the event **risk-management** plan, which includes the crowd management and crowd control plans. (For more information, see Chapter 4 on risk management in *Planning and Managing Meetings, Expositions, Events, and Conventions,* by Fenich.)

Event Design/Layout

Designing the event layout carefully is a crucial first step in crowd management and helps avoid a lot of potential issues. For all events, the event professional must also leave space for entrances, bathrooms, and food concessions. Flow, space requirements, and seating are also important. These items are related to one another.

Making sure that attendees can move safely and easily throughout an event is called **flow**. Flow takes into account the entire event location as well as the event activities, which have varying space requirements. For example, a fair consists of midway rides, games, food concessions, and displays. A midway ride requires a significant amount of physical space for the ride itself, a safe zone around the ride, the mechanics, and an area where attendees line up (**queue**) to wait for their turn on the ride. Games, on the other hand, take up a lot less space and generally do not have a formal queue. Food concessions are subject to health and safety standards that could affect the space requirements, such as trash cans and hand-washing facilities. Queues for food concessions can be quite extensive, depending on the food being offered. Finally, displays require some sort of stands or casing to showcase items and may include a space around the displays and level ground to protect them from being knocked or tipped over and injuring attendees. For the most part, displays are set up inside a building or tent to offer some protection from the weather.

Now, think of the space requirements for a concert. The stage, or performance area, and the lighting and sound systems are contained in one area, which needs to be restricted to performers and event staff. There is a safety zone in front of the stage and audience seating facing the stage. In the past, many concerts offered general admission, or festival seating; there were no assigned seats. When the doors opened, or attendees were allowed to enter the concert seating area, there was a rush to get to the front in order to have the best view. This resulted in several cases of attendees being injured. Concerts held in the United States and Canada mostly offer assigned seating for events today; *music festivals* may not.

Then there are trade shows, which require very specific space parameters. It is common to have several different sizes of space to offer exhibitors. There can be quite a bit of variety among exhibitors, with some requiring utilities (electricity, water, and gas) and/or audiovisual support. Returning exhibitors, or those paying for larger spaces, will likely want prime locations, meaning the calculation of space must be carefully designed. The company ExpoCad has developed software that tracks hot and cold locations on a trade show floor. There is a trend in trade shows for interactivity, which means more additional space. The event professional must consider how to assign exhibitors to space so there is limited competition. At the National Restaurant Association Show held annually in Chicago, Coca Cola and Pepsi buy large, premium exhibit space but are never located next to each other.

Signage

Arguably the most effective crowd management technique an event professional can use is **signage**. Proper signage will eliminate the majority of problems/issues; when it's used in conjunction with barricades, it is extremely successful in directing attendees. There are three types of signs used in events: **identification**, **information**, and **directional**. Identification signage tells attendees the name of the event and its ownership. This is done by including sponsorship or host names with the event name. Identification signage is also included on each exhibit space in a trade show and above trade show aisles. Informational signage provides information and/or instruction to attendees. This can include changes to the event, details about an activity, or areas that are off limits. Directional signage is responsible for moving attendees. This can be done best with words and/or symbols. Keep in mind that if attendees are international, symbols are less likely to be misinterpreted. Signage must be clear, concise, and simple. Wording should be short and to the point, using common language, in a font size that is easy to see. The size and location of signs must also be carefully weighed. A sign needs to be large enough to be seen by attendees; otherwise the message will be lost. Placing multiple signs in high-traffic areas will increase the chance they will be seen by attendees. It is very important to place directional signs in parking areas to assist attendees in finding the event site. When placing signs outdoors, make sure to protect them or use materials that are resistant to the elements such as rain.

As with so many other aspects, signage needs to be tailored to the requirements of the event and/or event activity. For example, place cards are used at meal functions to indicate seating arrangements. Name signs are placed on stands or taped to the floor in exhibition space to indicate exhibitor space. Name tags are frequently used at meetings and conferences to identify attendees. Banners are used at social-life cycle events, like graduations, to convey a congratulatory message.

Although there are different requirements for events, there are some common signs that should be included at all events. Exit signs should be prominent and lighted. Announcements should be made over a public address system at the beginning of the event to ensure that attendees know where exits are located. Washrooms should be clearly identified, as should parking areas. Administrative, security, and first aid location signs should also be prominent and include directional signs from multiple areas of the event site.

Entrance/Exit Protocols   Another important consideration for crowd management is the event entrance/exit protocols. Regardless of the event, it is necessary to create a system to allow entry and exit from the event site in an orderly fashion as well as to prevent overcrowding or unauthorized attendees. This is generally done by security personnel. The priorities are to control the number of people in the event and to create a safe and secure environment. Controlling the number of people in the event is done through credentialing and queuing.

Credentialing refers to the documents or proof that need to be provided by individuals in order to gain access to an event site. This can be in the form of an invitation, a ticket, cash paid at a ticket booth, or a name badge that has been issued by the event organizer. It also includes requirements for re-entry: When attendees leave the event site, are they allowed to re-enter? If so, what must they do? For an event without pre-registration, it is very important that the credentialing system include a method of counting attendees who enter and exit the site. This will help ensure optimal capacity and thereby optimal safety.

Queuing refers to the manner in which people line up to gain access to an area. This can be the event site as a whole, specific activities such as registration, or exiting an event site in times of crisis. A well-developed queuing system can avoid crowding, shoving, and stampedes and make the event site safer. Queuing can be done through the use of barricades, signage, or entertainment, depending on the number of attendees attempting to gain access to the site. The barricades can be ropes or gating—they may include the type of barricade used in most U.S. banks. Anyone who has visited Disney or an event with rides has likely experienced queuing of this type. The design of this queuing can also assist in reducing the amount of attendee frustration. It is common to see barricades set up so that lines wind back and forth. This allows attendees to continue to move (albeit slowly, at times). Signage can also reduce the frustration associated with waiting. Using an event that has rides as an example, signs that read "Wait time 10 minutes from this point" are common. This type of information lets attendees know what is happening and what to expect.

Providing entertainment for attendees in line can distract them from their wait. This may include jugglers, acrobats, strolling musicians, or monitors with event information.

Name badges are a common form of credentialing for all types of events. These badges take many forms. For conferences, meetings, and trade shows, they usually show the attendee's name and company. For festivals, concerts, or other public special events, they generally show the name of the activity that the individual can access. A recent trend is to include radio frequency identifier (RFID) technology. Originally designed to assist farmers in tracking the movement of livestock, this technology has been adapted for use in a variety of other situations, including the events industry. It consists of a chip embedded in the name badge that allows event professionals to know how many people are in different areas of an event as well as track their movements throughout the event. Not only can this information help event staff forecast where potential problems are in terms of overcrowding, but it also allows emergency personnel to know how many people are at the event if there is a problem.

RFID technology does have significant advantages for crowd management; however, there are concerns as well. The biggest concern is privacy. The RFID chip can be programmed with personal information about the attendee. Scanners, which read the chip's location, can be programmed to extract this information. Further, if the name badges are not returned when the attendee leaves the event, the RFID chip can be used to continue to track movement.

Another queuing system uses numbers. This is common in U.S. government offices. A machine distributes sequential numbers to attendees; when their number is called, attendees can gain access to the event. This is not a preferable method of credentialing or monitoring crowd numbers, as the numbers are not returned when an attendee exits the event. This means there is no way to know how many people are currently at the event site.

Searches must be conducted in order to create a safe and secure environment. They are generally done by security personnel. Searches have a long history at sporting events (at soccer matches in Europe and at the Olympics, for instance). They have also been part of the admittance procedure for concerts and political events for years. After the September 11, 2001, attacks in the United States, searches have become more common for all types of events. A variety of techniques are used, from security personnel "patting down" attendees to metal detectors to advanced screening methods. These searches are not done solely to find weapons, but for any type of contraband, including drugs and alcohol. Their primary purpose is to find anything that could threaten the safety of anyone on the event site.

Regardless of the type of search or the personnel conducting the search, it is paramount to remember to be respectful of attendees. This means being courteous and polite, asking attendees to submit to the search, and conducting the search in a discreet manner. Asking permission to conduct the search is common courtesy. It allows attendees to feel as though they have an option. If they refuse to submit to the search, they can be denied entry; this is similar to searches conducted at airports. Anyone has the right to refuse to be searched, knowing that they forfeit the right to proceed further into the airport or to board their plane. Further, it is inappropriate to dump the contents of a bag onto a counter in plain sight of a crowd; instead, have a screen of some sort set up to protect the privacy of the attendee being searched.

Security

An event may involve many different types of security. In terms of crowd management, an event professional needs to consider lighting, barricades, and personnel. These are tools that can be used to direct attendees, keeping them out of areas that are unsafe or off limits, or used in times of crisis.

Lighting is used as a crowd-management tool in that it allows attendees and those involved in an event to see what is happening. If an area is not well lit, it usually discourages people from approaching; darkness can create a feeling of anxiety, as people do not know what is hidden in the dark. An unlit area can also encourage some individuals to explore and/or engage in inappropriate or dangerous activities. Floor lighting or lighting stands that illuminate an aisle can be used to direct attendees through an event. In the case of an emergency, lighting should be bright enough for everyone to see exits and any potential hazards. Spot lights should be avoided, as they can be blinding and may cause people to stampede to the lit area, particularly if it's an exit.

Barricades come in many shapes and sizes, from fencing to ribbons to false walls. Barricades are used to direct attendees toward a specific activity, to create a zone of safety, or to keep attendees away from an area of potential danger. The choice of barricades must match the event type. For example, parade barricades need to keep attendees back from the parade route without obstructing their view. This is best accomplished by wooden, concrete, or steel frames roughly three feet in height. In the case of a wedding, ribbons can be used to reserve seating for family or special guests. Concerts generally use barricades to keep the audience back from the stage. This is done to protect the performers (from attendees jumping up on stage) and to protect the audience (from being squashed against the stage).

At many smaller events, volunteers, often called **ushers**, supply security. It is very important to remember that volunteers are not qualified—and should therefore never be asked—to do more than monitor an event site. They should never attempt to break up an altercation or restrain event attendees. Not only could this lead to injury for attendees and volunteers, but it could also lead to legal disputes. These volunteers should be identifiable to all attendees through the use of a uniform of some type.

Third-party security firms are one option for creating and maintaining a safe and secure environment. Make sure to thoroughly investigate a security firm prior to hiring it, including obtaining references from former clients. If possible, attend an event where personnel from the firm are working so you can observe their behavior. A security firm should have various forms of insurance, including automobile, comprehensive general liability, and special equipment. In addition, ask for the firm's qualification criteria for employment and look for security-specific training and education. Finally, ask to see proof that the firm has the necessary licenses and approval to operate in the city/state/country. This license will be issued through a local/state government. (In California, it is issued through the Department of Consumer Affairs.) It is also a good idea to have a combination of male and female security personnel, in case searches are necessary. Having a female **security guard** conduct a pat down and/or search of a purse will make female attendees significantly more comfortable.

A police presence may be desirable state for the event or may be required by local legislation. Notification of a required police presence will be given when the permit/license for holding the event is submitted to local government. Another option is to hire **off-duty police** to provide security for an event. The biggest advantage of hiring off-duty police is that they are trained to deal with crowds as well as able to arrest any lawbreakers. The biggest disadvantage is that they may be called away if there is a situation that requires a large law enforcement presence.

Other Considerations

Like every other part of an event, effective crowd management relies on good communications between everyone involved. An overall communication plan needs to be developed for an event and applied to each aspect of planning, such as crowd management. Communication procedures and policies should be written up and included in the event documentation. They should also be included in any and all training manuals for event staff and volunteers. Hands-on training for communication equipment should be part of staff and volunteer training sessions. (For more detailed information regarding on-site communication, see Chapter 14 in this book.)

A multitude of other elements could be considered for a crowd-management plan; however, they are not always applicable to every event. Some, like protocol requirements or transportation, are very event specific.

Protocol   **Protocol** requirements are applicable to political events with visiting dignitaries, international business events with special guests, and weddings. They include elements such as styles of address, flag placement, greetings, and receiving lines. Each of these elements varies significantly depending on the dignitary and the event. For example, when greeting the president of the United States, it is appropriate for the individual to shake hands and address him as "Mr. President." On the other hand, when greeting royalty, protocol dictates a bow or curtsy; if a member of royalty offers his or her hand, the individual should gently touch, but not shake, hands. Royalty is addressed as "Your Majesty" or "Your Royal Highness."

Books on cultural differences, such as Robert Axtell's *Do's and Taboos Around the World*, are fantastic resources for these types of events. In terms of crowd management, the event professional in charge of these types of events will work in close collaboration with the individual's personal security and protocol offices. Although event professionals will work with many third parties and partners when planning an event, the difference for these types of events is that there will be systems and procedures in place for the individuals that will have to be integrated.

Transportation   Transportation is unique in that some form of transportation will be required for attendees to get to the event; however, it is not always within the scope of the event professional's responsibilities. It is something that needs to be investigated during the site inspection. The event professional should note the types of transportation available. These include airports and associated airlines, buses, trains, subways/metros, taxis, shuttles, and rentals.

The Conference on Protocol

A few years ago, Ambassador Capricia Penavic Marshall, chief of protocol of the United States, convened the inaugural Global Chiefs of Protocol Conference at the U.S. Department of State. The event drew more than 100 officials from 77 countries to refine their craft of protocol: from planning international summits and working with media to the intricacies of giving official gifts and engaging the diplomatic corps. The ambitious agenda included a session on international meetings and conferences, during which Destination Marketing Association International (DMAI) addressed the value of working with official destination marketing organizations for successful meetings and events.

Deputy Secretary of State Tom Nides noted in his welcoming comments that he assured attendees they cannot overstate the importance of face-to-face meetings. Looking someone in the eye, shaking their hand, taking their measure—these things really matter. Ambassador Marshall called these traditionally inconspicuous officials "hosts of history," and encouraged them through the learning sessions to use every tool in the diplomatic tool box to plan successful events.

Transportation options vary greatly depending on the country. For example, public transportation in the United States and Canada tends to be plentiful and reliable within metropolitan cities; however, travel between cities and states/provinces can be slightly more problematic, with limited options and time schedules. In particular, air travel can be very costly (a flight from Toronto, Ontario, to Vancouver, British Columbia, may cost in the area of $800 in the summer months) due to the limited airline options. Travel between countries in Europe tends to be easier and cheaper. (Eurail offers affordable train passes with many packages for travel within a country or between several countries.) In addition, many charter airlines offer affordability and convenience. Regardless of whether booking travel is part of an event professional's responsibilities, this information will need to be gathered in order to pass on to attendees.

When the event professional arranges all forms of transportation, he or she will need to understand all aspects of travel from the attendee's home country to the event site. Issues such as airlift, traffic patterns, and load capacities of the vehicles used, and the creation of a shuttle schedule, are part of efficiently transporting attendees. One of the more common transportation responsibilities for event professionals is to book flights. Similar to arranging a room block, it is possible to negotiate a reduced rate with an airline through the group sales office of the airline. In order to do this, it is necessary to collect travel dates/requirements from attendees.

When arranging travel for attendees, it is important to keep in mind a company's corporate travel policies. After September 11, 2001, many corporations and businesses developed travel policies. Although these can vary, it is common for the policy to restrict the number of "C" level, or executive, personnel allowed to travel together. Further, the president and vice president of a company are usually asked to travel separately.

When having to arrange transportation for attendees, an event professional should make use of existing transportation as much as possible in order to reduce the carbon footprint of events. There are cases when an event professional will be required to charter flights. Considerations when booking charter flights include access to airports and price. These flights can be booked through larger airlines or private companies. Not all airlines have access at every airport, so this is the first thing that needs to be investigated. Charter flights allow a greater flexibility in departure times; however, this comes at a cost. A flight from New Hampshire to Las Vegas in January for 14 people would cost approximately $88,000. Often destination management organizations (DMOs) or convention and visitor bureaus (CVBs) can help event professionals with transportation requirements.

Parking is one aspect of transportation that should never be overlooked. An understanding of available parking, including location and fees, is crucial to developing an event program. It will help to determine arrival and departure patterns for attendees.

One thing to keep in mind is that during a crisis, all event resources are put at the disposal of agencies such as the Federal Emergency Management Agency (FEMA) and/or the local branch of Homeland Security. In fact the FEMA website is an extremely valuable resource for determining the potential risks for an area and developing a risk-management plan.

Crowd Control

As mentioned earlier, crowd control refers to actions taken when a crowd becomes, or shows signs of becoming, disorderly and/or dangerous. A crowd-control plan should be part of every risk-management plan. Every risk-management plan, and crowd-control plan, needs to be tailored to the individual event. An important part of any risk-management plan is the inclusion of triggers. A trigger is an early warning system that a problem is about to take place. Triggers allow event professionals to be proactive.

For example, a crowd of people gathering in one location could indicate the potential for a fight. If security disperses the crowd at this point, it is likely that the fight will be avoided. Another example would be the sky becoming darker. This would indicate a storm moving in and that the evacuation plan needed to be executed.

The main purpose of a crowd-control plan is to move people out of danger and into a safe environment as quickly and orderly as possible. The first thing to always remember in a crisis or emergency is to stay calm. Keep your voice neutral but firm and give instructions in a concise manner, using simple words and short sentences. Display the confidence and leadership that are inherent in event professionals; doing so will help keep others calm and allow safe evacuation.

The second critical piece of a crowd-control plan is communication. Communication protocols (including equipment and the message) need to be developed and practiced with event staff. For large events, it is a good idea to have walkie-talkies/radios and megaphones on hand. It is common in an emergency for phone lines to get jammed because of the volume of calls being made. Walkie-talkies/radios allow the event team to communicate with each other. Headphones keep conversations among the event team members private. Megaphones do not rely on electricity, so they can be used to get attendees' attention and give instructions. Make sure extra batteries are part of the on-site materials for an event and that they are carried by anyone with a walkie-talkie/radio. Smaller events may not need a megaphone in order to communicate with attendees, but walkie-talkies/radios are still recommended.

The evacuation strategy must be conveyed to attendees. It is important that the message be simple and easy to follow and delivered in a neutral and firm manner. An individual should be chosen prior to the event as the spokesperson. This person should have a clear voice, be articulate in the language(s) of the attendees, and convey confidence and calm. The message should be pre-written, read verbatim, and repeated. The message should be repeated every one to three minutes depending on the severity of the situation. Again, it is crucial that the individual delivering the message stay calm.

Prior to an event, the event professional will have scouted all access points and devised an evacuation strategy. A crowd-control plan should always incorporate several exit strategies. When developing these strategies keep in mind two elements: lighting and instinct.

Indoor events tend to be more limited in evacuation options, as there are a finite number of doors and windows. In an emergency, power may be cut off. If the event is being held in a location with no natural light, it will get very dark. Darkness can increase attendees' panic, meaning an alternate source of light must be used. Ideally, emergency lighting can be incorporated into the event design, similar to the floor lighting in airplanes. Flashlights should also be included in the emergency kits that are part of the on-site event materials. Most indoor locations have exit signs over the doors and some form of emergency lighting; make sure these signs are not covered when creating the event environment.

In theory, moving people in an outdoor location seems much simpler. However, this is not always the case. In fact, it can actually be significantly more dangerous. Wide-open spaces make it much more difficult to control the manner in which people move, especially if they are panicked. They increase the potential for stampede. One way to control the crowd is to use barricades. Ideally, the event site would have wooden or steel barricades on-site that could be moved quickly to create an exit path. If this is not possible, using event staff is another alternative. This also solves the potential problem of communicating with a larger crowd. Have the staff create a human barricade and direct people to the nearest exit.

Lighting can be an issue for two reasons: There may not be emergency lighting outdoors, and it will have to be brought in. The second issue is that during the day, emergency lighting is not visible. Signage becomes an event professional's best friend.

In a panic situation, people do not think rationally. Instead, they go on instinct. It is instinctive to move away from danger. An individual's first thought is usually to exit from the same location he or she entered. If all attendees entered through the same door, it will cause utter chaos if they all move toward that door at the same time. Event staff must be trained to direct attendees to alternate exits, especially if one exit is blocked. Again, staying calm is crucial to dealing with people who are operating on instinct.

SUMMARY

Crowd management is a crucial part of event planning and production. Specifically, it is important to have a risk-management plan. Crowd management is different from crowd control. The main purpose of crowd management is to ensure the safe and secure movement of people prior to, during, and exiting an event. The first two steps of crowd management are knowing the event goals and knowing the event attendees. Without these steps, it is impossible to create an effective crowd-management plan. Although each crowd-management plan needs to be tailored to the individual event, there are some common considerations covered in the chapter. These include site inspections, event design/layout, signage, entrance/exit procedures, queuing, security, protocol, and transportation. Finally, a crowd-control plan must be developed as part of crowd management and risk management. The main purpose of a crowd-control plan is to move people out of danger as quickly and orderly as possible.

Now that you have completed this chapter, you should be competent in the following Meeting and Business Event Competency Standards:

MBECS Skill 21: Develop a Plan for Managing the Movement of Attendees

Sub skills		
21.01	Develop admittance credential systems	
21.02	Select crowd-management techniques	
21.03	Coordinate accommodation and transportation	
21.04	Manage protocol requirements	

KEY WORDS AND TERMS

The definitions for the keywords are based on the Glossary developed by the Convention Industry Council and can be found at http://www.conventionindustry.org/StandardsPractices/APEX/glossary.aspx/.

crisis
crowd management
crowd control
Americans with Disabilities Act (ADA)
ingress
egress
emergency

security
evacuation plan
risk management
flow
queue
signage
identification
information

directional
credentialing
ushers
security guard
off-duty police
protocol

REVIEW AND DISCUSSION QUESTIONS

1. What is the difference between crowd management and crowd control?
2. What types of barricades can be used? Indicate the most appropriate barricade for a given event.
3. What are important considerations in designing the signage for an event?
4. Describe some lighting issues associated with developing a crowd-control plan.
5. Communication is a critical part of event planning. Describe how communication is used in crowd management and crowd control.

6. What different types of security can be used in events? When should they be used?

7. What are crowd-control triggers? Give examples for different types of events.

8. What are some of the important considerations when designing an evacuation plan?

9. Write a script for an evacuation announcement.

10. Describe some transportation options that should be investigated during a site inspection.

11. What are the three types of signs that can be used at events?

12. Describe different techniques that can be used for queuing.

ABOUT THE CHAPTER CONTRIBUTOR

Linda M. Robson, PhD, is an assistant professor in the School of Hospitality Management at Endicott College in Beverly, Massachusetts. She has over 30 years of experience as an event planner, having planned a variety of events in Austria, Czech Republic, Switzerland, New Zealand, Canada, Italy, and the United States. She completed her master of tourism administration degree at George Washington University and her PhD at the University of Waterloo in Canada. Her research interests include the event industry, risk, and risk perception. She also holds an event management certificate from George Washington University and the special event coordinator designation from the Ontario Tourism Education Corporation. She has been a speaker and has published in several academic and industry events and publications.

Financial Management

CHAPTER 11

Managing the finances is a critical element in producing meetings and events.
Kurhan/fotolia

Chapter Outline

INTRODUCTION

Accounting, in the simplest term, is the process of assessing a business entity in monetary terms. Financial accounting is the process in which financial transactions of the entity are recorded to create **financial statements**. These financial statements are tools in managerial accounting, which is the analysis of financial statements to monitor the financial stability of the entity and to make business decisions.

There are five types of accounts used in reporting financial transactions: assets, liabilities, owner's equity, revenue, and expenses. Assets include items such as cash, inventory, and equipment that the entity owns and uses to produce **revenues**. Liabilities are the monies owed to others. These include payroll payable, notes payable, and accounts payable.

A payable is created any time goods or services are rendered and not paid at that time. Owner's equity is the claim that the owners of the entity have to the assets of the entity. In a publicly traded company, this includes stockholders who have purchased stock in the company. In a sole proprietorship, owner's equity is the amount that the owner invested to start the business. Revenue is the income, or funds, that flows into an entity. This could be for goods or services provided. While assets include the cash received, revenues are earned in a specific time period. Expenses are the funds that flow out of an organization for goods or services during a period of time. The difference between a liability and an expense is that a liability is still due, where an expense has been incurred.

Financial Statements

The success of meetings and events is often assessed through profitability—and **budgets** and income statements (also known as profit and loss statements) are the primary tools used in the assessment. The formula used in both budgets and income statements is revenue minus expenses equals profit (or loss if expenses are greater than revenues). It must be understood that a budget and an income statement are financial statements that show the profitability of the entity over a period of time, such as a month, quarter, year, or any specific period of time, including the time frame for planning and executing an event.

The balance sheet is another important financial statement that indicates the effectiveness of the management of the entity. The balance sheet shows the financial condition of the entity by indicating the status of its assets, liabilities, and owners' equity. The balance sheet formula is assets equal liabilities plus owners' equity. A balance sheet indicates the status at a point in time, such as the end of the business day on the last day of a month.

Financial Reporting

In terms of reporting financial transactions, prior to creating a financial plan, an organization chooses to report either on a *cash basis* or *accrual basis* accounting. In cash basis, the inflow and outflow of cash is reported when it is received or paid. In accrual basis accounting, the reporting of the cash flow is reported in the period in which it is earned or used. For instance, if booth rental fees begin to arrive 11 months prior to an event in cash basis accounting, the rental would be applied and reported on the income statement in the month the funds arrived. In accrual basis accounting, the funds would be reported on the balance sheet as unearned revenue and remain there until reported on the income statement until the event occurs.

Based on **generally accepted accounting principles (GAAP)**, even if an event is held in a location with a different currency than the organizer, it is important to note that financial statements must maintain the use of a single currency. Additionally, they should not be reported until the exchange into the base currency is made, since exchange rates change constantly.

MANAGING THE BUDGET

Once the goals and objectives are determined for a meeting or event, the next step is to create the budget. A budget, or expected revenues and expenses for an event, estimates one of three outcomes: make a profit, break even, or operate at a loss. The type of organization hosting the event will often indicate the desired outcome. Fund-raising events for nonprofit organizations or profit-based organizations seek to make a profit from events being held. Corporations may host events (such as training) where they expect to operate at a loss or may host events (such as incentive events) where they actively seek out sponsors to offset the cost of the event in order to break even. Social

OSU Football Fiesta Bowl

Susan Anderson, CMP

In 2012, the Oklahoma State University Cowboys played in their first Bowl Championship Series (BCS), the Fiesta Bowl, in Scottsdale, Arizona. The OSU Foundation, in conjunction with OSU Athletics (hereafter referred to as planner), hosts a breakfast each year when the football team plays in an NCAA Bowl game. The planner's first choice in selecting the location for the breakfast is to host the event at the hotel housing the football team. This property is selected by the Bowl coordinators. When requesting space, the planner used historic data to tell the sales manager to expect 400 attendees, which the property could accommodate. But because the historic data was based on non-BCS bowls, the planner did not realize how much the numbers would change. Once the invitations were sent to the invitees, it was quickly realized that attendance was not going to be even close to what was expected. Within three days, the number of RSVPs stood at 500. The planner contacted the event manager to discuss a larger space—since about 700 guests were now anticipated. The hotel event manager was not sure if they had the space to accommodate the additional attendees and indicated that he would see what they could do. In the meantime, the planner began to look into other locations. This is not easy when one is in a town where a BCS Bowl is taking place: all the hotels were booked, including their event space. When the planner spoke with the event manager the next day, the planner had to inform the event manager that the numbers were at about 900 and increasing rapidly. The planner really wanted to hold the breakfast at our team's hotel. The planner was very happy with the service of the hotel but realized she would have to find another location or get very creative with what the hotel could offer. The planner and the event manager jointly decided to make this event happen at the property and began brainstorming during a conference call. The planner was given photos of the hotel grounds as well as its dimensions. Additionally, the planner went online to see aerial views of the hotel. Between the hotel leadership and the OSU events team, the planner would certainly have to be creative and think outside the box. In the meantime, the RSVPs had grown to 1,200 and were still coming in with five days until the event. The planner arrived at the hotel three days prior to the event and met with the hotel leadership, as it had not been finalized exactly where the event would be held at the hotel. In the planners' favor was the Arizona weather—and most of all—that the hotel staff wanted to make this happen. After about an hour of discussion, a decision was made to hold the entire event outside, in spaces that had never been used before. Additional food, equipment, tables, chairs, linens, staffing, and audio had to be included. The final count came in at 1,500. The event is still talked about today. This was a successful partnership with the hotel and the planners that resulted from a need to adjust budgets, staffing, logistics.

Provided by Susan Anderson, Oklahoma State University Foundation

events, such as weddings, do not have revenue sources and will therefore operate at a loss. This is not to say that a budget is not important for events that will operate at a loss. Estimating and monitoring expenses are important to ensure that the amount budgeted for an event is not exceeded.

As stated earlier, a budget is set up with the equation revenues minus expenses equals profit or loss. Revenues may include tickets sold, **sponsorships**, advertising sales, booth rentals at expositions or conventions, donations, grants, or other miscellaneous revenue sources. These revenues are listed as separate line items on the budget and will be summed up as total revenue.

Expected expenses are also listed as separate line items on the event budget. These might include space rental, equipment rental, linens, labor, insurance, advertising and marketing, food and beverage, printing, and any other expected expenses. These are totaled and subtracted from total revenue to determine the expected outcome for the event. See Figure 1 for an example.

When preparing a budget for an event, the best scenario is to use previous financial statements and historical data. If the event is being held for the first time, a best practice is to find a similar event and group and ask the event professional for any available data to begin to create a budget. This will help ensure that most line items are included and not forgotten. Compiling information for all possible revenue centers as well as expense categories needed to conduct the event should be used to create a budget. The first step is to estimate expenses. Actual amounts should be used if available regardless if using historical, a like event, or an original budget. Making estimates on expected expenses using actual information from suppliers will ensure that the budget is reliable. Only when an event professional knows the expenses to be incurred can the necessary revenue amounts be determined. If the revenues needed to reach the goals set by the organization are not possible, either the expenses need to be adjusted or a decision regarding the viability of the event needs to be made. Note: It is best to add an expense **overage** of 10 percent in order to allow for increases in prices or for unknown expenses.

A wedding/event professional described a bride's dream wedding not being a possibility: "The bride had it all planned in her mind. She wanted to have an outdoor wedding using multiple tents with extravagant flowers, tuxedos, and servers using crystal and silver serving pieces moving among the guests. It would have been beautiful, but the budget her father gave her would only cover a third of the cost. The tent rentals alone were over $20,000. She had to rethink. She was disappointed, but the event was still memorable. She got many of the things on her wish list, but had to forgo some of the extravagances."

FIGURE 1
Janabelle's Jamboree Budget

Revenues	
Ticket Sales (400 @ $25)	$10,000
Advertising Sales	$820
Sponsorships	$2,200
T-shirt Sales (250 @ $15)	$3,750
Total Revenue	$16,770
Expenses	
Printing	$500
T-shirts (250 @ $8)	$2,000
Entertainment	$4,500
Labor	$1,000
Venue Rental	$3,500
Insurance	$275
Misc. Expenses	$1,250
Total Expenses	$13,025
Profit (Loss)	$3,745

Direct vs. Indirect Costs

Expenses can be defined as either direct or indirect costs. A direct cost is one that is a result of holding the event. For instance, T-shirts sold as concessions are direct cost. If there were no event, there would be no need for the T-shirts. Indirect costs are those that would occur whether the event is held or not. For instance, if an association has an event professional on staff, the salary would be paid regardless if a specific event were held or not. When budgeting for an event, it is important to determine if indirect costs will be included.

Fixed vs. Variable vs. Semivariable Costs

Direct costs can be further separated into **fixed**, **variable**, and **semivariable costs**. A fixed cost is one that does not change regardless of the number of attendees. For instance, when the band for *Janabelle's Jamboree* was hired, they had a fixed price of $4,500. This negotiated price would be the same whether 1 or 500 people attended. Conversely, the cost for the T-shirts is based on how many are ordered. Note: Discounts are often available when ordering in larger quantities. Other costs associated with variable costs can make the cost a semivariable cost. These include shipping and handling. An example of a semivariable cost might be the rental of chairs for an event. If the chairs were $2 each, but there were a $100 delivery charge, it would be a semivariable cost. If the event professional ordered 50 chairs, the cost would be $200, appearing to be a cost of $4 per chair. If 250 chairs were ordered the cost would be $600, appearing to be a cost of $2.40 per chair. The delivery charge is the fixed portion; the per chair price is the variable portion.

These are all important concepts to understand when using the budget to analyze the performance of an event. A fixed cost can only be reduced if changed, such as reducing the amount of time that the entertainment plays or choosing a less expensive option. Since a true variable cost changes with the attendance, it is viewed and evaluated as a percentage of the attendance revenue. If the attendance numbers are trending low, the variable cost can sometimes be changed to reduce the percentage, such as choosing a less expensive entrée for a dinner. Either or both of the previous scenarios can reduce a semivariable cost.

MANAGING CASH FLOW

Receivables are amounts that are due to be paid for services or products provided to attendees, exhibitors, or sponsors. This might include booth rentals or sponsorships that have been reserved but not yet paid. It is vital for an event professional to keep abreast of the status of receivables. Receivables often drive the cash flow of an event, and ensuring that they are paid in a timely manner is important to maintain the ability to pay the costs associated with the event. Providing goods and/or services without first receiving the funds opens the organization up to incurring bad debt, which could jeopardize the ability to pay invoices and other payables.

Payables conversely are the monies due to others for goods or services rendered. Examples of payables might be labor, drayage charges, or any other expenses that are paid after the fact. Note: Many companies require partial or full payment in advance. This might include printed materials that are specific for an organization or an event. This demonstrates the importance of managing receivables. If an organization gets the reputation of being a slow payer, the less likely it is that vendors will allow them to charge in the future.

Inventory, an asset, is the physical goods that an event professional will use in producing the event. This might include collateral printed material, equipment, or items for sale as concessions. As a whole, inventories are minimal for events that are held in locations other than the home location. Most décor, equipment, and furnishings are rented to avoid the need to ship the items to and from the meeting/event destination. The rentals can be a fixed cost, such as computers for registration; or variable, such as pipe and drape based on the number of exhibitor booths.

Although budgets for events are typically reported on a single financial statement, the revenue, expenses, assets, liabilities, and owner's equity often occur over an extended period of time. It is important to create and evaluate the financial statements prior to the event to ensure that the event is on track with the budget and to catch discrepancies in a timely manner. It might be that expenses for one event were inadvertently charged to another or that funds received were not applied to the correct receivable. It is equally important to monitor that the expenses for the event are posted to the financial statement. An expense that was inadvertently left off the financial statement but then discovered and added after the event could change the financial outcome of an event and cause stakeholders to question the ability of the event professional in proper event management.

MANAGING BUDGET PERFORMANCE

As stated earlier, monthly or quarterly financial statements are important gauges of the financial activities of a meeting or event. The line items as well as totals should be compared to budget to measure progress. If it is a repeat event, comparison to the previous event is important as well. This will indicate if benchmarks previously set are being met. By monitoring the financial activities with budget and previous events, event professionals will be able to make adjustments as needed. It is important to remember that a budget is a fluid document that should be adjusted when the original figures are found to be inaccurate estimations.

Managing Revenues

As discussed and demonstrated above, various revenue streams can be identified for meetings and events. It is often the event professional's duty to insure that the procedures are in place to receive the funds from the sources identified. Obviously ticket sales or attendee registrations fall under the purview of the event professional and must be monitored on a continuous basis to ensure that the potential attendees are communicated with and are actively recruited for participation. Additionally, other funding sources should be managed as a component of the event professional's duties. This might include applying for and securing of grant funds.

Funding sources include industry-based associations, government entities, or industry partners. The revenues can either be in the form of cash or like kind with donations of goods or services to hold the event. In terms of grants, applications including budgets, letters of recommendation, business plans, and the benefits to the participants may be required to apply. In applying for a grant, it is vital to provide the required information. Missing information will often result in a grant application being disregarded. An industry partner may be willing to support an event to promote its products or services to attendees. It is not uncommon for suppliers to an industry to be willing to subsidize events in exchange for advertising and promotional exposure.

An event professional for a large restaurant company revealed: "It wasn't difficult to get food distributors and beverage companies to agree to participate in supporting our incentive trip for our managers. They had the opportunity to promote their products through food and beverage offerings at the event. They got the most bang for their buck by demonstrating their products to 750 general managers at the same time. We had the benefit of event funding as well as like-kind donations to reduce our food and beverage cost. It was a win–win."

If a grant is the primary source of revenue for an event, securing it will occur at the beginning of the planning process immediately following a preliminary budget. Sometimes grants are revenue sources that are supplementary to the primary revenue stream and are discovered during the planning process. While most grants are broad enough to accommodate a range of proposals, they are typically for a specific purpose. Event professionals should not assume that the grant can be adapted to their goals and objectives of the meeting. Therefore, it is important for event professionals to understand the purpose and specific requirements to qualify for a specific grant. Additionally, a grant "request for proposal" or RFP must be followed precisely. Many grant applications are discarded by granting agencies because of lack of adherence to the grant application requirements.

Some convention and visitors bureaus (CVBs) offer grants to events that bring a substantial number of room nights to their city or region. The grant amount may be variable depending on the number of room nights. The room nights are typically tracked through room blocks at the contracted hotels. It is very important for participants to book inside the block(s) in order to get the full benefit of the grant.

Follow-up reporting is a typical requirement of any grant. The granting agency provides specific directives for reporting how the grant was used and the benefit that the grant provided. Again, it is vital for the event professional to provide all required documentation and a report that shows the activities that the grant match the grant application and stipulations.

Managing Expenses

Prior to and during an event, it is vital to ensure that what was ordered for an event is received. An event professional needs to ensure that the quality and quantity of orders placed are received as ordered. This is done through precise record keeping and checking in deliveries when they are received. If items are missing or damaged, it should be reported immediately. An order should not be accepted and signed for if it is incorrect or damaged. The quality of goods and services provided should also be closely monitored. If goods are not of the quality ordered, they should be returned to the supplier to be replaced with the items as they were specified and ordered. If time constraints will not allow the goods to be replaced, the provider should be contacted immediately and a reduction in price should be negotiated. It is important to note, however, that if an item was ordered incorrectly (for instance, with a spelling error that came from the copy submitted by the event professional), it is not the responsibility of the supplier to provide a replacement at no cost. This emphasizes the importance of having multiple individuals proof items that are to be custom printed.

An event professional recounts an issue that she had: "I had always had really good service from this particular production company. I didn't have any qualms about letting them come in overnight to set up the pipe and drape for our trade show. Image my surprise when I walked in the next morning and the drapes were wrinkled and many were dirty. We didn't have any choice but to use them since the production company was located more than an hour away and the exhibitors were set to start moving in within the hour. I was embarrassed, to say the least. Although I was given a partial refund, I lost my trust in the company and probably won't use them again. Also, I will always have someone on the premises during setup. I learned my lesson."

Although a budget may reflect a cost for a budget line that was accurate at the time of budgeting, budgets are often created years before the event is to take place. This may seem unrealistic, but remember that a budget must be created to determine if the event is feasible after the goals and objectives are set. An event professional may not be able to secure the expected line items as originally specified and therefore should be up-to-date on other options that would achieve the same result as the specification but at a lower cost, in order to maintain the budget. Sometimes the option might be sourcing other providers while other times it might involve finding an alternative product that has a lower cost.

A new event professional explained: "Although they had always used the same company to provide the awards for the gala, I was able to find a local source that was competitive on price, but didn't cost me anything for shipping. Also, by using some of his award stock inventory, I was able to save even more. Not only was I able to stay within budget, I cut that line item by a third and was able to compensate for some items that were coming in above budget."

Another excellent method of managing expenses is to provide accurate counts for food functions; a stakeholder sees money go to waste when there are empty seats at food functions. Historical data will help the event professional estimate the number of attendees who will not show up for an event, although sometimes the location will have an impact on the count. If the event is being held at a location where there are few other dining options, it is likely the count will be closer to the attendee count. If there are many activities and dining options in the area, the count could be lower. One method to more closely estimate count is by asking attendees who have signed up for the entire event to indicate which food functions they will attend. Tickets to those events can then be provided accordingly. Another might be to provide all full attendees with vouchers for the meals and ask them to exchange them for tickets for the meal functions prior to the time that the final count is due to the facility. Additionally, the event professional should have an accurate count of those in attendance. When tickets are taken at the door, it is easy to verify against the count that is provided to the facility. While an event will be responsible for paying for the number guaranteed for the event, the event professional should ensure that any number above the guarantee is accurate. This is especially important in a buffet, where the facility may go by plate count and not head count. One thing to note is that an event professional shouldn't under-guarantee based on historical data alone; other information should be gathered. The satisfaction of attendees as well as risk of future attendee participation could be at stake.

An attendee at a large conference commented: "It was awful. We had our dinner tickets, but when we got to the ballroom, there weren't any spots left. I will say that the event staff got tables set up pretty quickly, but it was obvious that they didn't have enough food. We got what appeared to be small pieces of chicken cut off of the end of larger pieces. I paid for full conference attendance but got a gala dinner that amounted to a chicken nugget on my plate. We had to eat again after we left."

Some key factors to measure against budget are attendee registrations, exhibitor registrations, and sponsorships. These revenue sources will directly impact the funds available to pay the expenses incurred for an event. If any are trending to be lower than expected, changes to expense lines may be necessary. Another key item that should be monitored, which is not on the budget, is room pickup at contracted lodging facilities. If the contracted room block is not filled, the organization will likely be responsible for attrition fees. Attrition fees are not typically a budget item and can result in a large expense for an event. If other expenses arise that were unplanned, it is important to determine if they can be covered by an additional revenue source or an adjustment to an expense category or be absorbed by current revenue streams. Again, this emphasizes the importance of an expense overage line item on the budget. See Figure 2 as an example of budget monitoring.

As you can see in Figure 2 (a simplified event budget), the fund-raising dinner is scheduled to occur in 30 days, and several factors need immediate attention. Although donations have come in higher than expected, ticket sales are considerably lower. The event professional estimated that if they were able to sell 500 tickets for last year's event at $150, they should be able to sell 450 tickets for $200. So far, only 375 tickets have been sold. The first thing that should be evaluated is the ticket sales pattern from years past. If ticket sales typically remain strong up until the day of the function, then ticket sales may not be a problem. It should be closely monitored daily, however, so that informed decisions can be made. Options might include increasing communication to previous attendees to drive attendance or launching other marketing efforts to increase sales.

Another issue that is obvious is lower than expected sponsorships. This too should be compared with the pattern from previous years. It should be determined if sponsorships that have been promised but have yet to come in are collectable. It is important to note that sponsorships often include their names on printed materials. It is important to collect the sponsorships in a timely fashion so that services that are provided are actually deserved by payment of sponsorship. This is also important when contracting for exhibitors. Exhibitors should not be allowed to attend and exhibit at the trade show without payment in advance. It is often difficult if not impossible to collect once the event is over. Additionally, if exhibitors are allowed to choose their location within a trade show, the incentive of paying in a timely manner is to receive an optimal location choice. If exhibitors know that they might be relegated to a less

FIGURE 2

Fundraising Dinner 30 days prior to event

REVENUES	Actual to Date	Budget	Last Year	Variance	Percent to Budget	Variance to Last Year	Percent to Last Year
Ticket Sales ($200 ea.)	$75,000	$90,000	$75,000	-$15,000	83%	-	100%
Donations	$21,000	$18,000	$18,000	$3,000	117%	$3,000	117%
Auction	$50,000	$50,000	-$50,000	$50,000	0%	-$50,000	0%
Sponsorships	$12,000	$17,000	$15,000	$5,000	71%	-$3,000	80%
TOTAL REVENUE	$108,000	$175,000	$158,000	-$67,000	62%	-$50,000	68%
Cost of Sales ($50 ea.)	$18,750	$22,500	$20,000	-$3,750	83%	-$125,000	94%
GROSS PROFIT	$89,250	$152,500	$138,000	-$63,250	59%	-$5,625	65%
EXPENSES							
Printing	$4,750	$3,500	$3,000	$1,250	136%	$1,750	158%
Entertainment	$6,000	$5,000	$4,500	$1,000	120%	$1,500	133%
Décor	$12,000	$10,000	$9,500	$2,000	120%	$2,500	126%
Labor	$2,200	$6,000	$4,000	-$3,800	37%	-$1,800	55%
Venue Rental	$11,000	$11,000	$12,000	-$1,000	100%	-$1,000	92%
Misc. Expenses	$5,250	$7,000	$5,000	-$1,750	75%	$250	105%
TOTAL EXPENSES	$13,025	$42,500	$38,000	-$29,475	31%	-$24,975	34%
PROFIT/LOSS	$76,225	$110,000	$100,000	-$33,775	69%	-$23,775	76%

than choice spot if they do not pay their exhibitor fee quickly, they are more likely to be prompt with payment.

Since the auction is held the night of the event, it is difficult to assess if there will be any issues. If it appears that tickets and sponsorships will not make budget, the auction might be an area to concentrate extra effort in order to secure additional funds. While the event professional may be responsible in securing auction items, it could be the duty of another department or committee. Communication is key in determining if the auction items are likely to secure the budgeted amount of revenue. If the event professional is responsible for securing auction items, he or she should consider the audience when making requests. While a silent auction is a relatively easy fundraising activity on the day of the event, a live auction for high-value items is likely to raise more funds. A good auctioneer can be the difference in mediocre and outstanding fund-raising. When looking for an auctioneer, ensure that recommendations are sought from other like groups that have had experience with the auctioneer. Not only can the auctioneer create excitement for auction items, but if they are familiar with the organization and particularly some of the attendees, they can push them to continue to bid and create competition within the group.

In terms of expenses, printing as well as entertainment and décor are already over budget. If any of these expenses were contracted at the budgeted amount, the event professional should determine why the amount paid was higher than the contract. While it could be that an expense was inadvertently overbilled, it could also be that the event professional asked or agreed to additional products or services, which incurred additional cost. While labor is currently lower than budget, it should be determined how much additional labor will be used. This is important in order to determine if the current figure is accurate or if adjustments need to be made. It might be that by utilizing volunteers instead of paid staff, the line item could be sufficient. Additionally, while miscellaneous expenses are currently under budget, previous year's financial statements should be evaluated to determine the extent of last-minute expenses.

If it is determined that revenue centers will not make budget, and since most of the expenses listed are difficult to reduce by a significant amount, it is important to look at any areas that are negotiable. The per plate price of $50 could be discussed with the caterer: Could the price be reduced in order to make additional profit? It is important, however, to assess whether the reduction might negatively impact both next year's attendance due to quality concerns or discourage bidding during the auction if the attendees became dissatisfied with the value for the ticket price paid.

If after research is conducted and the expectation for significant improvement in ticket sales or sponsorship is unlikely, stakeholders—including groups such as a board of directors, executive officers, or others who have a financial responsibility for the organization—should be contacted to determine a plan of action.

Authority   It is important to note that adjusting budgets as well as signing contracts may not be in the scope of authority for the event professional. An independent event professional hired to plan and execute the event may be required to have stakeholders in the organization sign all contracts or other documents that will encumber funds or may have limited authority to sign up to a specified dollar amount. Also, depending on the level within an organization, an event professional may or may not have signing authority. It is likely that an event coordinator will have less authority to sign than a vice president of meetings and events. Note: Although authority to sign may not be given to an individual representative of the organization, it does not mean that the organization will not be responsible for the signed agreement. It is very important to clearly communicate to all parties who have authority to sign contracts and require strict adherence.

MANAGING MONETARY TRANSACTIONS

Cash Handling Procedures

In order to assure that incoming funds are attributed correctly, it is important to set cash management procedures. This is especially important on-site where temporary or volunteer workers may have **cash handling** responsibilities. The use of technology has increased the level of control available to event professionals. Requiring that all transactions be conducted through the event website via credit card limits not only cash control issues but also liability for handling credit card information. Limiting worker access to cash or credit card numbers limits the availability of theft or fraudulent behaviors against the organization or the attendees. The best practice is to only accept credit cards if on-site registration is permitted. If a great deal of cash or checks are expected, the best practice is to station a paid staff member at registration and implement an electronic system to print receipts with proper storage for funds received. This could include a cash register or cash box depending on the amount of cash expected. Regardless of storage method, there must be a checks and balances system ensuring accuracy. If a cash bank is provided to the registration personnel, the individual responsible for the cash should count the drawer in the presence of the event professional or designee and sign a form indicating that the bank amount matches that which the event professional indicates was provided. At the end of the individual's shift, again the bank should be counted and matched with the receipts for payments received minus refunds given. The remaining balance should match the initial bank that was provided. These signed forms should also accompany the funds to be deposited. As an additional precaution, the individual who collects the money from the revenue centers should complete a form indicating the cash received but not be the one to complete the deposit slip or take the funds to the bank. Understandably, in small operations this may not be possible. However, every effort should be made to ensure that all funds received are deposited in the appropriate account.

In the case of a suspected fraudulent activity, it is important to first curtail the activities that are suspected to be fraud. Once this has occurred, compilation of accurate information that indicates that fraud has occurred should be gathered, and appropriate stakeholders should be informed. This might include the legal department at the organization, financial and executive officers in the organization, or company officials if the fraud involved an outside contractor. Only after the fraud has been unequivocally confirmed should a decision be made whether to contact law enforcement for further action.

Reporting to Stakeholders   While monitoring budgets, cash handling, and other financial responsibilities are important during the event, the event is not really concluded until all financial documents are completed that accurately report the activities of the event. It is vital that the event professional assures that all revenues have been received and recorded and that there are no outstanding invoices that have yet to be paid. Close monitoring to ensure that all financial transactions are complete must be done prior to wrapping up the final financial documents to submit to stakeholders. These documents will include, but may not be limited to, an income statement, with budget to actuals reported; a balance sheet; any documentation required for grants received showing that requirements were met; or other documentation or reports required by the stakeholders.

SUMMARY

There is a proverbial "bottom line" in meetings and business events: making money. More specifically, this means that revenues must exceed expenses or, in a corporate setting, that the ROI must justify the expenses. The only way to accomplish this is to use appropriate financial accounting processes when on-site. Thus, the event professional must know the basic principles of accounting and the five types of accounts used in reporting financial transactions. These concepts are used to develop and then monitor the budget. Equally important is managing cash flow to ensure that the sponsor or organizer of a meeting or event has sufficient cash on hand to pay bills. Implicit in the budget are performance goals or benchmarks that are achieved when the event professional controls revenues and expenses. When on-site, it is critical for the event professional to establish and monitor cash handling procedures. Lastly, financial results are reported to the stakeholders.

Now that you have completed this chapter, you should be competent in the following Meeting and Business Event Competency Standards:

MBECS Skill 8: Manage Budget

Subskills		Skills
8.01	Develop budget	
8.02	Establish pricing	
8.03	Establish financial controls and procedures	
8.04	Manage cash flow	
8.05	Monitor budget performance	
8.06	Revise budget	

MBECS Skill 9: Manage Monetary Transactions

Subskills		Skills
9.01	Establish cash handling procedures	
9.02	Monitor cash handling procedures	

KEY WORDS AND TERMS

financial statement
revenue
budget

generally acceptable accounting
        principles (GAAP)
overage
sponsorship

fixed cost
variable cost
semivariable cost
cash handling

REVIEW AND DISCUSSION QUESTIONS

1. What is involved in financial management?
2. Differentiate between fixed, variable, and semivariable costs.
3. What is GAAP?
4. What are the accounts used in reporting financial transactions?
5. An income statement is also known as _____.
6. What does a balance sheet show? How does an event professional calculate it?

7. What is the difference between *cash basis* and *accrual basis* accounting?
8. What is the equation for calculating a budget?
9. What is the difference between direct and indirect costs?
10. Describe proper cash handling procedures for a meeting or event.

ABOUT THE CHAPTER CONTRIBUTOR

Sheila Scott-Halsell, PhD, is an associate professor and associate director in the School of Hotel & Restaurant Administration at Oklahoma State University. She has served in various leadership capacities for Meeting Professionals International and for ICHRIE. She was co-investigator for the groundbreaking research study on millennials supported by a grant from the Education Foundation of PCMA.

Marketing and Sales in Meetings and Business Events: With A Focus on What Happens On-Site

CHAPTER 12

Learning Objectives

After completing this chapter, the reader should be able to:

- Implement sales plan and objectives
- Conduct sales activities
- Determine sales platforms
- Manage marketing materials
- Produce marketing materials
- Distribute marketing materials
- Manage meeting or event merchandise
- Determine merchandise pricing
- Produce merchandise
- Distribute merchandise
- Monitor merchandise sales

The selling of merchandise is a large part of many meetings/events. dbrus/fotolia

Chapter Outline

INTRODUCTION

Marketing can be defined as the scheme of planning and executing the conception, pricing, promotion, and distribution of ideas, goods, and services to create exchanges that satisfy individual and organizational objectives. This sentence has been broken down for better understanding below.

A scheme can be thought of as a series of steps or a course of action. Planning is the research and homework necessary to intelligently decide what to do. Execution means to perform a task. Conception is the act of creativity. The price set for attending an event or purchasing products at the event, hopefully, is what the customer is willing to pay. Promotion is about communicating information to inform, persuade, or remind. Distribution in this context is the location of the meeting/event and the delivery of the idea, goods, or service. Exchange is giving something in return for receiving something. In this context, exchange requires two parties: the individual (attendee) and the organization (the sponsor of the meeting or business event). For the individual attending the meeting or business event, the objective is to satisfy a need or want. The objective of the organization holding the meeting/event is to generate revenue and/or enhance the image perceived by customers. As a result, we can say that marketing is satisfying a customer's needs in a way that is profitable both to the individual and the organization.

If you ask a person what marketing is, you may receive an answer that really describes the sales or advertising functions within an organization. In fact, in many industrial organizations, sales professionals have titles like "marketing representative" or "marketing associate," although the job has a sales focus. For the purposes of discussion in this chapter, marketing is recognized as a strategic or long-term process. Activities such as trade shows and other similar business events, personal selling, and the merchandising and sale of products affiliated with the meeting or event are tactics that are developed as a result of strategic marketing.

Meeting and business event marketers determine what the needs and wants of their current and prospective customers are through analysis and research, scrutinize their strengths to develop a market strategy, select specific markets to serve by focusing on a specific group of individuals to satisfy, then create products, events, communications, or other marketing strategies to best satisfy those needs and wants. One strategy for meeting the goals of the business organization is to hold a meeting or business event. In fact, the marketing for this meeting or business event will evolve directly from the purpose for holding the event.

In this chapter, we will outline the process a business meeting and event manager (hereafter referred to as event professional) might follow to create a marketing action plan for an upcoming meeting or event. We will also discuss the sales activities that take place during business meetings and events and that provide some "banked memories" after the event is over.

DEVELOPING A MARKETING ACTION PLAN FOR MEETINGS AND EVENTS

A marketing action plan serves as the road map for undertaking the marketing process and guides the event professional. First, by creating a plan, the event professional is undertaking a key element of management. This plan, based on the goals and objectives of the organization, is written in such a way that valid measurement of performance is possible. Next, the event professional conducts research about his or her organization, the business world outside of the organization, competitors, and customers. Based on the analysis of this information, the event professional develops a marketing strategy, which guides the execution of marketing activities or tactics, such as the business event, personal selling, and merchandise sales. Lastly, because of the dynamic and ongoing nature of the marketing process, the performance measures described above are used to control the marketing tactics and evaluate the overall plan.

Strategic Planning: Goals and Objectives

Every organization, at its highest level, begins a strategic planning process that defines the mission of that organization. The mission, then, guides the long-term strategy, which is translated into goals and measurable objectives for the organization. Marketing goals are written in such a way to achieve the overarching goals of the organization. They can be related to increasing awareness for a product or service, increasing sales for that product or service, new product or service development, and/or targeting different markets. Objectives are those specific and measurable elements related to the goal. Once these goals and objectives for the organization have been formulated, the strategic marketing planning process can begin.

Goals and objectives are written for a meeting/event in such a way to describe the reasons for holding the event and the outcomes expected for the event. These goals and objectives assist the event professional in developing the marketing action plan by describing what need will be satisfied for the attendee (goal), and by what measure the marketing activities can be assessed (objectives).

Marketing Research

Marketing research helps uncover information in three different areas: 1) customer and competitor profiling; 2) opportunities and problems facing the organization, and 3) evaluating how an organization's marketing activities relate to the goals and objectives set forth. For example, the event professional uses market research to assess the target market for the organization's product, service, or reasons that they would attend the event. A profile of these target markets can be developed to determine what their current and future needs might be in the context of a meeting/event.

Customer Profile/Target Markets

The purpose of the meeting/event may be important to the organization or professional who created it, but without people in attendance, it will not be a successful meeting/event. In order to maximize the people in attendance, a profile of the target meeting attendee or customer likely to attend the business event is required. Before a target market and attendee profile can be established, market segmentation must take place. Market segmentation is the act of separating customers or attendees into distinct groups, making it easier to tailor the product, service, meeting, or event to the needs of that particular group. Table 1 summarizes market segment variables important to the event professional:

TABLE 1 Market Segment Variables

Variable (consumer/business)	Examples
Geographic (residence and business location)	Country or International region, country region, city, postal code, census density
Demographic (consumer and business)	Age, gender, income, occupation, occupation level (executive vs. front line staff), education/training, generation, nationality, organization annual sales, organizational number of employees, industry, relationship to organization (customer, distributor, member)
Psychographic (consumer and organization staff)	Social class, lifestyle (timid vs. adventurous), personality (extroverted vs. introverted)
Behavioral (consumer and organization staff)	Buying frequency, buying readiness (no awareness to loyal customer), buyer role (user vs. decision maker), buyer attitude toward event, and purpose or benefits of attendance (education, business problem solved, network with peers)

The profile of the attendee must be aligned with the purpose of the meeting or event, consequently making marketing tactics easier to develop, implement, and control. The value and benefits of attending the meeting or event should be readily clear to the profiled attendee, and should answer the attendee's question, "What's in it for me?" Within the attendee profile, answers to the following questions should be also considered:

- What tangible and intangible features of the meeting/event attract the attendee?
- What is the most important benefit of the meeting/event?
- What media do attendees use for information related to purchase decisions?
- What event merchandise offered will be in great demand?

The targeted profiles then guide the marketing strategy and tactics to be created for the meeting or event. For example, an entertainment event held in conjunction with an annual international industry convention would likely profile global executives of certain revenue-size companies who make the final purchase decision. These executives may be considering the company's products to purchase for the first time, or repurchase. The event offers the organization the opportunity to communicate a persuasive (based on the most important benefit) or reminder (based on the features which most are most attractive) message to these executives, based on their readiness to purchase. The type of entertainment would be planned based on certain demographic (such as age) and psychographic (such as personality) variables. Any merchandise offered to attendees would provide that lasting marketing message in the form of something tangible.

Competition

No marketing plan should be started without the competition in mind. A competitive analysis is designed to compare the products and services of the event professional's organization to those of the competitors. This comparison of the competition might even be an analysis of the meeting/event itself. Competitors may be direct or indirect in their relationship to the event professional's organization. For example, within an industry trade show, there may be many organizations selling similar products or services, which describes **direct competition**. An example of direct competition for an event might be multiple wedding or bridal shows conducted in a metropolitan market area. **Indirect competition** is also known as substitute competition. Rather than attending a live event, a future bride may choose to use a virtual wedding planning tool on the Internet, or a smart device.

One of the ways to evaluate the competition is to develop a competitive profile. This profile evaluates the strengths, weaknesses, and competitive advantage of each competitor. The first step in creating this profile is to identify those competitors that offer the most serious threat to the professional's meeting/event. While there may be many competitors in the market place, typically five or fewer are most perilous for the professional's organization or event. Once that has been accomplished, the following questions should be addressed for each competitor:

- What products or services do they offer? How are they superior to yours?
- Who is/are their customer target(s)?
- What is their unique selling proposition? How are they different?
- What types of media do they use?
- What are their most effective marketing programs? What are their weakest marketing programs?
- What are their strengths and weaknesses?
- Where are they vulnerable? What actions does this suggest for you?

Once the most important competitors have been identified and evaluated, the event professional is wise to develop a competitive matrix. It provides an easy-to-read portrait of the meeting or event's competitive landscape and the position of the organization's products/services or meeting/event in the marketplace. By analyzing the competition and its strengths and weaknesses, the event professional is able to plan selling activities, develop marketing materials, and create promotional products that align with the marketing strategy of the organization.

Positioning and Branding

In today's world of many products and services, the messages that point out the features and benefits those products and services have to offer are overwhelming. Therefore, marketers must practice segmentation to narrow their target market and to understand the perceptual processes a consumer employs to filter the nearly 250 advertising messages received per day; by doing so, they simplify their messages to impress the customer. Positioning is a technique whereby marketers first seek to understand the mind of the customer and communicate the word, concept, or idea that rings true for the customer. That idea can be an innovative product or service or the solution to a problem. The event professional must then position the idea or solution of the meeting/event in the mind of the prospective attendee. Typically, the position for a meeting/event is the theme that is communicated.

A brand is a name, term, design, symbol, or feature that differentiates one seller's product or service from those of other sellers. Brands are made up of many elements, including:

- Name
- Trademark or logo
- Slogan
- Colors, graphics, shapes, and fonts
- Sounds, scents, and tastes

These elements combine to form a "personality" that distinguishes the product, service, or company as part of the relationship with the customer, employee, or other stakeholders. This personality is a catalyst for the perceptions and feelings that stakeholders have about the brand. Each time an attendee or customer, employee, or other stakeholder interacts or comes in contact with the product, service, or company, that person has an experience. This experience can leave (hopefully) a positive image, which could lead to increased sales and repeat business. It is important, then, for the meeting and business event professional to develop the branding for the meeting or event so that it is consistent with the mission statement, goals, and objectives of the organization and the meeting/event.

Depending on the goals and objectives of the meeting/event, the professional may engage public relations and graphic design firms to develop an appropriate name and logo. The event professional uses this name, logo, and slogan wherever sales and marketing collateral come in contact with the attendee: on registration forms, save-the-date cards, confirmation notes, brochures, and so on. Furthermore, based on the goals and objectives of the meeting/event, the brand elements can be applied using strategic materials used to sell a product, service, or core idea. These strategic selling materials may be **SWAG** ("stuff we all get"), such as pens, memory sticks, or other office supplies. More targeted collateral such as brochures, informational CDs, and white papers provide those important "takeaways" that help inform, persuade, or remind the attendee of the meeting or event. In the case of targeted collateral, these items may in fact be a part of the product or service the meeting/event is designed to offer.

The Marketing Mix/Integrated Marketing Strategy

The term marketing mix was first devised by Neil Borden, who suggested that the person responsible for marketing was a "mixer of ingredients" deigned to market a product or service. Those ingredients (known as the four Ps: product, pricing, promotion, and place) are the elements that a person responsible for marketing can control based on the target market and the internal and external factors facing the organization. The marketing mix in meetings and events can be considered at two levels: 1) a strategy that complements and integrates into the overall marketing strategy of the organization, and 2) a strategy developed for the meeting/event.

An integrated marketing strategy focuses on the communication related to the organization's event, or the specific communication designed to attract attendees or inform other stakeholder of the organization. Specifically, marketing communications overlaps with the positioning strategy and the promotional elements of the marketing strategy. As will be discussed later in this chapter, marketing communication at a meeting/event includes personal selling; product merchandising; retail sales; and the positioning statement, which convey a unique selling proposition and value to the customer/attendee. Ultimately, marketing communication seeks to achieve the following goals, based on the attendee's readiness to buy: 1) create awareness, 2) develop interest, 3) generate desire, and 4) stimulate action (these four steps spell "AIDA").

The integration of such activities requires a message consistency that builds on and reinforces each other. This consistency leads to success in the application of the marketing mix strategy. Integrated marketing communication requires the consistency of both the implicit message of each mix element and the explicit message of each marketing communication. What follows is a discussion of the traditional marketing mix elements: **product, price, promotion**, and **place** (or distribution).

Product

A product is defined as that item that can be offered to a market to satisfy a want or need. Products can be tangible or intangible—the collateral or physical takeaway of a meeting/event would be tangible, whereas the educational outcome, an experience, or other service-related components would be intangible. The service product occurs on four different levels: 1) the core product, 2) the facilitating product, 3) the supporting product, and 4) the augmented product. The core product can be thought of as what need the attendee is seeking to satisfy by attending the meeting/event. The core product can be directly linked to the purpose of the event, or what benefit the attendee derives from the meeting or event. The facilitating product is that level of product that enables the individual to attend the meeting/event or purchase the products offered at the event.

The supporting product or service is that product or products that add value to the core product. Consider supporting products to be the amenities that a meeting/event offers, either complimentary or for sale, to enhance the perceived value of the meeting or event on the part of the attendee. Supporting products and services assist in the differentiation of one meeting or event from another. Finally, the augmented product can be thought of as what is offered to the attendee as well as how it is offered. The augmented product includes the theme of a meeting/event. The themes and branding of the event and its products go hand in hand.

Pricing

As with the event and its products and services, price can be expressed on two levels. First, it can be defined as the amount a customer pays to attend the meeting or event. This is commonly thought of as the registration fee. On the second level, price can be stated in terms of the amount an attendee pays for any merchandise offered to the attendee prior to, during, or after the meeting or event. Pricing is an important element of the marketing mix because it is the only element that contributes to revenue; the other elements are costs. In setting prices, for either an event or merchandise, the event professional can follow a similar process: 1) Identify the target market and how it perceives value, 2) determine the price sensitivity of the target market, 3) comprehend the financial goals and pricing objectives of the organization, 4) determine costs, and 5) set prices.

The target attendee's perception of value is related to how the meeting, event, or merchandise will satisfy its needs or requirements. The core product is central to the perceived value by the attendee. In planning the meeting/event, professionals must take into account those features that add value or benefit to the target attendee. Along with a firm understanding of the target attendee's perception of value is the need to understand the degree of price sensitivity of the target attendee. This sensitivity can be the result of a variety of scenarios: 1) The attendee must pay for the meeting/event themselves; 2) there is a unique value or outcome of attendance that minimizes sensitivity to price; 3) there is an exclusivity of the event or merchandise that adds value; 4) there are lower cost substitutes, such as virtual meetings, which satisfy the need of the attendee equally well.

It is the responsibility of the event professional to understand the financial goals and objectives of both the organization and the event. For example, a nonprofit organization may wish to use an event to raise money, thus requiring a specific pricing philosophy. For-profit organizations, when holding internal business meetings, typically choose a "break-even" pricing philosophy by charging company attendees whatever the costs of holding the event may be. Finally, pricing may be set to make a profit.

Promotion

Promotion provides customers with information and knowledge in an informative and persuasive manner communicated in one or more ways, known as the promotional mix. The promotional mix includes six elements: 1) advertising, 2) personal selling,

3) sales promotion, 4) public relations, 5) merchandising, and 6) direct mail/digital-social media. The promotional mix is also known as integrated marketing communications; this means that the event professional will integrate the six promotional mix elements in such a way to offer a clear, consistent, and compelling message to the target attendee.

To develop an effective promotional plan for a business meeting, event, or merchandise sales, the event professional must follow these steps:

- Identify the target attendee(s) and their preferences for receiving marketing communication.
- Determine the promotional objectives: to inform, persuade, or remind.
- Design the messages for content, structure, and format.
- Select the promotional mix element or elements suited to the situation.
- Select the message source or spokesperson that will provide the most credible message.
- Evaluate results through measurement and feedback.

Meeting and event promotional materials should create a distinctive message based on the theme of the event. Promotional messages to each target attendee segment should convey the clear and consistent message discussed earlier. First and foremost, the promotional message should emphasize the benefit of attendance or of purchasing the merchandise. One of the most powerful promotional messages is a testimonial from a past attendee or buyer. When creating a persuasive message, the event professional should be specific, keep sentences short, and use powerful adjectives to add excitement. In any promotional message, it's important to make it easy for the customer to buy the product. Therefore, registration information, contact information, and frequently asked questions should be part of any brochure—paper or digital.

Each promotional element has positive and negative attributes. For example, advertising can reach many buyers and repeat a message many times. Unfortunately, advertising offers an impersonal message and is quite expensive. The use of sales personnel helps develop relationships with target attendees or buyers of merchandise through the personal interaction that takes place. However, the use of sales personnel is the most expensive promotional tool. Sales promotions and merchandising are commonly used to motivate the purchase of merchandise, but can also be used to stimulate registration for meetings and events. Public relations are the most effective form of communication because of its believability and message by a qualified third party. The use of direct marketing allows for a widespread and nonpublic message. Furthermore, social media offers a message that can be immediate, customized, and interactive.

Promotional campaigns can be successful through essentially three ways: 1) A successful promotional campaign can attract new attendees or new buyers of event merchandise; 2) promotional campaigns can attract attendees to return more frequently or purchase merchandise more frequently; 3) a promotional campaign can be successful by motivating target attendees or loyal attendees to influence their colleagues or friends to attend the meeting/event. In the context of merchandise, a successful promotional activity will motivate the attendee to purchase more merchandise.

To summarize, the promotional plan should outline no more than three benefits to each attendee segment. The plan should specify the materials and activities that will communicate these three benefits. The plan should undertake an integrated approach by having a consistent, clear, and compelling message in each of the promotional activities. Each promotional element should have a consistent look and feel; this aids in strengthening the recognizability of the meeting/event and the sponsoring organization. This look and feel is a direct indication of the brand identity of the organization, which was discussed earlier in this chapter.

Place/Location

In the context of the marketing mix, place can be defined as the location for the meeting/event. Location also plays a role in the process of making event merchandise available to the consumer or target attendee. The choosing of a location falls under the meeting planning element of site selection. There are important marketing implications that relate to the location of the meeting or event. How and where event merchandise is placed for sale is also a strategic decision.

When identifying the space for event merchandise, the event professional should consider high-traffic areas. This could be a pre-function area with pipe and drape booths or a designated meeting space near the high-traffic areas. How the merchandise is laid out is a matter of control and storage. Depending on staffing and security concerns, merchandise can be made easily accessible to attendees on shelves, or displayed out of reach with requests for the merchandise made to sales personnel.

Merchandise can be arranged in many ways. The most common method is with similar items adjacent to each other. Shirts are placed next to shirts, hats next to hats, and so forth. Another method of arrangement is price lining; items are arranged based on the similarity of price. This can be especially effective when the style and variety of items are limited in number, and sales personnel provide items over the counter. Finally, vertical merchandising arranges items in similar colors, taking advantage of the human eye's natural movement.

Partnerships/Co-Branding

Partnerships or co-branding are cooperative marketing strategies that associate single products or services with more than one brand or organization. The purpose of such activities is to combine the strengths of each organization to maximize the penetration of and promotion to the target attendee market. Partnership/cross-promotion activities can enhance the image of the organization(s) involved, minimize marketing expenses assumed by each organization, and result in the most successful marketing campaigns.

Important to the success of the cross-promotion and co-branding activities is the selection of appropriate strategies for a win–win situation for each partner. The message communicated to the target attendee must be consistent with the image of each partner and resonate with the target attendee. Finally, the co-branding activities and strategy must result in the best possible return on marketing investment (ROMI).

Measures of Performance

The goals and objectives of the marketing activity help guide the measures or metrics to be used to evaluate performance. These metrics can be related to revenues and profit, attendance, satisfaction, and return on investment. While there may be only one reason for holding the meeting/event, marketing measures of performance will help the event professional determine which strategies and tactics were most successful in achieving the goal. The use of metrics and key performance indicators helps ensure the consistency of marketing activities.

Measures of performance related to revenue and profit may include sales based on registrations, sales based on ancillary goods (other products and merchandise), and profits from the event. Attendance metrics may include the overall number of attendees and the number of exhibitors. Satisfaction metrics may be related to intent to attend again, quality of room accommodations and/or food and beverage offerings, and quality of programming. Finally, performance metrics may be calculated based on the return on investment to the sponsoring organization. Within these measures of performance, elements such as change over a prior year may be taken into consideration. No matter the metric used, it must be specific and easily measured by the business meeting and event-planning professional.

Marketing Calendar

When the event professional is creating a marketing calendar, it's helpful to use the *journalistic six* checklist. By following the "who, what, when, where, why, and how?" technique that journalists use, the event professional can determine critical dates and coordinate activities with other aspects of meeting or event production. This provides more details to staff members, therefore preventing misunderstandings, missed milestones, and marketing action plan errors.

Asking "who?" helps determine the market segment to be targeted by the activity. Consequently, there may be multiple answers. Asking "what?" defines the strategies and tactics to be implemented by target market. These activities will be based on the goals and objectives set forth at the beginning of the planning process. Specific dates for implementing the tactics can be listed on a spreadsheet, which answers the "when?" question. The "where?" question addresses both the geographic area to focus on, and specifically, what media (or non-media) should be used for marketing and promotion tactics. By linking the strategy, tactic, and objective, the event professional and his/her staff can understand "why?" this tactic was implemented. Finally, the "how?" question satisfies the need to direct and control the budget for marketing activities.

MARKETING TACTICS FOR MEETINGS AND EVENTS

Principles of Sales for Meetings and Events

Within the promotional mix, personal selling is a key part of marketing strategy that relies heavily on the interaction between the salesperson and the client or prospective client for the purpose of creating, developing, and strengthening a business relationship. Personal selling is more important than other forms of promotion because of the interpersonal nature of the selling relationship. While advertising is the most common form of promotion, personal selling has an element of persuasion that advertising and other one-way forms of marketing communication do not exhibit. Therefore, personal selling involves oral and written communications between a salesperson and a prospective customer, or customers, for the purpose to inform, persuade to purchase, and or remind them of the products or services the salesperson's company has to offer.

A salesperson at a business event or trade show can take on many roles. The salesperson can be a demand creator seeking new sales leads from existing or new customers; a missionary, with the intent of creating goodwill and educating existing or potential customers on the products or service the salesperson's organization has to offer; or an order taker or customer service representative. Business events and trade shows are an efficient way for personal selling to take place. Based on the goals and objectives of the business organization, trade shows and corporate events can be the perfect way to bring the salesperson face-to-face with current and potential customers.

Personal selling can be seen as a six-step process, from identifying potential clients to service and delivery after the sale. The salesperson seeks to develop a long-term business relationship with the potential client during this process. The first step in the process is "access," or the identification of sales opportunities from current customers or potential customers. In this step, the salesperson uses various methods such as cold calling, networking at business events, and attendance at trade shows to develop a pool of prospects, or "leads." The second step is "establish," or the establishment or inquiry into the needs of the prospect. In this step, the salesperson begins to develop a business relationship through the identification of the prospect's need for the product or service of the company that the salesperson represents. The third step is sometimes called "present," or the demonstration of the products or services the company has to offer. This demonstration is based on the information the salesperson collected in the second step of the sales process. The fourth step in the sales process is the handling of resistance to purchase and the negotiation of the terms of the sale. The resistance a salesperson might face can be mild or severe based on how well the salesperson collected information about the prospect earlier in the process. Once the resistance has been overcome and the negotiations successfully completed, the salesperson then closes the sale or receives a signature on the contract. The last step in the sales process is the service that the salesperson provides as part of the delivery of the product or service for which the prospect contracted.

The unique nature of selling at business events requires a set of skills unlike the traditional sales contact. In the traditional sales process, prospects must be identified through "cold calling" and other contact collection methods. The business event or trade show reverses this process by bringing the prospect to the salesperson. Because there are many attendees, the goal of the on-site salesperson is to speak to, and collect information from, as many attendees as possible. While on-site salespeople have a typical attendee profile available to them, the role in the buying process that each attendee plays varies. Consequently, on-site salespeople must assume that each attendee is a potential buyer; the on-site salesperson must take little time collecting personal information and maximum time uncovering the attendee's needs and buying objectives. One of the advantages to on-site sales is the exhibit and marketing materials readily available to the salesperson. As a result, forms of proof, which are important in the sales dialogue, are readily available. This may not be the case in the traditional sales contact. Business events are loud environments with many distractions—they are an energy-sapping situation. Therefore, on-site salespeople must possess tireless energy and an outgoing personality with a lot of enthusiasm. In any sales dialogue, but especially at a business event or trade show, it is best for the salesperson to listen intently and take good notes.

Whether he or she is working at a trade show, business event, or merchandise booth at a fair, the successful on-site salesperson demonstrates certain personal behaviors and qualities, which can be described as either intrapersonal or interpersonal.

Intrapersonal

- Appropriate and comfortable clothing and shoes
- Excellent personal hygiene
  - Does not chew gum
  - Does not have bad breath
  - Wears appropriate jewelry
  - Avoids excessive scents
- Has attentive posture
- Has an interested demeanor
  - Hands are out of pockets
  - Arms not crossed
  - Is not using electronic devices
- Wears a name badge on his/her right shoulder

Interpersonal

- Sincerely greets all attendees
- Speaks in a clear, easy to hear voice
- Asks questions and takes notes
- Doesn't interrupt an attendee
- Never ignores an attendee
- Maintains direct eye contact and has a firm handshake

The on-site salesperson must mentally and physically prepare him- or herself for an environment different than the traditional sales contact. In fact, some sales professionals liken business event selling similar to upscale retail sales, similar to working at Neiman Marcus or Tiffany. Impeccable grooming, excellent manners, ethical behavior, and business-like demeanor will serve the on-site salesperson well.

The Sales Plan and Objectives for the Business Event   The on-site marketing and sales activities at a meeting/event require some advance planning, (which was covered earlier in this chapter). In choosing when and where to participate in a trade show or hold a business event, the marketing organization must be clear on the demographics and psychographics of the target market. Furthermore, the marketing organization must be aware of the sales practices of competitors. This information will help clarify the unique selling proposition, or position of value, the target market will experience compared to the marketing organization's competitors.

Based on the sales communication objectives of *inform* and *persuade* discussed earlier, there are a variety of objectives that an organization might develop as a plan as part of a trade show or business event:

Inform

- Introduce a new product
- Build awareness for the company
- Educate current customers of new product features
- Recruit new employees
- Acquire market and competitor intelligence
- Identify prospective customers
- Publicize the organization's achievements to media

Persuade

- Acquire sales leads from prospective and current customers
- Make sales demonstrations
- Sign contracts
- Retain current customers

The type of sales tactics used by the on-site sales team will be a function of the target market profile (discussed earlier) and the outcomes desired. The outcomes or key performance indicators (KPIs) that the sales team is responsible for will include the number of contacts made during the event, the number of qualified leads for future contact, and the number of contracts drawn up or closings. When evaluating who should be a member of the sales team at a meeting/event, the following criteria should be used:

- Level of knowledge of the product/service being sold
- Level of experience of selling, both at business events and in general
- Personal qualities: friendliness, enthusiasm, and confidence
- Degree of persistence

Once the sales plan and objectives have been developed and the sales team has been identified, a meeting should be held with the sales team to discuss the sales plan. This meeting could be in the form of a training session that discusses an overview of the business event, a description of the target audience/attendees, the key performance indicators that the sales team will be evaluated on, and specific sales tools and tactics to be used with the target attendee.

Conducting Sales Activities

We've already covered the personal selling process—which is based on a more traditional sales call method that may take multiple contacts with the individual and many hours. Selling at a business event or trade show, on the other hand, involves a single contact with multiple individuals for a matter of minutes or seconds. Therefore, selling at a business event or trade show emphasizes the first three elements of the personal selling process: access, establish, and present. With these three elements in mind, the salesperson seeks to access the attendee through conversation, establish whether the attendee has strong potential for future sales opportunities, and if so, present information and discuss the next steps for furthering a business relationship. These steps might include an appointment, delivery of marketing materials, and/or a demonstration at the event.

There is a five-step process that salespeople can use for engaging attendees at a trade show or business marketing event: engagement, qualification, discussion, information acquisition, and disengagement. In the engagement step, the salesperson seeks to start a conversation with the attendee. Typically, this conversation is begun with an open-ended question such as "How are you enjoying the event?" Once the conversation is underway, the salesperson has generally 30 seconds to 1) describe the product/service, 2) offer a unique selling point, 3) emphasize a benefit for the attendee, and 4) ask the attendee for additional time to discuss/present.

In the qualification step, the salesperson seeks to answer four questions about the attendee: 1) How strong is their interest in the salesperson's product or service? 2) Do they have a need for the product or service? 3) Do they have the budget for the product or service? and 4) What job function and authority to purchase does the attendee hold? Qualification questions can uncover a profile of the attendee and his or her company or focus on the buying process and challenges the attendee faces in his or her organization. These questions will be based on the key performance objectives set forth in the sales plan. If the attendee is not qualified for further conversation, the salesperson will then disengage. If the attendee is qualified, further discussion is the next step.

The ability to ask the right questions at the right time is an important skill for the on-site salesperson. Generally, questions can be categorized into open-ended and close-ended; close-ended questions work best in a business event or trade show environment when a salesperson is seeking to qualify the attendee. Open-ended questions become more important after the attendee is qualified. The topic areas of these questions typically fall into one of three areas: technical questions, buying-process questions, and client motivation questions.

In the discussion step, the salesperson presents features of the product or service that may be of interest to the attendee. Given that the attention span of the attendee is short in this environment, the salesperson should limit the discussion to no more than three features and their corresponding benefits to the attendee. If, after this brief conversation, the attendee shows stronger interest, a presentation may be appropriate. The presentation can incorporate product samples, informational brochures or other marketing collateral, video presentations, and/or other forms of technology for the purpose of demonstration. It is important that this information is integrated with other marketing and promotional activities.

Once the discussion is complete, the salesperson must acquire the information necessary for future communication. This information will include contact information, the preferred method of contact (e-mail, telephone, personal sales visit), and the next step to be taken by both the attendee and salesperson. Other information, such as specific product or service interest, a time frame for purchase, and the current product or service use may also be part of the information acquisition step. It is important for the salesperson to remember that the old adage "time is money" applies to selling at a trade show or business event. As a result, only the required information or information that will help lead to a sales closing should be acquired. Personal conversation should not be undertaken. The disengagement step takes place once all the information has been gathered and the next steps for both the attendee and salesperson have been agreed upon. Body language and closing phrases such as "It was a pleasure to speak with you today" or "Thank you for your interest" while shaking hands is an effective way to disengage with the attendee.

Successful salespeople at business events and trade shows have some things in common. First, they seek to identify the needs of the attendee; as a result, they discuss benefits that are important to the attendee. They do this by asking the right question at the right time. Next, they stay focused on the sales plan developed by the company, eliminating wasted time. Further, they ask the attendee for action, whether that be for a future appointment or an actual sale. Finally, they understand that rejection is not personal and should be welcomed; it saves the salesperson's time and avoids wasted effort in the future.

Rejection, sometimes called objections or resistance, can come in one of five forms. The primary rejection by the attendee is need based. In this case, the attendee has no need for the product or service. This is the most difficult objection to overcome. The most common rejection voiced by attendees is that the price of the product or service is too high. This rejection is easiest for the attendee to voice, but is rarely the real reason for rejection. The third form of rejection is based on the characteristics of the product or service. For example, the hotel may be suitable for a business event in other ways, but the meeting space is too small. Another form of resistance is the source of the product or service. Source objections are generally based on brand. Brand-loyal customers are less likely to purchase from a competing brand. Finally, time rejections come from the attendee who needs time to think about the purchase. Time rejections in the meeting and event-planning industry can be based on the availability of space on a certain date or time.

On-site salespeople can use a variety of techniques to close the sale. Closing the sale does not always mean a signed contract or transaction. At business events or trade shows, "closing the sale" often means a "trial close," where the on-site salesperson moves the sales process to the next step. This step may be a presentation or an appointment for further discussion. In some cases, the attendee has come to the event with the purpose of purchasing or of signing a contract. In this case, the on-site salesperson must be ready, using closing techniques, to influence the attendee to consummate the sale. This influence requires a "closing" technique, given the situation.

The "close" is essentially asking the attendee/customer for the sale. It can be direct, such as "I would like to have your business; please sign this contract and we can set up delivery for next week." Other methods for closing the sale will depend on the attendee's buying objectives and the context in which the sales dialogue has taken place. The most common method is a summary of the buying objectives that the attendee/buyer has, and the benefits that the on-site salesperson's product or service has to offer. Another method, based on the confidence of the salesperson, is the assumptive close. In this technique, the salesperson will say something like "When you become an expert at using our product, you will find other ways it can meet your needs." This method puts the attendee/buyer in an "owner" position.

The alternatives method is another way that on-site salespeople may close the sale. After understanding the attendee's buying objectives, two product/service options may become obvious. In this situation, the salesperson asks which option is more appealing to the buyer, and based on this information, focuses the sales dialogue on that particular product/service until the attendee/buyer is ready to sign a contract. Still another method, similar to the alternatives approach, is the balance sheet approach. This technique is best when the attendee/buyer is considering the product or service from an alternative company. Using this method, the salesperson outlines the positive and negative aspects of his or her product or service and that of the competitor. Obviously, the salesperson must be very knowledgeable about the competitor. Using this technique, the salesperson guides the buyer to the conclusion that the salesperson's company offers the best solution to the buyer's needs.

Finally, the special concession closing technique is used frequently at business marketing events and trade shows. This technique offers an incentive for purchasing during the event. The concession appeals to one of the three types of resistance an attendee/buyer might express: 1) price, 2) time, or 3) product/service. In this closing technique, the salesperson offers a concession in the form of an "event discount" on price, a limited time offer (typically during the event), and/or additional product features or services. The concession emphasizes a quick decision on the part of the attendee/buyer. This technique provides the on-site salesperson with "something to sell" besides the product or service; this helps stimulate desire and action on the part of the buyer.

Once the sale has been consummated, the service and details surrounding the sale are negotiated and payment methods and credit terms are arranged. Any fees related to the shipping of products or materials required for the service are finalized. Delivery or pick up of the product or dates for the service to be provided are arranged. During this phase of the sales process, upselling and seeking referrals are important. A professional salesperson will ask for referrals as a means for gaining new prospects. Upselling is the technique of offering additional products or services that will satisfy needs that the buyer had not considered. This is similar to offering a dessert to a dining customer.

Determining Sales Platforms

The sales platform is the technique or strategy by which the meeting/event sponsor sells its products or services. Consider the sales platform to be the "transfer mechanism,' or the channels of information and distribution, in which attendees/buyers receive the products or services in which they are interested. These distribution channels may be direct from the seller, or indirect through an intermediary. The sales platform is the element for which the sales and marketing initiatives for a product or service are a function of the marketing goals for the event. For example, the organization may use marketing events to roll out new products. In this case, direct contact with company salespeople and other executives inform attendees about the product and persuade them to take further action. In this particular case, the sales platform is more strategic in nature.

Sales platforms for sports and entertainment events can be both direct and indirect in nature. Tickets, along with merchandise and other saleable event materials, can either be sold through the organization or through third-party distribution and merchandising companies, such as Ticketmaster and Event Merchandising, Inc. Thus, as discussed earlier in the chapter, the decision of how products and services (if appropriate) are to be sold must also take into consideration the target market and the suitability of the sales platform for the products or services to be marketed. Various issues, such as printing/production costs versus exclusivity of distribution by a third-party company, play into the decision. Whatever the decision, it is important for the organization holding the meeting/event to acquire contact information about the attendee for future research, marketing, and control purposes.

Once sales platform considerations have been made, other infrastructure decisions follow. First, how will access and egress—in the form of gates and security points—be set up for the event/merchandise sales areas? The use of credentialing to insure security and access by the appropriate people is an increasing concern. The equipment to be used for sales transactions must be arranged, including credit card authorization devices, handheld barcode readers, and handheld or computer-based sales recording devices. If cash transactions are allowed, the size of the "bank" or "float" must be decided. Depending on the complexity of the event, the prices charged, and the likelihood that attendees will use cash, the bank for each cashier station could be as low as $50 or as large as $400. Specifically for merchandise sales, the quantity and quality of the products offered must be considered based on the target market segments. Certainly, the image of the organization holding or sponsoring the meeting or event should be taken into account when selecting the quality of the merchandise.

Event professionals must be on guard for unauthorized on-site and remote sales and other activities that infringe upon the rights of the organization holding the meeting/event. Such activities are known as "ambush marketing,' where a non-authorized individual or organization associates him- or herself with the organization holding the event without paying a fee for sponsorship or licensing. The licensing of merchandise or souvenirs can be a substantial revenue source for the organization holding the meeting/event. Counterfeit merchandise or proclaiming association with the organization holding the event without paying sponsorship or licensing fees can have negative effect on the brand of the event and organization.

While conducting sales activities, it is possible for inappropriate behavior to take place on the part of the on-site salesperson. Such activity might be against social standards, such as improper etiquette. This is especially important in the international environment. Understanding the proper cultural practices of each country in which the organization conducts business is a must. Other unacceptable activities may be based on regulations of the industry in which the marketing organization belongs or regulations of the trade show or organization holding the event. Industries in foreign countries also have regulations that are different than those in the United States. Furthermore, illegal or unethical activities may take place. These activities might include the acceptance of bribes or payoffs. In the international marketplace, however, these activities may not be considered illegal or unethical. In each case, it is essential that each salesperson adhere to a code of conduct and that the sales organization examine causes and take corrective actions.

Managing Marketing Materials

The attraction of meetings and events is the ability to bring together the attendee/buyer and the sales representative of the company. The dialogue that takes place allows the on-site salesperson to inform, persuade, and remind the attendee about the features and benefits of the organization's products and services. Further, it allows for networking and the discussion of work-related issues. While these conversations foster a business relationship, the attendee/buyer will also receive information from the marketing materials provided by the organization. Based on the goals and objectives of the organization and the event, these materials, also called sales collateral or sales aids, provide the attendee/buyer with information, samples, or other giveaways that help remind them of the organization after the business event or trade show. The giveaways are typically called SWAG, or "stuff we all get." These can be printed marketing materials, such as brochures, data sheets, and customer testimonial letters. They can also be electronic tools, such as video demonstrations or company commercials provided on DVDs or available on company websites or YouTube. The SWAG may consist of pens, cups, key chains, baseball caps, paperweights, magnets, T-shirts, balloons, buttons, or other generic products. When determining what items would be appropriate for SWAG, the marketing organization must think about the characteristics of the target market; some attendees will want very little SWAG. On the other hand, there are specialized items that other target attendees will find useful or valuable. These materials help provide the "banked memories" and a reward for speaking with the on-site salesperson.

Producing Marketing Materials

A number of steps must be carried out to ensure the success of the marketing materials used at the meeting/event. First, specifications must be developed for each item that offer a specific set of requirements about how each marketing item is to be designed, created, and delivered. Next, vendors must be located and solicited. Many vendors of marketing materials are, in fact, representatives of the company that will actually produce the materials. There are thousands of companies that produce promotional materials and products. Therefore, it is important for event professionals of the marketing organization to research various vendors based on the goals of the organization and event, the purpose of the marketing materials, the quantity and quality of the materials required, and the budget allocated for such materials. Other factors in vendor selection relate to shipping: the location of the vendor relative to the event and/or the attendee (shipping costs), expertise in handling overseas shipments (customs documents), and expertise in shipping large quantities.

When a vendor is selected, a timeline for design, creation, approval, and delivery must be developed. Particularly with promotional products, there are a number of issues related to design that can impact whether a product can be created. Printing and embroidery on clothing are limited to what the decorating equipment can handle. Costs for custom work or brand-name retail products can be very high, well outside the budget. The type and quality of the artwork offered for the materials to be produced have an impact on the overall quality of the finished product. Thus, the event professional must monitor the quality of the production process, from design to delivery.

When producing marketing materials, the location of the event can impact the selection of promotional materials, based on local custom, climate, and so on. If the materials are produced internationally, the event professional must consider the additional costs of a customs broker and/or an international freight forwarder (some IFFs are brokers) to the delivery costs. Finally, shipping costs based on the size and weight of the materials must be considered. Logistically, another consideration for shipping is whether the marketing materials are being delivered directly to the event or to the event professional first.

Distribution of Marketing Materials

Marketing materials are designed to be distributed to the attendee who has been qualified as a potential buyer of the product or service. As a result, how the items will be delivered to the attendee must be determined. For example, printed materials may be made available to all attendees at the event, whereas promotional products may be distributed only to attendees who reach the discussion step described earlier. In other cases, brochures and other marketing materials may be delivered *after* the event as the reward for providing the on-site salesperson with contact information.

Depending on the goal of the meeting/event, a "pillow gift" may be an appropriate reward or marketing item. A pillow gift is a marketing communication or token of appreciation from the organization holding or sponsoring the event that is left in or just outside an attendee's room. Usually integrated with the overall plan for the meeting, event, or convention, the pillow gift may be edible or inedible, wearable or nonwearable, serious or humorous, and destination specific or universal. These items are designed to provide a memory of the event or offer marketing communication about the products and services of the organization.

The logistics of the distribution marketing materials involve four important activities. First, a delivery method is established for each marketing item. As previously mentioned, certain marketing materials are used as sales aids and are distributed to attendees before and during the event. These materials help reinforce the marketing message while the event is taking place. At a trade show, a data sheet may be beneficial as marketing collateral so the attendee can make comparisons with other organizations at the event. The vendor of some promotional products may also provide "fulfillment." Fulfillment can include the warehousing and distribution of the promotional product. The attendee contacts the vendor, usually at a website that represents the marketing organization. The materials are then sent to the attendee, based on his or her wishes. In the case of pillow gifts, hotel staff distributes/delivers such items. Obviously, valuable gifts must be placed inside the room. Typically, non-edible items are delivered by bell staff, while edible items are delivered by room service staff. Other printed marketing materials can be left outside the room. The industry standard for such deliveries is $1 per room.

The next element of distribution logistics to be adopted involves the distribution schedule. This too, is integrated with the overall plan for the meeting, event, or convention. Distribution can be set up by both time and day. The schedule for distribution is really based on the message to be emphasized, the target attendee, and the theme of the meeting, event, or convention. All marketing communication materials and products are designed to inform, persuade, or remind. Therefore, the timing of such distributions must also coincide with the goal of the marketing action plan: to create awareness, develop interest, generate desire, or stimulate action (AIDA).

Finally, the marketing materials must be organized and assembled for distribution. There may be a need to stuff folders if there are brochures and other printed materials. Materials must be placed within any carry bags or other types of containers. Vendors will do this for a fee. In some cases, depending on the size of the event, it is easier (and cheaper) for the organization's event professionals and marketing department to undertake such activities. Once the materials have been organized and put together, they must be transported to the site of the event, or the facility where they will be distributed to attendees.

MANAGING MEETING OR EVENT MERCHANDISE

The sale of goods or services from the organization holding the event or a business at the trade show to the attendee is defined as retailing, for our purposes. In fact, the sale of such merchandise at the meeting or event provides the organization holding the event or the business at the trade show with an excellent source of income. This merchandise is usually valued for the banked memories of the event that it provides. These items include clothing (hats, shirts, outerwear, etc.), celebrity photographs, and commemorative collectibles (pins, other "special edition" items, etc.). Businesses displaying at trade shows can extend their retail operations on a smaller scale, presenting those items likely to be most popular with the target attendee. Managing the sale of event merchandise requires the development of a retailing plan that incorporates the four Ps outlined at the beginning of this chapter. The first element of that plan is the goal that the organization formulates by selling merchandise. These goals can include 1) strengthening the attendee's association with the brand, 2) increasing revenues through supporting products, 3) increasing banked memories or the "legacy" of the event, 4) creating awareness about the organization or event, and 5) augmenting the event experience. The merchandise offered may help achieve all of these goals. Whatever the goal, the strategic elements of the product, price, promotion, and place must be well thought out to achieve an appropriate return on marketing investment.

Product

The products to be sold during the meeting or event must align with the goal and theme of the event. The quality and quantity of the items offered will be based on the target audience. Typically, merchandise offered at events is limited in the number of options, keeping inventory management easier. However, larger quantities of each item (especially sizes of clothing!) must be maintained. For example, when ordering 12 dozen T-shirts (a traditional quantity), industry experts recommend requesting two dozen small, four dozen medium, four dozen large, and two dozen extra large. Thus, inventory management is an essential part of the retail strategy. One reason for purchasing merchandise at an event is the desire on the part of the attendee to associate with the brand, whether that is an organization, a celebrity, or a sports team. Licensed products are those linked to the organization, celebrity, or sports team. They can be considered "official" or "authentic," therefore adding to their value and desirability. Event professionals may wish to license the logo and slogan of their event to vendors as a means of producing officially licensed merchandise. By doing so, the brand image is protected, and the royalties received by the event organization are based on the revenues generated through the sale of merchandise or other services.

Pricing

To price merchandise, the event professional must calculate the direct and indirect costs of producing that merchandise. The profit percentage required by the organization must also be taken into account. When determining prices, the event professional must also consider the desirability of the product. Products that are authentic or licensed by the sponsoring organization usually command a higher price. When setting the prices for each type of merchandise, the event professional must: 1) set price points for each target market segment, 2) consider the quality of the merchandise to be sold, 3) ensure that the price matches the perceived value of the item to the attendee purchasing the product, and 4) evaluate the opportunity for merchandise sales prior to, during, and after the meeting or event.

Promotion

Promotional activities for the retail sales of event merchandise include **personal selling**, internal advertising (also known as merchandising), external advertising (such as online), and sales promotions. Depending on the goals of the event, event retail salespeople may be cashiers and order takers or sales consultants. Advertising placed at the point of purchase (or within the retail sales environment) is considered merchandising. Merchandising is designed to create an awareness of particular available products near shelves of products, at the entrance to the retail space, and near cashier locations. External advertising connected to event merchandise may be on the event or company website on a "store" page or tab. E-mail may be used to direct the attendee to the company or event website store. Sales promotions, such as "buy one get one free" or discounts can be used to incent the purchase of event merchandise. Sales promotions can be used in conjunction with other promotional activities (advertising, merchandising, and direct mail).

Place: Location/Distribution

The place element of the merchandise retail strategy has three levels. At the top level, it must be determined *who* will distribute the event merchandise. Depending on the size and complexity of the event, professionals may negotiate with third-party companies to handle merchandise sales. These third-party companies can also set up payment methods, credit card processing, and inventory management. At the next level, *how* the merchandise will be made available to attendees and the public must be considered. Live sales locations, kiosks, stands, or larger areas should be used during the event and at critically selected specific sites within the venue. Online stores available before, during, and after the event provide another channel of distribution. Finally, "brick and mortar" retail establishments may be used as a means of distribution. On the base level, *where* the merchandise is located will have an impact on sales. The location on webpages, shelves, and arrangements within the live retail sites will have an impact on sales volumes. Finally, it must be decided *when* merchandise is to be made available to the public. For example, some merchandise may only be available during the event to preserve its legacy or commemorative status.

Merchandise Procurement

Once the event merchandise to be sold has been identified, procurement must develop the specifications for the merchandise. Merchandise specifications consist of a set of requirements that a product satisfies that are identified by the event professional. The budget to be spent on such items should be set as pricing determinations are made. Characteristics such as color, sizes, manufacturer (if appropriate), and details specific to the item must be included. Next, the vendor source must be identified. Typically, vendors that offer national or international brands, along with private labels, are best suited for event merchandise procurement. Event professionals may be required by their companies to follow procurement guidelines by soliciting a request for proposal from multiple sources, depending on the quantities needed. Similar to the procurement of promotional products, the event merchandise desired may be coming from an international location. With that in mind, it is best for the event professional to identify a vendor source with import and export expertise.

Merchandise Licensing

As mentioned earlier, event professionals can license the logo of the event or their company to vendors for the purpose of selling products affiliated with the event. The licensing process serves many purposes: It protects the image of the event or company brand, it offers additional marketing channels that event professionals might not have access, and it limits the investment required for producing merchandise. Another value of licensing is the ability to minimize counterfeit or unauthorized replicas of the branded merchandise. Typically the event licensing process follows these steps: 1) the event professional chooses the products to be licensed (shirts, caps, etc.); 2) the event professional seeks out vendors and negotiates a license; 3) the event professional approves the products for sale; and 4) the vendor sells licensed products to the public and/or authorized retailers. Licensing fees can be fixed or variable, depending on the quantity of merchandise sold. Licenses help the event professional monitor internal and external sales, which can help prevent unauthorized sales or the sale of counterfeit merchandise. Event professionals who carry out license agreements are wise to use mystery shoppers and other confidential sources to discourage fraud by unauthorized sellers.

SUMMARY

The "Ps" of marketing are the basis for all marketing, sales, and promotion activities in meetings, expositions, events, and conventions. While they first come into play in the "planning" stages of a meetings or event, they are also involved in the production of an event. The event professional then implements the marketing and sales plans. Marketing research is used to identify the target market(s) for the meeting or event and the profile of potential attendees. This enables the event professional to develop "branding" for the event, for merchandise and for tangible products. These products are then "positioned" to provide the highest level of sales and revenues. When on-site, principles of sales for meetings and events are employed and, at the microlevel, marketing tactics are deployed. The sales plan is implemented by the sales staff, who must exhibit high levels of both interpersonal and intrapersonal skills. Personal selling is key on a trade-show floor or at an exhibitor's booth. Sales platforms must be determined, and marketing materials and merchandise produced and managed.

Now that you have completed this chapter, you should be competent in the following Meeting and Business Event Competency Standards:

MBECS Skill 26: Manage Marketing Plans

Subskills		
26.06	Implement Marketing Plan	

MBECS Skill 27: Manage Marketing Materials

Subskills		
27.04	Distribute Marketing Materials	

MBECS Skill 28: Manage Meeting or Event Merchandise

Subskills		
28.02	Determine pricing	
28.03	Control brand integrity	
28.04	Produce merchandise	
28.05	Distribute merchandise	

MBECS Skill 31: Manage Sales Activities

Subskills		
31.01	Implement sales plan	
31.02	Conduct sales activities	
31.03	Determine sales platforms	

KEY WORDS AND TERMS

marketing
direct competition
indirect competition
SWAG

product
price
promotions
place

sales platforms
personal selling

REVIEW AND DISCUSSION QUESTIONS

1. What are the Ps of marketing? How many are there?
2. What is situation analysis and how is SWOT employed in it?
3. How are the concepts of positioning and branding applied to meetings, expositions, events, and conventions?
4. What are the roles that a salesperson at a meeting or event may take on?
5. What is the five-step process that salespeople can use for engaging attendees at a trade show or business marketing event?
6. Discuss the different sales platforms that can be used in meetings and events.

ABOUT THE CHAPTER CONTRIBUTOR

Jeff Beck, PhD, is an associate professor in the School of Hospitality Business at Michigan State University, where he teaches courses in sales, marketing, and meeting and event planning. He is widely published in academic journals, including research on marketing ethics, revenue manager profiles, and consumers' experiences in hospitality.

CHAPTER 13 Public Relations

Learning Objectives

After completing this chapter, the reader should be able to:

- Understand the importance of strategic public relations as it relates to meetings and events
- Develop, manage, and evaluate a publicity plan
- Develop and manage media relations
- Understand the importance of getting the community involved in public relations efforts
- Develop/enhance the meeting/event's image, and maintain it in a positive manner at all times

Login/fotolia

Chapter Outline

INTRODUCTION

What Is Public Relations?

Public relations is defined as the effective management of relationships and communications in order to influence behaviors and achieve objectives. As it relates to the meetings and events (hereafter events) industry, public relations can be defined as the "presentation of an event via the media or other outlets, stressing the benefits and desirability of such event" (CIC, 2011). All events involve public relations strategies, some at a smaller scale, others at a bigger scale.

Public relations activities involve much more than media relations. They include all communications and the development of relations with all event publics from attendees to sponsors, speakers, the community where the event will be held, the government, and the organization members and leadership, among others. It also involves managing a crisis or unexpected situation in a way that the event image remains positive and therefore attractive for constituents.

Professional relationships, just like friendships, grow and strengthen with time and collaboration. In that sense, the relationships built today with the community, the media, organization members, attendees, sponsors, vendors, and other people involved in the execution of the event plan will likely last for years, making the event organization smoother, and probably more successful, each year.

Why Is Public Relations Important for Event Professionals?

The event professional can have the most wonderful event ever planned in the world, but if people don't think it is wonderful, then their efforts are useless. Public relations is a fundamental element of the event's marketing plan and will help control, to a certain extent, people's perceptions regarding the event.

Communicating to stakeholders the benefits of attending an event, and helping them form a positive perception of it, is key to achieving success. There are many competing events occurring at any given time; the attendees and sponsors may decide to support any of them. The event professional's job is to persuade these people to make the decision of supporting their event rather than the others. In order to ensure support, organizers must develop a marketing campaign that will probably include both advertising and public relations strategies.

Although both relate to marketing, public relations and advertising are two different things. Advertising is what is said about the event through paid channels. On the other hand, public relations has to do with managing, through building relationships, what others think and say about the event. Different to advertising, public relations involves third-party opinions regarding the event. In that sense, the publicity and word of mouth they generate can be more valuable for people and have more credibility than conventional advertising. For example, it is not the same to watch an ad announcing Susan G. Komen's "Walk for the Cure" as the best fund-raising event in town as it is to listen to an interview during a credible news show with a breast cancer survivor giving testimony, through the media, of how the funds raised with this event gave her a chance of survival. Although both intend to achieve the same goal, the latter is more credible and therefore more powerful.

People's perceptions will define what they think about an event and consequently what they say to others. The more people are reached with a positive message, the more chances there are that they will pass the message along to those who believe and trust them. If those people who are passing the messages on could be passing them to potential sponsors and supporters, the idea of public relations becomes even more appealing.

Developing Public Relations Goals and Objectives for a Meeting or Event

All plans need a set of goals and objectives to serve as a guide. The public relations plan is not the exception. Setting clear specific, measurable, attainable, realistic, and timely (SMART) public relations objectives will certainly help event professionals develop and manage a strong publicity plan, select the appropriate outlets, communicate with all stakeholders, and of course measure the return on investment (ROI). Before setting public relations goals and objectives, it is important to know the answers to three very important facts:

1. Who are the event professionals communicating with (the publics)?

When they refer to the **publics**, they refer to all the people who will be involved with the event (e.g., attendees, sponsors, exhibitors, organizers, vendors, the community), and all those people/organizations with whom they would like to develop a relationship.

2. What does the event strategic plan look like?

During the strategic planning phase, event professionals will create the blueprint for the event. A theme will be conceived, goals and objectives will be set, and a date and venue will be selected. Event professionals will also research who the publics are and what the value of the event is for them, what factors will drive them, and so forth.

Before starting our public relations efforts, it is very important to allow time for strategic planning. From that process, the event professional will get important information that will set the groundwork to develop the messages that will be sent to the "publics." The public relations plan must support the event's goals and objectives and should include a set of clear and consistent messages. These communications are geared to create a positive perception of the event. The idea is to inform and persuade people, not to confuse them. For example, if people are told that a fund-raising gala will support breast cancer research but is then changed to lung cancer research, it is likely that people will get confused. That confusion will create frustration, which will in turn lead to a loss of credibility with stakeholders who will spread negative comments through word of mouth. Word of mouth is very powerful and can rapidly destroy an event's reputation. Creating perceptions is difficult, but changing them is even harder.

3. What is the public relations budget and which resources are available to implement the plan?

Although public relations efforts do not involve a fee, like advertising, there are a number of resources that the event professional will want in order to successfully implement a public relations plan. Any plan will be worthless if it lacks the financial resources to implement it and to cover the unexpected/unforeseen events that may occur. For example, if a publicity plan includes a press conference, the event professional will probably need to invest in developing and printing materials for a press kit; secure a room in which to hold the press conference; and, depending on the scope. arrange for audiovisual equipment and refreshments. Even when the value of the media coverage that results from the press conference is much more than what has been spent on the small details, there must still be a budget to make that happen.

Public relations activities are time-consuming and require a lot of follow-up. Therefore, before deciding on a plan, the event professional must know if there is enough staff to implement the plan, and most importantly, if the staff is prepared to successfully implement it.

Defining the Publics

Who They Are The publics are those people involved in any way with an event, the audience that the event professional is trying to reach with the message and/or to build a relationship. It is very likely that the event's publics will be defined during the strategic planning phase. (For more information, see Chapter 2 in *Planning and Management of Meetings, Expositions, Events, and Conventions,* by Fenich.) However, the event professional will probably want to reach other groups that may help spread the word among the event's publics.

How They Can Be Reached Communicating effectively with different groups of people can be challenging, especially if it is not understood what is driving them to the event. The publics can be segmented into different groups with similar behaviors and motivations. For example, a certified public accountant (CPA) may decide to go to the CPA annual convention because he is looking for continuing education in his discipline; Bank of America may decide to participate as an exhibitor with the idea of promoting the bank among thousands of CPAs that will hopefully bring more business; and the local newspaper may decide to cover the event because it is projected to have a strong economic impact on the local economy.

Event professionals must devote some time and effort to research and understand the event's "publics" and their motivations to support/participate in their event. Since media relations are key to generating publicity, it is important that event professionals see the media as one of their publics, or target markets.

How to Communicate with Them There are many different outlets to communicate our message. However, not all of them may be appropriate. To be effective, communication outlets must be selected carefully based on research of the different target markets or "publics." While some people will prefer to receive communications via e-mail, for example, others may prefer fax. Each public may prefer a particular type of communication, and the plan should seriously consider those preferences.

DEVELOPING AND MANAGING A PUBLICITY PLAN

The publicity plan must be developed based on the event's needs; it must be designed to reach the publics and achieve the public relations objectives that have been stated. The ultimate goal of the plan will be to generate enough publicity to create a positive image for the event and garner the public's support. The plan should outline the following: the public relations objectives, the tactics that will be employed to achieve each objective, dates when each tactic is expected to be implemented, who will be in charge of implementing it, and the budget allocation for each particular tactic.

Selecting Appropriate Media and Communications Outlets Based on an Event's Needs

The event professional can choose to send a message to the public through a number of different media and communication outlets. However, choosing the most common outlets (e.g., television, radio, and social media) is not guarantee that the audience will listen. Remember, not everyone thinks and acts alike, and not everyone thinks of an event with the same goal in mind. Therefore, understanding the publics—the way they communicate and the way they prefer to accept communication—is key to selecting the communication outlets that will become the backbone of the media plan. For example, attendees may prefer to receive communications by e-mail, while sponsors would rather check the event's website or call the event professional directly. Attendees probably don't care about having the event covered by local media, while sponsors would probably be extremely interested in that kind of exposure.

Selecting the right type of communication outlet will save time, money, and effort, will ensure the right message reaches the right people, and may even secure the support of future sponsors. Thus, taking some time to research the publics and their preferences will likely help more than making decisions based on the event professional's own perceptions.

Generating Messages: The Five Cs Rule

A public relations plan will include a set of messages that are aligned with the event's goals and objectives and are intended to:

- Inform people about the event;
- Persuade them to support/attend it and/or;
- Remind them about the benefits associated with participating and/or being involved.

The messages that will be sent must be carefully selected and strategically developed to create a positive image and communicate what is really wanted. When generating messages, it is important to remember the five Cs rule. Messages should be:

1. **Clear:** The idea is to inform, persuade, or remind people, not confuse them. If the event professional tries to communicate too many different things, they may end up not communicating anything.
2. **Clean, or simple:** Messages should be as simple as they could possibly be. People have many distractions, and complex messages may not be understood as intended.
3. **Consistent:** If the event professional is not consistent with the messages that he or she sends, people will get confused or simply lose confidence in what is said. Confusion creates frustration, and frustration leads to negative word of mouth, which could be devastating for an event.
4. **Correct:** Whether the information to be communicated is good or bad, it should always communicate the most current/accurate news. Communicating accurate information will help establish relationships of trust, even when the news is not as good as we may like. Lying or sending inaccurate messages is not an ethical practice and will destroy the event's reputation, sooner or later. Once credibility is lost, it is very difficult to get it back, so making sure that the correct message is sent is the way to go.
5. **Credible:** A credible message is key in generating the attention of the publics. Credibility fosters trust, and trust often generates support.

Generating Messages with Little Time   Unfortunately, things don't always go as planned, especially on-site with the event underway. As much as the event professional tries to plan ahead and project anything that could impact the event's execution, sometimes he or she must confront unforeseen situations. While following a plan is desirable, being flexible when these arise is very important. In these cases, managing communications strategically and as quickly as possible will minimize the damage and likely help protect the event's image.

Identifying and Developing Resources

Public relations is about communicating with people. Unless the event professional can talk personally with all the event's constituents, they will likely need to develop a number of resources in order to help achieve the event's public relations goals. Many of those resources, which range from print materials to electronic media campaigns, will be developed with the idea of getting the attention of the media, as they will play an important role in sending the event's message, especially to the local community. Those resources include press kits, websites, fact sheets, stationery, social media communications, email blasts, merchandise, equipment for a media room, and so on. Although many of these resources will be used to try to generate publicity or "free" coverage of the event, developing them can take a great amount of time and effort and definitely costs money. Therefore, planning ahead is necessary to ensure that there is enough time, money, and staff to successfully implement the plan.

Print Materials   In this age of technology, print materials are still in demand and will help event professionals get the event's message across. Not everyone will look at a website or accept e-mail blasts from anyone. Print materials can attract the media and give them the information they need to write an editorial or develop a public service announcement (PSA) to draw people's attention. Remember, newspapers, radio stations, and other media have not been involved in the event's planning and therefore have not captured any of the details.

Follow these guidelines when developing print materials for an event:

- Abide by the **attention, interest, desire, and action (AIDA) principle** (discussed in Chapter 12). Print materials are meant to capture the attention of the intended market and should be developed with this in mind. The materials should lead the audience to develop an interest in the event and the desire to support it. They must also ask the reader to take action. To this end, if the materials are designed to generate publicity, they should include a contact for media inquiries.
- The materials should be aligned with or reflect the event's image, with a design that conveys the event's look and feel.
- The materials should be developed by a professional. Not everyone knows how to combine colors and graphics or produce an appealing layout. Hiring a graphic artist to design the event's materials will ensure an appropriate layout and high-quality printing.
- The materials should be easy to read, not too cluttered, and with terms the audience can easily understand. They should be detailed enough, but not too long.
- Any graphics should be of good quality (printing wise) and assist in sending the right messages.
- If the material will be faxed or photocopied, they should look good in black and white.
- Always have someone read through the materials to look for spelling, punctuation, and informational errors. Printing costs can be very high, and finding an error after they are printed may be expensive.
- Allow enough time for printing. Lead times will vary depending on the complexity of the material and the printer. Having a little extra time will allow you to make corrections if need be.
- Make sure the printing and the paper are of high quality; this speaks for the event professional and for the event.

Before deciding to print materials, you should consider the role they will play in the effectiveness of the campaign and whether there is a green alternative to achieve your communications goal. People often throw printed materials in the trash before they have even read them. In that case, the event professional will have wasted time and money, as well as acted irresponsibly toward the environment, without achieving the intended goal.

Electronic Media   These days, most people have access to some type of electronic device. Text messages, event websites, and social media are a trend that the event professional should follow. Besides being green and cost-effective, electronic media is a great way to send a message and one of the best outlets for reaching certain demographics.

Most events have web pages where people can register and get updated information. This allows constituents to be connected anytime from anywhere in the world.

E-mail blasts, blogs, and social media are also excellent ways to communicate messages and keep people engaged. In fact, most events today have a Twitter or Facebook page where event professionals create a buzz and can even get feedback. The networks are so powerful that it is possible to reach millions of people with just a click. Never before has it been possible to connect with people in such a way.

When designing electronic media, remember these pointers:

- Their design should be aligned with the event's image.
- They should be easy to read and easy to navigate.
- There must be someone in charge of updating them daily (e.g., a web page or blog) and making sure all the information delivered is accurate.
- When developing web pages, try to find a URL that is logical and easy to remember. For instance, the website address of the consulting firm Fenich & Associates LLC is www.fenich.com.
- Social media is all about the capacity to get people engaged. These are not information clearinghouses, but rather a way to establish virtual relationships with people. Therefore, creating the pages is not enough. The event professional will need to appoint someone to manage these pages. This can be time-consuming work.
- When sending e-mail blasts, the messages should be short and concise and personalized, if possible.

Electronic media can be an excellent way to generate publicity. However, it is not necessarily the right outlet for reaching all audiences.

Materials for the Press   Once the event professional has managed to get the attention of the press, it is important to provide them with the information they need to write powerful editorials. A **press kit** is the most common tool developed for the press and may include:

- Press release or news release (see Exhibit 1).
- Fact sheet: This document contains important information about the event that is too lengthy to include in the press release. It may include the event date, time, venue, a list of participating celebrities/government officials/VIPs, attendee demographic information, information about the impact that the event will have on the host community, a list of ancillary events that will be held as part of the main event, any local cause the event is supporting, and any other information that may help the press to write an editorial or develop a PSA.
- Information regarding the host organization: What they do? Why are they hosting the event?
- Pictures or images that the press can use as part of an editorial. These images should convey details about the event and must be available electronically with good printing resolution. The event professional must ensure that he or she has the rights to publish those images and that he or she is passing those rights to the publication (magazine, newspaper, web page, etc.)
- Video: If a video is available with powerful graphics or even an ad, it is a good idea to add it to the press kit.

Print materials reflect the corporate or professional image. Therefore, providing error-free, high-quality materials with a professional layout will likely generate better results. Many publications today will request this information electronically, so creating them in Portable Document Format (PDF) is also advised.

INTEGRATING PUBLIC RELATIONS WITH ADVERTISING AND PROMOTIONS

Public relations must be closely related to the event's marketing plan. After all, the ultimate goal of the publicity plan as well as advertising and promotions is to draw people's attention to the event in a positive way. It is very possible that some of the materials developed for a particular promotion or advertisement will also be used to enhance public relations efforts. Also, relationships with stakeholders will stem from all public relations interactions (negotiation processes, phone interactions, planning meetings, dinners at promotional events, and so forth.) For example, the event professional may include in a press kit a brochure that was meant to be an "advertisement"—and the press may turn the information from this brochure into publicity.

DEVELOPING AND MANAGING A PUBLICITY CAMPAIGN

A strong publicity campaign should be aligned with the event's marketing goals and objectives and should generate buzz about the event, draw the attention of the media, and develop a positive image about the event among constituents.

Unless the hottest celebrity in town is supporting our event and has spoken openly about it, the press is not likely to show up at the event, write editorials, or talk about it (for free) unless we solicit such coverage.

When communicating with the media, the event professional must:

- Make sure your database is updated with the right contacts. If a press release about a sporting event is sent to the editor in charge of politics, it will likely end up in the trash.
- Keep the message short, compelling, and "newsworthy." Editors get solicitations from many organizations and do not have time to read long, complex stories. If the headline does not catch their attention, they probably won't read it.
- Follow up. The event professional should call an editor after sending a message to see if it was received.
- Be accommodating. The press expects certain accommodations, especially if they are on-site covering the event.
- Think strategically. There are certain times when it is best to contact the press. For instance, reporters are usually busy Monday mornings catching up with the events of the weekend. Therefore, scheduling a press conference then may not be a good idea. And if there is a national emergency, the media turn their attention to it; so scheduling a media conference when there is something else happening may not be effective.

There are various tools to generate publicity, including:

- ***News Announcement* or *Press Release***: A release should be sent to the media when there is "new" exciting news regarding an event. This "story pitch" can also be used to build interest by releasing bits and pieces of information at a given time with the idea of capturing people's attention. For example, when *Dancing with the Stars* announces a new season, they do not release the names of all the artists that will be participating at one time. Instead, they release the name of one artist at a time, which causes a sense of suspense that both media and the public love.

- *Press Conference*: A press conference should only be organized when there are important announcements to make and when there is a magnet to attract the media. For instance, if a celebrity is supporting an event and will be at the press conference, that may lure the press to attend. Organizing a press conference requires a considerable investment of time and money, as the event professional contacts the media, follows up with them, and makes sure to build a space that can accommodate their needs. But even if we invite and then follow up with the media, we cannot ensure attendance. A press conference with no audience will not generate any publicity. By making the wrong decision, the event professional risks losing the resources he or she has invested.

- *Media Tour*: A media tour occurs when the designated spokesperson goes to a number of key cities announcing the event or communicating the designated message. The tour is planned in advanced and interviews are prearranged to ensure coverage. The execution of a media tour requires a major investment of time and sometimes a great relationship with media outlets to even get the appointment. The media are interested in stories that will create interest to their audience, so securing appointments can be challenging if the story pitch is not strong enough. Having a celebrity or a well-known industry leader as the spokesperson is always a plus.

- *Media Blitz*: This intense media campaign is intended to reach the masses with a particular message in a short period of time. An example is when the event professional announces the event every single day, many times a day, through all the available media outlets (TV, radio, Internet, etc.) for a period of two weeks. This strategy is helpful only when the professional is prepared to support the mass response that may result from it. So, before planning a media blitz, the event professional must ask what would happen if millions of people started calling the next day to register for the event or to buy admission tickets. Is the organization ready to accommodate and successfully manage them?

- *Social Media Campaigns*: Facebook, Twitter, and other social media are emerging as one of the best and most cost-effective strategies to reach the publics and build interest. Many people connect to these regularly and they have, to some extent, the wonderful power of word of mouth. When a communication is sent through social media, the people who get the message may re-send it to their friends, causing the information to be disseminated exponentially.

- *Newsletters and Events*: People tend to think that only mass media outlets such as TV and radio can help them generate publicity. Nothing is further from the truth. Announcing an event in an association's newsletter or local activity may build a buzz. For example, publicizing an event directed at U.S. pediatricians through the American Association of Pediatricians newsletter may be a better strategy than announcing it on a morning TV show. Although the TV show draws a larger audience, it is very likely that more pediatricians will be reached through the newsletter.

DEVELOPING AND MANAGING CONTACT INFORMATION

Many promotional efforts fail even when the promotion itself generates interest. The reason for this is because the contact information provided is not accurate or because the event professionals are not prepared to manage the ensuing requests. For instance, if an event professional sends a news release to the media, the media outlets may contact the professional for more information. To do so, they will probably refer to the contact information provided. If that information is not accurate, they will not be able to connect with event organizers. Likewise, if the person contacted is not ready to talk about the event and provide details, he or she will probably lose the opportunity for coverage. Remember these rules:

- Provide accurate/correct information (people may not find a website if even one letter of the URL is wrong).
- Have a process to receive and answer requests quickly. Requests must be answered within 24 hours.
- Provide various mechanisms for communication (e.g., website, e-mail, voice mail, and fax). Due to busy workloads or time zone differences, people may not be able to connect with the event professional during office hours. In this case, having an e-mail address or a website that lists event details will certainly help. When there are international delegates, include the country code or a toll-free number.
- Make sure the contact person is knowledgeable about the event, ready to answer any questions, and available to do so quickly and efficiently.

UNDERSTANDING THE IMPORTANCE OF PROTOCOLS

Events can be as diverse as the world itself. They may draw together different people with different backgrounds and different positions. Professional speakers, celebrities, prime ministers and presidents, corporate CEOs, kings and queens, Muslims, Christians, Jewish, Americans, Asians, Latinos, just to name a few: Each bring with them different traditions and protocols they expect the event professionals to understand and follow.

Dealing with protocols and cultural differences can be challenging and time-consuming. Nevertheless, no matter what the event is about, the event professional must be ready to manage all these differences properly and, especially, with respect and professionalism. After all, this is a very important aspect of maintaining the positive image that the event professional strives for. The only way of achieving this goal is by taking the time to understand the differences and the protocols that each group has and ensuring that both the staff and collaborators (e.g., suppliers, volunteers) are also aware of them and ready to comply.

Let's use the Olympic Games opening ceremony as an example. Here, presidents, prime ministers, royalty, and officials from over 200 countries gather to welcome exceptional athletes to the major sporting event celebrated worldwide. Each brings a different set of protocols and expectations; accommodations must be made to ensure all participants are secure and feel respected and welcomed to the host country: That is indeed the spirit of the Games. The protocols are clear: The Olympic Committee president always starts his speech by addressing royalty and the country officials first. The athletes from Greece always open the parade, in honor of the first Olympic Games celebrated in Athens; participating countries walk along behind in alphabetical order; and the host country delegation closes the parade. Failing to comply with these protocols may result in serious issues of security. As the media reports on breaches of conduct, participants may appear to be disrespectful and unprofessional before not only the delegates but also before the whole world. One small mistake will most likely damage the relationships that event professionals have cultivated for so long and may considerably hurt their image.

CREATING AN ASSESSMENT PLAN

Plans are as wonderful as our ability to follow them and assess their effectiveness. They are strategically designed to deliver our success. However, plans are developed ahead of time, sometimes many years before the event, when situations that might occur can only be guessed at. During implementation, things can change, and the event professional may need to adjust the plan accordingly. Thus, an assessment plan must be created and used to make these adjustments. Putting together and implementing a plan takes time and effort. When doing so, remember the following:

- **Return on Investment (ROI):** If we invest more than we get in return, then the plan is not working properly. When we talk about investment, we don't only refer to money alone, but also to time and other valuable resources. For instance, an event professional may plan on holding a press conference; he or she will spend hours trying to get media to attend and spend money developing and printing a press kit and preparing the event—hoping this effort generates publicity for their event. However, if all that effort does not generate enough publicity to offset the money spent, then it can be said that it was not a good use of resources. You would not pay $100 for something that is only worth $10. Likewise, when event professionals design a plan, they need to make sure they are not investing more than they get back.
- **Performance Indicators:** To determine whether the event professional is on the right track and if the plan is working properly, he or she needs to establish milestones, or key performance indicators (KPI). In other words, there must be a mechanism to assess if the professional is going in the right direction. There are many different ways to measure effectiveness. For instance, the effectiveness of a media tour can be assessed by comparing website hits before and after the tour. If there are more hits after the media tour, and there has not been any other promotion during that time, the professional can assume that the website hits increased as a result of the media tour. In other words, the effectiveness of every public relations strategy implemented can be measured to assess. Well-designed, SMART objectives also serve as a great measure. For example, an event professional said that he or she would like to have at least 10 media outlets represented in a press conference. As soon as the press conference is finished, he or she will be able to assess if the objective was achieved or not.

DEVELOPING AND MANAGING MEDIA RELATIONS

The media play a key role in our publicity plan, as they are responsible for generating the publicity we look for. The catch is that we can't control whether they will support our event. Nevertheless, we can help them decide whether to support us by developing positive (and hopefully long-lasting) relations with them.

The first thing to know when working with the media is that writers and editors specialize in different areas. Therefore, the contacts for sporting events and political events are probably different. The contact method we use is important—some writers like to be contacted by e-mail, while others prefer fax—but it is also important to establish a relationship with the right person. The editor in charge of political events will only cover your event if it is of interest to his audience and if it relates to his or her area of expertise. If you contact an editor without knowing his or her area of expertise, your communication will likely be ignored. Depending on the event, the media may be all over you or not interested at all. Different strategies can be used to keep them informed and interested.

News Releases

A news release or press release is a story, written in third person, that helps communicate important information about a particular event to the media so that they can write or talk about it. During the event planning process, a series of releases can be sent to the media to start generating interest and building excitement. A release can be sent alone by fax or e-mail or distributed as part of a full press kit.

News releases often follow the format presented in the template below.

EXHIBIT 1   **News Release Template**

[Event Logo or Company Logo]

Contact Name: FOR IMMEDIATE RELEASE

Work Phone:

Mobile Phone:

E-mail:

Facebook or Twitter

HEADLINE GOES HERE; SHOULD BE WRITTEN IN CAPS AND MUST BE CATCHY
Subtitle goes here in "Title Case" and should describe the headline

(City, Date) The opening paragraph should briefly describe the main message we wish to communicate and clearly state why this information is relevant and newsworthy for the media.

The body usually contains two or three paragraphs describing our event in a short and yet descriptive and compelling way. Each paragraph should focus on only one idea and contain a few sentences. Sentences should be kept short. The use of hyperlinks and catchy keywords is highly recommended.

The last paragraph should contain the host organization's information. The same paragraph can be used in all communications.

The pound signs (###) centered on the page mean that the body of the message is complete. After this, you may add a note reminding the reader whom to contact should they want more information or to schedule interviews and how to contact that person (i.e., phone, email, twitter, etc.).

When writing a news release, the event professional should:

- *Think Like a Reporter:* Reporters receive hundreds of these communications; they will not pay attention to them unless they offer something that makes their jobs easier, like a story that can attract their audience. Unless that is achieved, reporters will likely ignore the event professional, not return their calls, and not make a decision about covering the event.
- *Develop the Story from the Reporter's Perspective:* When we write, sometimes we erroneously assume that others know everything we do. It is likely that reporters will not recognize the event name when they get the release, Even if they do, they will not know the details, as they have not been part of the planning process.
- *Make Sure to Include Important Details:*
  What is the event all about?
  When will the event take place?
  Where will it take place?
  Why is this newsworthy?
  Who will be there?

- *Get to the Point and Provide Unique Information:* Including a quote from a well-recognized industry leader may be attractive to the media. Twisting the story to touch people's hearts is almost always a winning formula.
- *Make Sure the Message Sent Is Clear, Easy to Understand, and Accurate*
- *Write Persuasively, But Do Not Lie:* Lying is not ethical and will put the event professional in a difficult position sooner or later.
- *Make Sure the Communication Does Not Have Grammatical Errors:* Sending communications with errors make an event profession look unprofessional.

Once the news release is written, it needs to be distributed. To do so:

- Set up a database containing the names and contact information of media outlets that should be approached. The database should contain (at a minimum): the name of the reporter or editor, area of expertise, e-mail, fax, phone, and the way he or she prefers to receive communications. Obtaining this information can be time-consuming and frustrating. Therefore, the event professional should collect this information ahead of time and have it ready when it's time to send the communication.
- Send communications soon after writing the release, so that the information is still new when the media gets it.
- Use the proper way to communicate with the media. If they prefer fax, then use it.
- Address communications to the correct person.
- Follow up by phone the day after sending any communications to make sure they received the news release. That way, you can find out if they are interested in covering the event and answer any questions. Reporters are usually very busy and will not necessarily answer all the voice mails they receive. Practice patience; most importantly, be respectful and professional.
- Check the media outlets to see if they have written an editorial or have announced the event. That is another way to assess the effectiveness of the plan.

Selecting and Managing Spokespersons

Not everyone is capable of verbalizing a message properly or remaining calm and professional during a crisis. To that end, it is important to select a **spokesperson** who will be responsible for communicating with media about the event. Some organizations decide to find someone in-house to manage this, while others prefer to outsource it. Depending on the scope of the event, the person selected could be the president of the host organization or a public relations manager appointed to handle all event communications. In other instances, the organization chooses a celebrity speaker or someone renowned to manage communications, with the hope that this person will become a magnet for people and the media. For example, if the event professional is planning a National Culinary Fest, they may select a nationally renowned chef to be the spokesperson. A host organization's executive director may serve as the spokesperson for a nonprofit event, while the president of the Olympic Committee may be appropriate for the Olympic Games. In any case, the person in charge should:

- Be knowledgeable and available to speak about any situation or detail of the event when needed.
- Understand the message that is being sent and the image it is meant to portray.
- Have a proper image that is aligned with the hosting organization and the event.
- Be a good communicator, capable of communicating an idea clearly verbally or in writing and able to control his or her facial expressions and remain calm in any situation.
- Have the right combination of knowledge and character to establish a healthy relationship with the media.

If the spokespeople are not involved in the planning of the event, event professionals must meet with them regularly to inform them of what has been going on and the way the organization would like to handle it.

Attracting and Accommodating Media

Unfortunately, it is impossible for the media to cover every single event in town. Therefore, the event professional's job is to make enough noise as to get their attention. This requires only one little thing: providing them with something that is newsworthy.

The best way to attract media attention is to build interest by creating a series of stories and events that surround the main event. These activities must be outlined in the publicity plan. For instance, when an event professional brings a convention to a city, he or she may calculate the economic impact that the event will have on the local economy and communicate that to the local media. This is certainly of interest to the local community and may be a good way of getting its support. If the event supports a local charity, the professional can develop a story about the organization to generate interest among potential attendees or sponsors.

Once the event professional has attracted the media, he or she must be ready to answer all their inquiries and accommodate all their needs. To that end, there must be someone on staff assigned to answer media inquiries immediately. Voice mails and e-mails must be returned within 24 hours, remembering the media operate every day, including holidays. Some of the things expected from event professionals on-site are outlined below:

- A media registration area, separated from attendee registration.
- Someone on staff assigned to accommodate the media's needs. That person should receive members of the media during registration and introduce him- or herself as their facilitator, for whatever needs they have.
- Complimentary tickets for the media to enter the event as well as preferential access to special events, speakers, and sponsors.
- A media or press room with access to computers, Internet (Wi-Fi), phone, fax, electric outlets where they can connect their electronic devices, tables and chairs where they can sit and write their stories, and a small table in a quiet place to conduct interviews. It is always nice to provide a refreshment break in the media room.
- Someone prepared to provide the media with the latest, most accurate news as quickly as possible.

Once the event is over, a news release should be sent to media communicating the event's most important outcomes. It is a good idea to include some good-quality pictures they can use in their publications. Always remembering that in order for event professionals to be able to publish an image, they must have permission, not only from the photographer, but also from the individuals portrayed in the picture.

If people have been reading and hearing about a specific event for months, it is likely that they will be interested in the outcomes. If promoting a fund-raising event, the event professional should inform everyone of the amount of money raised and what it will be used for. That will help build credibility, which will in turn make the path smoother when pursuing media attention and community support in the future.

Saying thank you is always advised, not only to the media but also to all constituents. To that end, writing thank-you letters or e-mails may help enhance relationships with supporters and may even ensure getting their support once again in the future.

Table 1 provides some tips to accommodate and manage media before, during, and after the event.

TABLE 1 Tips to Accommodate and Manage Media Before, During, and After the Event

Before the Event

- Make sure to communicate with the right editors and/or reporters.
- Use their preferred way of communication.
- Follow up by phone after sending a news release.
- Build interest by creating stories around the event.
- Treat media with respect and professionalism.
- Follow protocols and make media aware of them.
- Appoint someone to be the contact person for all media inquiries.
- Answer media inquiries immediately.
- Invite the media to the event and provide them with complimentary tickets.

During the Event

- Have a media registration area, separated from attendee registration.
- Make sure someone is available on staff to accommodate the media's needs and provide the latest news.
- Have a pressroom equipped with Internet and computer access, phone, fax, electric outlets, and so on.
- Have a quiet place available for conducting interviews.
- Provide access to speakers, sponsors, and other VIPs.
- Provide preferential access to special events.

After the Event

- Send a press release with event's most important outcomes.
- Send pictures to reporters and editors.
- Call supporters and thank them for their help.

ESTABLISHING AND MANAGING RELATIONS WITH ALLIES

The best way to have a smooth experience in any destination is having allies: people who understand the industry and are familiar with the local culture, policies, and processes, and can serve as facilitators. The event professional may establish relations with government officials, local industry leaders, suppliers, and other stakeholders. In fact, having a partner in the host city is becoming the trend because it facilitates negotiations and provides guidance in the planning process. Those partners not only understand the culture, language, and way of doing business in the host country but also serve as liaisons with local suppliers, members of the community, government officials, and even members of the media. For example, years ago, a U.S.-based health organization was holding its annual meeting in Lisbon, Portugal. After years of planning, managers headed to Europe for the event. They had shipped materials ahead of time, including a laptop they were going to use at the registration desk. When the shipment arrived in Portugal, government officials thought the group wanted to sell laptops and so they held all the materials in customs. With a language barrier and no relationships in the country, the event professionals had no way of getting the materials (agenda books, name badges, registration lists, signage, etc.) in time for the event nor time to re-create all those materials. Because the organization had a local partner who spoke Portuguese fluently and had a relationship with the government, the event professionals were able to get their materials in time to welcome over 200 attendees to the meeting.

It is not what you know, but who you know. Having local allies will open doors locally and could help secure funding, local support, good prices, appropriate venues, volunteers, and much more. They will become the eyes and ears in the host city. Establishing and cultivating relationships with them is strongly advised.

DEVELOPING AN IMAGE AND MANAGING A CRISIS

Perceptions are images that we create in our head about people, places, events, organizations, and so forth. We have a perception of pretty much every person we know, and even of those we do not know. Our experiences help shape those thoughts and so does the culture, norms, and beliefs that rule our life. Some people may argue that perceptions are not necessarily real. Perhaps they are not. What matters is that when they are real in our head, they definitely drive our actions.

It is the event professional's responsibility to create an image of the event in the minds of the publics, so that they can in turn decide to support the event. In this sense, an event is like any other product in the market. However, there is one difference: Controlling all the details that come together in a live event is virtually impossible.

All these strategies sound great on paper, and they may work beautifully if everything goes as planned. Unfortunately, we cannot control what people think or how they act and neither can we control what the media will say about an event. The more people hear about a particular issue, the more they will pass along the message. And if the news is negative, the message will be passed 10 times faster. Therefore, the meeting professional needs to be ready to react quickly when a crisis strikes.

For example, years ago, Mexico had a serious outbreak of the swine flu. The rise in the number of cases and the deaths caused by it were all over the news, not only at the local level but internationally. People started saying that going to Mexico was dangerous; this in turn caused thousands of individuals to cancel their travel plans to that country. The truth was that the outbreak was controlled rapidly and precautions were implemented, so that going to Mexico was as safe as it had always been. Mexico was hosting a number of international conventions at the time and could not risk their cancellation. Officials from the Mexican tourism office and the convention bureau got together with the event professionals and immediately drew up a communications plan. Because the event professionals were able to react quickly and had established relationships with the Mexican government and the media, they were able to start a publicity campaign that prevented major cancellations and repositioned Mexico as a safe convention destination.

Projecting what is going to happen in the future is hard, but being ready to react quickly when something unexpected happens may mark the difference between success and failure. A way of projecting what may happen is by monitoring the environment both internally and externally. That may give good indications of how to prepare. Let's say that the U.S. president has been confirmed to speak at an opening session. The event professional has followed all protocols. But because the president is so busy, the odds of him not being able to attend are high. If the event professional knows this, he or she can choose to be proactive and prepare for the worst. What if the president has to cancel an hour before the session? The answer is called Plan B. That plan must be comprehensive because finding a replacement will not eliminate people's disappointment of not having the president address them, as they had expected. Besides finding the replacement, event professionals must strategize about the way in which they will communicate the news to their audience and the way they will handle disappointment.

Being proactive (and thinking about what the worst-case scenario would be) is the best way to prepare for unforeseen situations, as opposed to reacting when something happens and being forced to make decisions quickly without considering the repercussions. Therefore, thinking about all the issues that may impact the event execution is essential (even if there is a drafted plan) in case things change unexpectedly and the drafted plan no longer helps achieve the goals.

National Guard Convention

It was the summer of 2007, and Puerto Rico was getting ready to host the National Guard Association of the United States (NGAUS) Convention, the first citywide meeting to be held at the new state-of-the-art Puerto Rico Convention Center. Puerto Rico had made a substantial investment in a convention district in order to build an infrastructure that could support these types of meetings. The NGAUS Convention would bring approximately 3,000 attendees plus their families from all over the United States to the island for a period of four days. Attendees would occupy 17 hotels, using the eight major transportation suppliers of the island to capacity and injecting approximately $10 million into the island's economy. Based on the news that the convention was holding an exhibition of military equipment, some local residents developed the perception that the organization was coming to promote war and violence on the island. With that perception in mind, they created the Alliance Against the National Guard Convention. The organization provided transportation for a good number of local residents who were exercising their right to protest in various locations. They promised to protest in front of the convention center during the meeting's inaugural day and during the welcome reception that was to be held in Old San Juan, the island's historical district. This conflict generated a great deal of media attention. Ana María Viscasillas, former president and CEO of the convention center, and her staff were worried about the security of the NGAUS attendees and Puerto Rico's ability to deliver the smooth experience that was promised. She soon met with General Carrión, director of the National Guard in Puerto Rico and chairman of the convention's host committee, and together they drew up a strategic communications and community outreach plan. Being that politics is a hot topic on the island, Viscasillas and Carrión decided not to involve the government in the dispute (the government thus remained silent during the conflict). Understanding the power of media and communications, they went on a media tour that included all major local journals, radio shows, and television news shows. They knew other groups and organizations were watching to see how the conflict would be resolved before making a decision on whether to bring their own events to Puerto Rico. As the two major spokespersons of the campaign, Viscasillas and Carrión decided to use media outlets to educate residents regarding the value and benefits of bringing this convention to the island. They also explained to the locals how the National Guard serves as the Red Cross's right hand when it comes to national emergencies. By sending a series of press releases to the media, they managed to neutralize what the Alliance supporters were arguing. They sent the message to the other groups that Puerto Rico welcomes and values tourism. With government officials and the local police authorities on board, they were also able to change the welcome reception from Old San Juan to Central Park, where they successfully greeted 5,000 delegates. During the convention's opening day, there were small, peaceful protests that did not interfere at all with the event. The convention was flawlessly executed and the NGAUS representatives left Puerto Rico with a very good impression. In this case, a good public relations plan was key to achieving success.

SUMMARY

Public relations activities involve much more than media relations; they include all communications and the development of relations with all event publics. Public relations is a fundamental element of an event's marketing plan and help control people's perceptions regarding an event.

Public relations is different than advertising. Public relations involves third-party opinions of an event. In that sense, the publicity and word of mouth they generate can be more valuable for people and lend more credibility than conventional advertising. Before setting public relations goals, it is important to have a clear understanding of the event's strategic plan, who the publics are, and what resources are available to execute a public relations campaign. Creating perceptions is difficult, but changing them is even harder.

The publics are those people involved in any way with an event: all those who need to be reached with a message and/or with whom to build a relationship. Event professionals must devote time and effort to research and understand the event's "publics" and their motivations to support/participate in their event.

Selecting the right type of communication outlet will save time, money, and effort and ensure the right message reaches the right people. It may even secure the support of sponsors in the future. To be effective, messages should follow the five Cs rule.

While following a plan is desirable, being flexible and reacting quickly when unforeseen situations arise is very important.

Before deciding to print materials, consider the role these will play in the effectiveness of a campaign; consider if there is a green alternative to achieve the same goal. Electronic media can be an excellent way to generate publicity. However, it is not necessarily the right outlet to reach all audiences. Print materials are a reflection of the corporate or professional image.

The ultimate goal of the publicity plan is to draw people's attention to the event in a positive way.

Advertising and promotions have this same goal. Thus, public relations, advertising, and promotions must be closely related.

Dealing with protocols and cultural differences can be challenging and time-consuming. Nevertheless, no matter what the event is about, the event professional must be ready to manage all these differences properly, especially with respect and professionalism.

Plans are as wonderful as the ability to follow them and assess their effectiveness.

When event professionals design a plan, they need to make sure they are not investing more than they are getting in return. Well-designed SMART objectives are an excellent way to assess performance.

Attracting the media requires providing them with a newsworthy story. Once event professionals have attracted the media, they must be ready to answer all their inquiries and accommodate all their needs. To that end, writing thank-you letters or e-mails may help enhance the relationship with supporters and may even ensure their support again in the future.

Being proactive is the best way to get ready to handle unforeseen situations.

Now that you have completed this chapter, you should be competent in the following Meeting and Business Event Competency Standards:

MBECS Skill 30: Contribute to Public Relations Activities

Subskills		
30.01	Contribute to public relations strategy	
30.02	Contribute to publicity plan	
30.03	Develop media relations	
30.04	Contribute to implementation of publicity plan	
30.05	Manage crises and controversies	

KEY WORDS AND TERMS

public relations
publics
attention, interest, desire, and
  action (AIDA) principle
press kit

news announcement
press release
press conference
media tour
media blitz

social media campaign
ROI
spokesperson
perceptions

REVIEW AND DISCUSSION QUESTIONS

1. Why is it important to develop a public relations plan for an event?
2. How is public relations different from advertising?
3. What information is important to have before setting public relation goals and objectives?
4. Explain the "five Cs" rule for generating public relations messages.
5. Discuss the AIDA principle.
6. Mention five things that must be done when communicating with the media.
7. Mention four tools used to generate publicity.
8. Provide two reasons why it's important to comply with protocols.
9. What are performance indicators?
10. Discuss the steps needed to distribute a news release to the media.
11. Discuss the qualities or characteristics a spokesperson should have in order to be successful.
12. What should be done to attract the media to an event?
13. Mention how media should be accommodated before, during, and after an event?
14. Why should time be spent on establishing relationships with local allies?

REFERENCE

CIC. (2011). APEX Industry Glossary. Retrieved June 26, 2012, from http://www.conventionindustry.org/StandardsPractices/APEX/glossary.aspx.

ABOUT THE CHAPTER CONTRIBUTOR

Zoe Santiago-Font, MTA, CMP, is an associate professor in the José A. (Tony) Santana International School of Hospitality & Culinary Arts, Universidad del Este in Puerto Rico. She teaches in the area of meetings and events and is active in the Puerto Rico Hotel and Tourism Association and in the Puerto Rico chapter of Meeting Professionals International.

On-Site—Effective Event Communication

CHAPTER 14

On-site communication often involves head-mikes and two way radios.
lenets_tan/fotolia

Learning Objectives

After completing this chapter, the reader should be able to:

- Recognize the mission, goals, and objectives for effective business communication skills
- Develop a communication framework for effective on-site planning
- Determine the communications equipment, resources, and tools needed to properly execute the event
- Implement effective procedures and protocols for an event team in a crisis

Chapter Outline

INTRODUCTION

Principles and Practices of Business Communication

Among the many skills needed by event managers, good communication skills are a must: Managers must work well with others. Event managers might be working on two to three projects at a time, so their communication skills—verbal, **nonverbal**, conversation, written, Skype, e-mail, text messaging, social media, etc.—are critical. You cannot avoid miscommunication entirely, but you can reduce it using the proper tools. The event staff needs to be up-to-date, accurate, and detailed when receiving instructions, and providing feedback, for the functions that collectively make up the event. It is only effective communication skills that will help managers get their job done well and on time. Poor communication leads to wasted time and may even hamper the progress of the event.

How managers speak to their clients as well as the workforce will define the event professional's communication skills. One should not forget telephone etiquette, which is an important part of strong communication skills. Facing communication problems among internal and external stakeholders is quite common during event production. To keep problems relating to communication skills at bay, an event professional should strive to:

- Improve listening skills
- Overcome any language barriers
- Effectively read people's body language
- Use social networking to his or her benefit
- Influence his or her team to improve performance
- Identify any abusive personalities and know how to deal with them effectively
- Deal with conflict in the workplace

When event professionals have effective communication skills, half their job of hosting the event is done. Being courteous and polite while not losing patience can help leave a positive image on the client, even if he or she is fuming at you. One can always heal relationships and move ahead at work with simple, strong communication skills. Moreover, people will look forward to working with the event professional on future events, leading to continued business.

The importance of communication skills during event planning and production lies in the fact that the event professional will be working with lots of other people. Communication will be a part of the daily job; therefore, the event professional needs to be able to communicate well, both orally and in writing, with all involved. At the very least, good communication skills are needed in order to persuade all constituents to work together to successfully host the event.

Effective Business Communication Skills

Effective communication is highly under-examined. However, it is the essential ingredient for successful on-site operations and events. Through communication, stakeholders will understand their role and how they fit into the event. Communication begins during the *pre-planning* or *research stage* of the event, where the mission and goals are determined. Timely execution of all elements of the event will need to occur in order to achieve the event's mission and goals. During the *design stage*, meetings between event teams, vendors, and all stakeholders will ensure that all understand the event goals. During the *planning stage*, new ideas and concepts can be put forth.

FIGURE 1
Steps in the communication
process when producing
meetings and events.

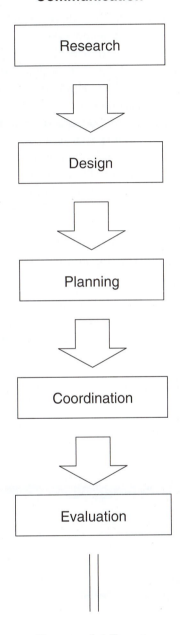

Communication

Therefore, an effective communication plan will keep all stakeholders current. During the *coordination* or *execution stage*, communication takes the form of constant monitoring of activities and follow-through regarding any changes that may occur. During the *post-event* or *evaluation stage*, communication takes the form of evaluations and feedback from all the stakeholders involved (e.g., attendees, sponsors, representatives from all facilities, and the event team). Figure 1 illustrates the role of communication in the five phases of event management.

DEVELOPING A COMMUNICATION FRAMEWORK

Three Stages of Event Communication

Pre-Event Communication The purpose of the **pre-con** (short for pre-convention) or pre-event meeting, which is held months before by a planning committee and/or just before the event at the primary facility where it will be held, is to provide an overview of the program, reconfirm and review event logistics, and discuss last-minute adjustments. The pre-con meeting also gives the event professional an opportunity to establish a rapport with the facility staff (they may not have been introduced as of yet). Lasting 24 to 48 hours, the meeting allows the event professional to give a brief history of the organization, its membership, and the event; offer highlights of the event; and identify board members and other VIPs who should receive room amenities, early or late checkouts, or other special services. Also, and this is an important note, this is the time to express an appreciation for the efforts of all concerned in partnering to ensure a successful event. These include oral and written skills as well as note taking and record keeping. An agenda should be developed before the meeting to inform attendees what will be discussed, keep them on track, and provide a record of the meeting.

In addition, the event professional should meet with his or her own staff to review responsibilities during this meeting and resolve any questions or problems the staff may have.

- Tip: The project plan (see Picture 1) is the primary tool for planning and reinforcing proper communication among all vested parties. It includes areas where the tasks, responsible parties, and follow-up notes can be written down.

On-Site Communication While the event is happening, there must be constant follow-up with all parties to ensure that the service has been delivered accurately

PICTURE 1
Project plan

	Project Plan		
Key code:	In Process	Complete	Past Due
Task	**Responsible**	**Due Date/Status**	**Comments/Outcomes**
Secure venue			
Schedule weekly core team planning meetings			
Create save the date & invitation			
Develop guest list			
Distribute information to team about initiative and event			
Create project plan			
Distribute project plan to team			
6 Months Prior			
Task	**Responsible**	**Due Date/Status**	**Comments/Outcomes**
4 Months Prior			
Task	**Responsible**	**Due Date/Status**	**Comments/Outcomes**

Project plan | Sheet2 | Sheet3

and all problems have been handled and any *fires* have been put out. The purpose of these meetings is to ensure that pertinent personnel are aware of the daily functions, the various requirements for each function, and any changes or additions that may have been made on-site. This is also a good time to review the effectiveness of functions that have already occurred and determine whether any modifications need to be made, midway through the event, to improve the outcome of remaining functions.

- Tip: Use a project plan for follow-up. Use a schedule, timeline, and/or agenda. Conduct a debriefing at the end of each day of the event.

Post-Event Communication   Two post-event (or **post-con**) meetings may be held. The first provides a vital source of feedback about the event that can serve as a reference for future events. This meeting is held on-site immediately after the event has been held. It is an opportunity for the organization to receive candid feedback from the frontline staff on how well the staff performed in the planning and management of on-site logistics. The second post-event meeting takes place with the heads of the event team 24 to 48 hours after the event to get feedback from a holistic perspective. There may be things that need correcting that can be useful in future planning.

It is also a good time to review outstanding invoices, highlighting any discrepancies or concerns and approving any outstanding changes. All facility and supplier staff members should be asked to provide feedback after the event. This includes the event team, sales professionals, food-and-beverage professionals, audiovisual professionals, decorators, and any other appropriate facility and supplier staff members. For example, sales professionals can provide feedback on attendees' use of technology and amenities; banquet professionals can let event professionals know whether they consumed more or less food and beverage than was guaranteed for particular functions. All participants should be encouraged to offer personal insights about what went well and what did not. Attendees should be surveyed during or after the event to ensure their needs and objectives were met. Thus, expertise in survey development, dissemination, and collection techniques is essential for the event professional.

It is important for event professionals to meet with their own staff to thank each member of the team and solicit feedback. Always compliment the individuals who contributed to the event. Then, move on to those aspects that went particularly well and should be repeated in the future. This often yields important information about a variety of issues, including staff involvement and participation in various aspects of the event.

If working with a planning committee of the organizing or sponsoring agency, event professionals should schedule a meeting with them as soon after the event as possible. Questions for this group could include: Were the event objectives achieved? Were attendees' expectations met? Exceeded? Was the venue appropriate for the event? Was the overall schedule of the event conducive to its objectives? What changes should be made for future meetings? As with other meetings, each person should be encouraged to speak candidly about what was and was not successful.

The event professional should complete a **post-event report (PER)** as well. The PER is the industry's accepted format for collecting, storing, and sharing accurate and thorough data on events of all types. It is available as a free download at www.conventionindustry.org.

- Tip: Use a project plan for post-event tasks and planning for future events.

Determining the Communication Needs of Meetings, Conventions, and Events

When determining the communication needs for a meeting or event, be sure to consider the specific needs of these different players:

Stakeholders: It is important to communicate with stakeholders, or the people who have a vested interest in the event. There needs to be a contact person for each element of the meeting or event to reduce miscommunication.

Staff: Use an organizational chart as a basis for determining staff member communication needs. Be sure to include management and training of volunteers with regard to communication.

Suppliers: The event suppliers need to know the goals, objectives, purposes, and agenda of the meeting or event.

Attendees: Communication is extremely important for on-site registration.

Like most professionals, an event professional will spend time communicating in some way with employees, coworkers, superiors, and clients. He or she must develop these skills in order to become a good communicator. The following are things to keep in mind as an event professional.

- *Listen* Everyone knows how, but many don't actively practice this skill. Some would say that humans were given two ears and one mouth for a reason: We must listen twice as much as we talk! Listening is the key to thoroughly understanding what is being said and being able to communicate effectively. Instead of deciding what you are going to say next, interrupting, or judging what is being said, focus on what is being said and process it. Stop talking and start listening.
- *Be clear and concise* Don't beat around the bush about what is being communicated: Make your point and expectations clear and concise. This ensures that you will be understood and your communication effective, regardless of the topic.
- *Repeat yourself* Whether you are speaking or sending an e-mail, repeating your expectations is the best way to ensure that you will be understood and that everyone will know the specifics of what you have communicated.
- *Use the right tone* Tone of voice can have a huge effect on what you are communicating. It is also easier to ensure that you are using the right tone when you are communicating in person. With today's inundation of **electronic communication**, tone can easily be misunderstood. When relying on electronic media to relay the message, make sure that your intended tone is clear.
- *Be careful with your body language* Your body language can convey the opposite of what you are intending. Be sure to say the right things with your body as well as with your words. As an event professional, it is important to pay attention to **body language**, both yours and your employees.
- *Proofread* Proofreading is a very important part of ensuring accurate and effective communication. Whether event professionals are drafting a newsletter, e-mail, or document about policy and procedure, proofreading helps make certain that they have properly and accurately written what they meant to say. In addition, skipping the proofreading step, even when the overall gist of the communication is clear, can show a lack of attention to detail and give the perception that the event professional is not serious about what is being said. Proofreading applies to all **written communication**, such as e-mail, and not just final reports.
- *Highlight the messages* When speaking with someone in person, it is wise to restate or highlight what was said. Exact words should not be repeated, but rather *paraphrased*. This shows that you were paying attention to the conversation and

fully understood what was being communicated. This will also help you remember the conversation as well as stay focused when you are spoken to.

- *Personalize it* Personalizing communication, whether in person or through e-mail, can help build trust between event professionals and their employees. To be a skilled event professional, it is necessary to establish trust and get to know the staff, employees, and volunteers. Occasionally making communication more personal demonstrates that you are interested in more than just the bottom line.

Remember that the best event professionals realize that communication is a two-way street and respect the opinions and concerns of everyone they are working with.

Determining the Message to Be Communicated

Internal Markets   Create a list of internal markets, which includes anyone inside the organization: the event company, the client, and the sponsoring organization. Determine who the staff, executives, employees, and suppliers are.

External Markets   Which part of the message do you want to communicate to the external markets, such as attendees, the public, the press, and government authorities?

The messages used to promote an event are extremely important. Usually there is limited advertorial space to convince all market segments to attend, so it must be taken advantage of. If there is enough time and a sufficient budget, it is a good idea to send these messages out to potential buyers, such as consumers, attendees, exhibitors, and sponsors.

Developing and Implementing a Flow Chart for Communication Responsibilities

Outline Distribution

- **Networks:** Many events have particular requirements for communication, which may even include the installation of a complete telephone communications network. Where there is a high level of demand on the communications network, the issue of bandwidth must be resolved, particularly if there is a significant amount of data being transmitted. A stadium often requires its own mobile phone base station owing to the number of people using mobile telephones, particularly at the end of the event.
- **Cell Phones:** Capacity of the wireless transmitters (Wi-Fi) must be analyzed and assessed. Given the increasing use of smartphones and tablets, having sufficient Wi-Fi capacity is critical. There is nothing worse than having the Wi-Fi crash during an important educational session because too many attendees were using it or for exhibitors to be unable to communicate with their home offices from their exhibit booth.

Hierarchy

- **Event Team Roles:** Who is responsible for what? Be sure to develop the communication and decision-making hierarchy for the meeting or event. An organizational chart is a helpful tool. It provides the following information: Who is immediately above and below each staff member and volunteer on the organization chart? Who speaks to and communicates with whom? Who is the decision maker at each level of the organization chart? The event professional does not want to be in a situation where the room monitor is giving orders to the service contractor.
- **Emergency Communication Plan:** The **emergency communication plan** is based on this hierarchy. In an emergency, who speaks to whom? Who is the

primary decision maker? Who is authorized to speak to authorities, to the press? The best spokesperson for dealing with the press may not be the event professional, but rather someone in marketing or public relations. The emergency communication plan should lay out the mechanisms for communicating with staff during an emergency. It cannot be assumed that all staff and volunteers have communication devices or walkie-talkies. Some event professionals come up with secret messages that can be broadcast over public address systems to alert staff to an emergency. An example of such a message is, "Will George Washington please proceed to meeting room 12?" While attendees will think this is a prank, staff members know that there is a fire in meeting room 12. (Franklin Roosevelt may indicate an electrical outage.)

The event professional is in charge of making sure that every detail of the event is set and that there are contingency plans for untimely incidences. Without a coordinator, teams will execute their own jobs during the project without thinking about the other teams. This may result in chaos. In event planning and production, learning to be a more effective communicator can lead to being more productive and professional on the job.

Setting Up Communication Channels

Consider the Entire Scope of the Meeting, Event, and Convention Needs   Event professionals are responsible for many areas of event planning and execution, which involve many different kinds of communication. Event professionals must:

- Call suppliers about food, beverage, and equipment rentals
- Confer with security guards and insurance agents to plan for risks associated with specific events
- Interact with entertainers (SEPs), catering personnel, event committee members, volunteers, and co-workers to plan events and coordinate activities
- Address audiences via public address system when conducting promotions
- Meet with clients to discuss the planning for upcoming events
- Communicate with supervisors, clients, and other public relations professionals to define the elements of marketing plans and the content of all marketing materials
- Interact with volunteers to motivate, train, and give recognition
- Interact with an audience to field questions or handle complaints
- Conduct media interviews
- Discuss event planning with clients and sponsors
- Talk to very important persons (VIPs) to clarify roles

Facilitate Flow   The event professional must facilitate the flow of communication among all stakeholders. The event professional acts like a coach in helping direct and motivate the entire team of staff, volunteers, and stakeholders. He or she should follow the mantra of "assign and check." Event professionals can't do everything by themselves, so they must assign certain communication tasks to other team members. However, assigning does not mean abdicating: They are still ultimately responsible for everything "on their watch" that is related to the event. The event professional cannot make the excuse that "So and so was supposed to do it—I assigned the task to him/her."

Verification Documents

- *Specifications Guidebook:* Electronic documents rely upon a power supply; if there's no power, there's no document. (And a flashlight is always a good idea in the event that there is no power!) In remote off-site locations and in many convention halls, wireless connections are not always reliable. Event professionals cannot risk being caught "in the dark" due to wireless interference, a power outage, damage to or loss of electronic devices, or other emergencies. There must be immediate access to a backup system. Copying documents to a flash drive or CD will suffice only if a working computer or mobile device is undamaged and unavailable. Even in today's seemingly paperless world, a hard copy binder still comes in handy. It is highly recommended that the event professional keep a hard copy binder on-site, at the ready. Copies should be made of all critical documents such as contracts, budget, function and exhibit specifications, change orders, checklists. Place these in tabbed sections in a binder, one section for each area of responsibility.

- *Production Book (aka operations manual, production binder):* This on-site reference manual covers every critical aspect of what happens "on-site." It lists the names and contact information of key staff, stakeholders, and vendors. This book should be available in both electronic and hard copy form—the latter for use during emergencies.

    Alternatively, a **contact list** can be developed in lieu of a production book. This contact list will contain the same type of information as the production book.

DETERMINING AND ACQUIRING COMMUNICATIONS EQUIPMENT AND RESOURCES

The event professional must be knowledgeable about **communications equipment** and resources—what is needed and where to get it (who can supply it). Yet decisions are made while being cognizant of the budget. The event professional must set realistic concepts and expectations and not put forth "pipe dreams" that the client cannot afford. Here are some of the common types of communication equipment.

- *Pager:* A pager is a small device that alerts the user to contact another party. It shows the name of the person who sent the page and where he or she can be contacted. Doctors were often seen using the small and unobtrusive pager; its size is why many event professionals still use one. However, the use of pagers is in decline as people send text messages from smartphones and tablets.
- *PA System:* A public address system is used to communicate with large groups of people. The system is usually "hard wired" and thus not affected by an intensity of usage. The event professional should make sure that a PA system has backup power supplies that enable its use during emergencies.
- *Computers:* Computers are the backbone of modern communication. Thus, having a firm grasp of desktop publishing software (e.g., Microsoft Office Suites) is invaluable to an event professional and essential for good written communication. Event professionals should consider where their information is stored, besides on the device itself. One alternative is external storage, often using a USB port. A newer alternative is web storage, often referred to as "cloud computing." Here, information is stored on a remote server and accessed via the Internet. The obvious advantage is that the data or information can be accessed from anywhere and by anyone with an access code. The downside is that it requires Internet access.
- *Walkie-Talkies:* These hand-held devices operate on radio frequencies. Each device can only communicate with another one on the same frequency. Communication is accomplished by simply holding a button. This is an ideal tool for an event professional who is communicating with staff.

The event professional must analyze the communication equipment needs of the event, taking into consideration the type and size of site/venue along with users, attendees, staff, and volunteers. These are some types of equipment sub-categories:

- *Emergency Personnel:* Different constituents require different equipment and resources. Emergency personnel need dependable, battery-powered communication devices. They may also require non-powered devices, such as semaphores, reflective batons, and even signs to help them communicate with and direct others during emergencies. The event professional should also assess the adequacy of emergency lighting and illuminated directional signage (battery-powered exit signs) in any venue being used. This "signage" serves as a form of communication equipment.
- *Attendees:* Communication with attendees will most often involve written and/or digital text, such as the event program, list of activities, and signs indicating what is happening in a given place and when. Presentations will require AV equipment, such as microphones and amplified sound, along with projection equipment. For more extravagant events, special effects, lighting, signage, and so on, will be used. Public address systems may also come into play.

Developing Guidelines

A key element in dealing with communication equipment relates to issuing and maintaining equipment. The event professional must determine who the users will be, how many users need to have what communication equipment, the frequency with which each will use each piece of equipment, and how intense the use will be. The other considerations are how the communications equipment will be maintained, by whom, and where. When the event professional has all this information, he or she can determine the communications equipment needs and develop guidelines that can be shared with key stakeholders.

Determining Appropriate Technology for Meetings, Conventions, and Events

Mobile Communication   A focus on sustainability and reducing waste means that event professionals must plan and execute on-site communication in the most efficient and effective way. As technology has evolved, the priority—and also challenge—for the event professional is in moving content onto mobile platforms. With the explosion of smartphones and tablet computers designed for mobility, stakeholders now expect immediate communication using these readily available and easily accessible devices.

The effectiveness of mobile communication devices can be explained by our increasing use of meeting-enhancing, online, and social networking tools, such as Twitter. A recent survey unveiled five key trends:

1. More demands from meeting professionals for innovative technology such as polling tools
2. A broadening scope of event technologies such as RFP and bidding software
3. Demands from delegates and speakers (especially younger ones who have grown up in a digital world) for increasingly sophisticated multimedia and other technologies that facilitate the flow of ideas between them and their audiences
4. A growing prominence of mobile applications
5. A growing adoption of events that combine in-person and virtual aspects

Internship Example 1
Communication and Event Planning Internship

Dentists Without Borders–USA | New York, NY

Industry: Nonprofit

Hiring Level: Entry

Are you looking for a fast-paced and challenging opportunity? Dentists Without Borders–USA (DWB) is looking for professional, creative, and motivated interns interested in gaining skills not usually found in the classroom. Get a jump-start on your career with hands-on, real-world experience while learning about the field of international nonprofit communication and marketing.

DWB–USA is a 501(c)(3) nonprofit humanitarian organization established to partner with developing communities worldwide to improve their quality of life through the implementation of sustainable dental programs, while developing globally aware and internationally responsible students and professionals. Currently operating in more than 45 countries, DWB–USA works with over 12,000 volunteers to install small-scale water, renewable energy, sanitation, housing, telecommunication, and other sustainable projects to those in need.

Communication and Event Planning Intern Job Description:

- Perform website maintenance and project development
- Assist in marketing duties, such as copywriting, editing, and research
- Conduct media outreach and follow-up
- Perform event coordination for the annual DWB–USA International Conference, including media relations, volunteer coordination, event development, and registration assistance
- Assist in writing event materials, press releases, and media advisories
- Undertake data collection and research as needed
- Perform administrative work such as copying, proofreading, and other basic duties on an as-needed basis
- Work directly with the communication event professional

Intern Qualifications:

- Must be enrolled as an undergraduate or graduate student in a course of study in communications, public relations, marketing, or similar area or have work experience in the field
- Ability to handle and prioritize multiple projects
- Excellent organizational skills and ability to work under deadlines
- Excellent people skills as well as solid written and **oral communication** skills
- Professional on the phone, in person, and in written communication
- Detail oriented; proficient at time management and multitasking
- Ability to work effectively and independently in a fast-paced environment
- Proficiency in data entry using Excel, Word, and PowerPoint software as well as Internet fluency
- Interested in nonprofit work

(Continued)

Commitment: Minimum of 20 hours per week, six-month commitment (internship duration can be made to match semester/summer length)

Salary: This is an unpaid internship; however, you may receive course credit

To apply for this position, please submit résumé and cover letter to:

Jenny Starkey, communication event professional at jenny.starkey@dwb-usa.org

Posting Date: January 2, 2012

Start Date: April 2012   **Application Deadline:** February 1, 2012

Start Date: September 2012   **Application Deadline:** August 1, 2012

PERSONAL COMMUNICATION

The focus of this chapter thus far has been on business communication and equipment. Event professionals must bear in mind that they will always be involved in personal types of communication. Personal communication can be categorized as formal and informal. While these techniques are self-explanatory, event professionals and their constituents must be aware of when and how to use each. Formal communication occurs in business settings, such as interacting with officials and dignitaries. Informal communication occurs within groups of peers in nonbusiness settings. It is critical that the correct technique be used in the setting where it is demanded. The two methods used for transmission of information are written and oral.

The importance of **oral communication** skills cannot be stressed enough. Due to the multifaceted nature of the meetings and events industry, the event professional will interact with various stakeholders to achieve the desired results. The oral communication summary is presented in a table that matches the types and purposes of oral communication.

- Tip: Reinforcement of the message is key. It can enhance safety and service, two essential responsibilities of the whole event team. The range of ways in which core messages can be reinforced are outlined in Figure 2.

FIGURE 2

Channels of communication for radio incident reporting

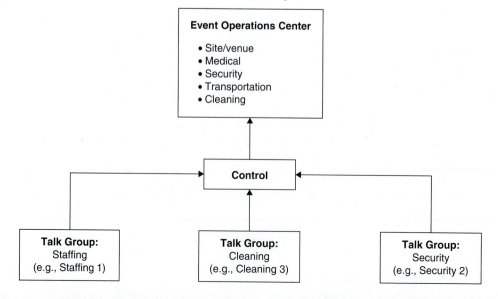

Communication with the Event Team

Here are some guidelines for improving communication within the event team:

Establish the level of priority: It is important to establish the level of priority immediately. Emergency situations are of course the highest risk for any event, and communication about an incident or potential incident should be given top priority.

Identify the receiver: By identifying the receiver, event professionals will be able to match their message to the receiver's needs, thus demonstrating empathy. The message will also reach the correct target.

Know the objective: Clarity in communication is often linked to the development of an action objective using action words or verbs. The use of certain "action" words to describe the action or task to be observed or evaluated is vital in developing good objectives. Some examples of action verbs are:

- To analyze
- To change
- To write
- To select
- To prepare

If event professionals know what they want to achieve and what words to use, they will be able to express themselves more easily and clearly. Stating a problem and its ramifications is often only the first stage. By indicating what needs to be done, the event professional can more easily achieve the objective and reach an agreed outcome.

Review the message in your head: In preparing to send a message, the event professional should structure the given communication effectively. It is also useful to review the receiver's likely response.

Communicate in the language of the other person: If examples and illustrations are used that the receiver will understand, the message will be more easily comprehended.

Clarify the message: This is essential if the receiver appears (from his or her nonverbal behavior or body language) not to understand the message.

Do not react defensively to a critical response: Asking questions regarding the reactions of the receiver of the message can help the event professional understand why he or she responded defensively.

Create a Plan and Team for Crisis Management

A crisis management plan (CMP) is a detailed guide outlining the policies and procedures to be followed in an emergency situation. The plan suggests that a crisis management team (CMT) and an evacuation team be assembled. The CMP's goals are to:

- Provide guidance to event professionals regarding appropriate procedures and resources.
- Protect the safety and well-being of all employees.
- Provide for the care of employees and their families through personnel services.
- Minimize post-traumatic stress reaction among employees.
- Ensure that accurate and appropriate information about the incident is conveyed to the appropriate audiences.
- Plan the orderly return of the workplace to a normal mode of operation.
- Outline preventative measures that should be taken in advance.

The crisis management team is the group responsible for responding to the emergency. This team could include the following personnel:

- Crisis event professional
- Administrative coordinator

- Operations coordinator
- Employee support coordinator
- Technical support coordinator

Figure 3 is the NATO phonetic alphabet created by the U.S. military. This phonetic alphabet is still used by event professionals in order to achieve clear communication.

FIGURE 3

NATO phonetic alphabet

Character	Morse Code	Telephony	Phonic (Pronunciation)
A	• —	Alfa	(AL-FAH)
B	— • • •	Bravo	(BRAH-VOH)
C	— • — •	Charlie	(CHAR-LEE) or (SHAR-LEE)
D	— • •	Delta	(DELL-TAH)
E	•	Echo	(ECK-OH)
F	• • — •	Foxtrot	(FOKS-TROT)
G	— — •	Golf	(GOLF)
H	• • • •	Hotel	(HOH-TEL)
I	• •	India	(IN-DEE-AH)
J	• — — —	Juliet	(JEW-LEE-ETT)
K	— • —	Kilo	(KEY-LOH)
L	• — • •	Lima	(LEE-MAH)
M	— —	Mike	(MIKE)
N	— •	November	(NO-VEM-BER)
O	— — —	Oscar	(OSS-CAH)
P	• — — •	Papa	(PAH-PAH)
Q	— — • —	Quebec	(KEH-BECK)
R	• — •	Romeo	(ROW-ME-OH)
S	• • •	Sierra	(SEE-AIR-RAH)
T	—	Tango	(TANG-GO)
U	• • —	Uniform	(YOU-NEE-FORM) or (OO-NEE-FORM)
V	• • • —	Victor	(VIK-TAH)
W	• — —	Whiskey	(WISS-KEY)
X	— • • —	Xray	(ECKS-RAY)
Y	— • — —	Yankee	(YANG-KEY)
Z	— — • •	Zulu	(ZOO-LOO)
1	• — — — —	One	(WUN)
2	• • — — —	Two	(TOO)
3	• • • — —	Three	(TREE)
4	• • • • —	Four	(FOW-ER)
5	• • • • •	Five	(FIFE)
6	— • • • •	Six	(SIX)
7	— — • • •	Seven	(SEV-EN)
8	— — — • •	Eight	(AIT)
9	— — — — •	Nine	(NIN-ER)
0	— — — — —	Zero	(ZEE-RO)

Some words with specialized meanings are used in radio communication throughout the English-speaking world as well as in international radio communication, where English is the lingua franca.

- **Affirm**—Yes
- **Negative**—No
- **Reading you five / Loud and clear**—I understand what you say.
- **Over**—I have finished talking and am listening for your reply. Short for "Over to you."
- **Out**—I have finished talking to you and do not expect a reply.
- **Roger**—I understand what you just said.
- **Copy**—I heard what you just said.
- **Say again**—Repeat; Please repeat your last words.
- **Break**—Signals a pause during a long transmission to open the channel for other transmissions, especially to allow any potential emergency traffic to get through.
- **Roger so far**—Confirm that you have received and understood the contents of my transmission so far.
- **Standby / Wait out**—Pause for the next transmission. This does not usually entail staying off the air until the operator returns, as they have used the word "Out," which indicates the transmission has ended.

MONITORING ON-SITE COMMUNICATION

Monitoring is the final key aspect of on-site communication at meetings and events. The event professional must keep track of and be up-to-date on what, when, and how something is being communicated. All established policies, protocols, and hierarchies must be adhered to. Equipment must be on hand when needed and in good working order. If any of the foregoing are not correct, the event professional must make adjustments and corrections. The event professional is the one ultimately responsible for every aspect of the meeting or event.

SUMMARY

The focus of this chapter was on communication, largely which takes place on-site. After a brief introduction, the discussion moved to developing a communication framework. We then identified the communications equipment and resources needed for a given event and how to acquire them. We discussed how to develop and implement communication procedures and protocols and closed with a discussion of how to monitor and the importance of monitoring on-site communication. The following chart (see Figure 4) synopsizes communication strategies.

FIGURE 4

Communications strategies chart

Written	Verbal	Visual	Behavioral
Training manual	Briefings	Photographs	Videos
Memo	Meetings	Displays	Working practices
Letters	Radio conversations	Models	Role modeling
E-mail	One-to-one discussions	Demonstrations	Nonverbal communication
Handbooks	Instruction	Printed slogans	Social networking
Staff newsletters	Telephone conversations	Posters	
Reports	Training	Videos	
Information bulletins	Word-of-mouth messages	Internet	
Checklists			

Now that you have completed this chapter, you should be competent in the following Meeting and Business Event Competency Standards:

MBECS Skill 25: Manage On-Site Communication

Subskills		
25.01	Establish communication framework	
25.02	Determine and acquire required communications equipment and resources	
25.03	Specify communication procedures and protocols	

KEY WORDS AND TERMS

nonverbal

pre-con

post-con

post-event report (PER)

electronic communication

body language

written communication

emergency communication plan

contact list

communications equipment

oral communication

REVIEW AND DISCUSSION QUESTIONS

1. What should an event professional do to keep problems relating to communication skills at bay?
2. What are the three stages of event communication?
3. What does PER stand for?
4. Whose needs should the event professional consider when producing a meeting or event?
5. What can an event professional do to improve his or her communication skills?

6. What strategies can event professionals use to develop effective communication between them?
7. What are the advantages and disadvantages of different types of communications equipment?
8. How does disaster planning fit in with communication?

ABOUT THE CHAPTER CONTRIBUTOR

Erinn D. Tucker, PhD, MBA is a professor in the School of Hospitality Administration (SHA) at Boston University (BU). She is directly responsible for the human resources management and meeting and convention management curriculum. She created and now administers the first event management program in conjunction with the BU study abroad office at the BU Washington, D.C., academic center, which focuses on government meetings and protocol. Tucker is a member of the New England chapters of Meeting Professionals International (MPI), the Professional Convention Management Association (PCMA), and the International Council of Hotel, Restaurant, and Institutional Education (ICHRIE). In addition, she serves on the Advisory Board for the National Black MBA Association Boston Chapter.

Tucker's work experience has crossed both corporate and educational institutions. She has worked in corporate sports marketing for RDV Sports and the PGA TOUR, and for General Motors R* Works in Atlanta, where she negotiated sponsorship agreements with multimillion dollar budgets. Her sales and marketing experience took her into the restaurant industry, where she was the special events event professional for Dave & Busters (formerly Jillian's Entertainment) in Charlotte, North Carolina. She has also hired and trained event service staff for sports teams, the Charlotte Bobcats and Charlotte Knights, which shaped and developed her practical human resources skills in the private sector.

Epilogue

CHAPTER 15

KNOWLEDGE CHECKLIST

Now that you have completed this book, you should be competent in the Meeting and Business Event Competency Standards that appears with a check mark (✓) beside them:

Meeting and Business Event Competency Standards (MBECS)	
Checklist as Related to Production and Logistics	
Domains/Skills	**Checklist**
A. STRATEGIC PLANNING	
1. Manage Strategic Plan for Meeting or Event	
2. Develop Sustainability Plan for Meeting or Event	
3. Measure Value of Meeting or Business Event	
B. PROJECT MANAGEMENT	
4. Plan Meeting or Event	
5. Manage Meeting or Event Project	✓
C. RISK MANAGEMENT	
6. Manage Risk Management Plan	
D. FINANCIAL MANAGEMENT	
7. Develop Financial Resources	✓
8. Manage Budget	✓
9. Manage Monetary Transactions	✓
E. ADMINISTRATION	
10. Perform Administrative Tasks	✓
F. HUMAN RESOURCES	
11. Manage Human Resource Plan	✓
12. Acquire Staff and Volunteers	
13. Train Staff and Volunteers	✓
14. Manage Workforce Relations	✓
G. STAKEHOLDER MANAGEMENT	
15. Manage Stakeholder Relationships	
H. MEETING OR EVENT DESIGN	
16. Design Program	
17. Engage Speakers and Performers	✓
18. Coordinate Food and Beverage	✓
19. Design Environment	✓
20. Manage Technical Production	✓
21. Develop Plan for Managing Movement of People	✓
I. SITE MANAGEMENT	
22. Select Site	✓
23. Design Site Layout	
24. Manage Meeting or Event Site	✓
25. Manage On-Site Communications	✓

(Continued)

Domains/Skills *(Continued)*	Checklist
J. MARKETING	
26. Manage Marketing Plan	✓
27. Manage Marketing Materials	✓
28. Manage Meeting or Event Merchandise	✓
29. Promote Meeting or Event	
30. Contribute to Public Relations Activities	✓
31. Manage Sales Activities	✓
K. PROFESSIONALISM	
32. Exhibit Professional Behavior	
L. COMMUNICATIONS	
33. Conduct Business Communications	